From Eastertide to Ecclesia

To Gabriella,
May Blessed Newman continue
to guide and enlighten you.
Donald Graham

DONALD GRAHAM

From Eastertide to Ecclesia: John Henry Newman, the Holy Spirit, & the Church

MARQUETTE STUDIES IN THEOLOGY
NO. 76
ANDREW TALLON, SERIES EDITOR

LIBRARY OF CONGRESS CATALOGING-IN-PUBLICATION DATA

Graham, Donald, 1961-

From Eastertide to ecclesia : John Henry Newman, the Holy Spirit & the church / Donald Graham.

p. cm. — (Marquette studies in theology ; no. 76)

Includes bibliographical references (p.) and index.

ISBN-13: 978-0-87462-795-4 (pbk. : alk. paper)

ISBN-10: 0-87462-795-8 (pbk. : alk. paper)

1. Newman, John Henry, 1801-1890. 2. Church. 3. Holy Spirit. 4. Jesus Christ—Person and offices. 5. Catholic Church—Doctrines. I. Title.

BX1746.G73 2011

262'.02092—dc23

2011041024

Cover art by Tessa Graham, entitled "fragrant white water lilies"

Indian River, Douro ON, Canada. Summer 2011

With a nod to the author's youthful Ontario cottage days, and drawing upon the spiritual symbolism of this family of flowers, this trinity of lilies suggests the surge from Eastertide to Ecclesia, while the red lily pad hints at the prior, related reality of Passiontide.

♾The paper used in this publication meets the minimum requirements of the American National Standard for Information Sciences— Permanence of Paper for Printed Library Materials, ANSI Z39.48-1992.

MARQUETTE UNIVERSITY PRESS
MILWAUKEE

The Association of Jesuit University Presses

CONTENTS

for Michèle

ACKNOWLEDGEMENTS

The writing of a book is similar to an adventure in Tolkien's *The Lord of the Rings* insofar as the writer, though a solitary, is also accompanied by a fellowship of those, seen and unseen, who make the journey possible, supply succour, and to whom the adventurer owes a debt of gratitude.

Along the way, the Rev. Dr. Ian Ker (Oxford) and Dr. Terry Merrigan (Leuven) extended friendship, advice, and encouragement, as well as inspiring me by the excellence and scope of their scholarship. In divers ways, the camaraderie, counsel, and faith of Dr. Danny Monsour (Lonergan Research Institute, Toronto), Dr. David and Theresa Beresford (Trent Univ., Peterborough ON), Chef Andrew and Julie Carter (The Queen and Beaver, Toronto) and The Hon. Mr. Justice J. Christopher and Lee Anne Corkery helped me to bear the burden of the day. When I was a 'stranger in a foreign land,' Sr. Mary Dechant FSO (Superior, The College, Littlemore), Dr. Petroc Willey (Deputy-Director, Maryvale Institute, Birmingham) and the Rev. Dr. Drew Morgan, CO (Superior of The Oratory, and former Director of The National Institute of Newman Studies, Pittsburgh) provided me with a place congenial to research, prayer and fellowship. The Rev. Dr. Aidan Nichols, OP (Cambridge) has kindly endorsed the fruits of my labour as worthy of consideration. My editor, Prof. Andrew Tallon, has made salutary suggestions, and presented my work in a pleasing, professional manner. To these, and *many* unnamed friends, I am grateful.

From the outset, my family – immediate and extended – has 'lived the adventure'. To my brothers, sister, and their families (especially, David and Kathy of the Warsaw 'Vanilla' Graham clan), and my in-laws, Jean and Louise Aquin, thanks for the helping our domestic church survive and thrive. Thanks so much to my niece, Tessa, for the beautiful artwork on the cover, and Mr. Greg Burke for back cover photograph. To my children – Aidan, Clare, Raïssa, Ambrose, Grace and Genevieve – your sacrifices, humour, and love have kept me afloat. We truly took the adventure together. To my own deceased Mom and Dad, thank you for my life, and laying down yours for mine.

Finally, and mostly, to my Michèle – wife, best friend, lover, dear-heart, and mother – I am grateful beyond telling for your patience, prudence, creativity, and the high honour both of believing in my abilities, and listening to the whispers of my heart. *Cor ad cor loquitur.*

ABBREVIATIONS

The abbreviations listed below for Newman's oeuvre are adapted from those used by Joseph Ricaby, SJ, in his *Index to the Works of Cardinal Newman* (London, 1914) and found in *The Letters and Diaries of John Henry Newman*. Unless otherwise indicated, references to Newman's oeuvre are to the uniform edition of 1868-81 (36 vols.) which was published by Longmans, Green, and Co. of London until the destruction of its stock during World War II. These are differentiated from other editions by the absence of a date or place of publication after the title. References to *Apologia pro Vita Sua, An Essay in Aid of a Grammar of Assent* and *The Idea of A University* are to the Oxford critical editions. Full information is provided in the bibliography.

OEUVRE

Apo. *Apologia pro Vita Sua.*
Ari. *The Arians of the Fourth Century.*
Ath. i, ii *Select Treatises of St. Athanasius,* 2 vols.
Call. *Callista. A Tale of the Third Century.*
Cons. *On Consulting the Faithful in Matters of Doctrine.* 1961.
DA *Discussions and Arguments on Various Subjects.*
Dev. 1845 *An Essay on the Development of Christian Doctrine.*
Dev. 1878 *An Essay on the Development of Christian Doctrine.*
Diff. i, ii *Certain Difficulties felt by Anglicans in Catholic Teaching,* 2 vols.
Ess. i, ii *Essays Critical and Historical,* 2 vols.
GA *An Essay in Aid of A Grammar of Assent.* 1985.
HS i, ii, iii *Historical Sketches,* 3 vols.
Idea *The Idea of a University.* 1976.
Jfc. *Lectures on the Doctrine of Justification.*
LG *Loss and Gain: The Story of a Convert.*
Mir. *Two Essays on Biblical and Ecclesiastical Miracles.*
Mix. *Discourses addressed to Mixed Congregations.*
OS *Sermons preached on Various Occasions.*
PS i-viii *Parochial and Plain Sermons,* 8 vols.
Prepos. *Present Position of Catholics in England.*
SD *Sermons bearing on Subjects of the Day.*
TT *Tracts Theological and Ecclesiastical.*
US *Fifteen Sermons preached before the University of Oxford.*
VM i, ii *The Via Media.* 2 vols.

POSTHUMOUS

AW *John Henry Newman: Autobiographical Writings*. 1956.

Campaign *My Campaign in Ireland, Part I*. 1896.

CS *Catholic Sermons of Cardinal Newman*. 1957.

Insp. *On the Inspiration of Scripture*. 1967.

JHNS i *Sermons on the Liturgy and Sacraments and on Christ the* Mediator. Vol i of *John Henry Newman Sermons 1824-43*. 1991.

JHNS ii *Sermons on Biblical History, Sin and Justification, the Christian Way of Life, and Biblical Theology*, vol.ii of *John Henry Newman Sermons 1824-43*. 1993.

KC *Correspondence of John Henry Newman with John Keble and Others 1839-1845*. 1917.

"Three Latin Papers of John Henry Newman: *Newman-Perrone on Development* (1847), *Theses on Faith* (1877) and *Proposed Introduction to the French Translation of the University Sermons* (1847)." 1995.

LD *The Letters and Diaries of John Henry Newman*. vols. i-viii (1978-99), xi-xxii (1961-72), xxiii-xxxi (1973-77).

Moz. i, ii *Letters and Correspondence of John Henry Newman during his Life in the English Church with a brief autobiography*. 2 vols., 1890.

NO *Newman the Oratorian: His Unpublished Oratory Papers*. 1968.

PN i, ii *The Philosophical Notebook of John Henry Newman*. 2 vol. 1969-70.

PVD *Prayers, Verses and Devotions* which includes *Meditations and Devotions* (1903) and *Verses on Various Occasions* (1903), 1989.

SE *Stray Essays on Controversial Points*. 890.

SN *Sermon Notes of John Henry Cardinal Newman, 1849-1878*. 1913.

TP i *The Theological Papers of John Henry Newman on Faith and Certainty*. 1976.

TP ii *The Theological Papers of John Henry Newman on Biblical Inspiration*. 1979.

OTHER

Holy Spirit Congar, Yves. *I Believe in the Holy Spirit*. Vol i-iii. 1997.

NJBC *New Jerome Biblical Commentary*. 1990.

NDT New Dictionary of Theology. 1987.

ODCC *The Oxford Dictionary of the Christian Church*. 1985.

TFT *Tracts for the Times 1833-41*. Vols. i-vi. 1841.

VCS *Veni Creator Spiritus: A Theological Encyclopaedia of the Holy Spirit*. 1990.

May we never speak on subjects like this without awe; may we never dispute without charity; may we never inquire without a careful endeavour, with God's aid, to sanctify our knowledge, and to impress it on our hearts, as well as to store it in our understandings.

Blessed John Henry Newman,
"The Mystery of the Holy Trinity,"
Parochial and Plain Sermons vi 360-1

FOREWORD

From Eastertide to Ecclesia: John Henry Newman, the Holy Spirit, and the Church is an important and original contribution to Newman studies. Donald Graham argues that for Newman the humanity of Christ is to his divinity what the human dimension of the Church is to the Holy Spirit that vivifies the Church. Newman once described the sacraments as "embodied forms of the Spirit of Christ"; similarly, the Church, which is the primordial sacrament, can be called "*the* embodied form of the Spirit of Christ".

Donald Graham begins by showing how Newman abandoned an Evangelical ecclesiology of the Church as the invisible union of believers and came to accept baptismal regeneration and the Catholic idea of a visible sacramental Church. In his Trinitarian theology Newman insisted on both the distinctness of each of the three Persons of the Trinity and consequently their differing roles in the economy of salvation. Arguing that Newman scholars have failed fully to appreciate Newman's understanding of the role of the Holy Spirit in both the life of Christ and of the Church, Dr Graham draws our attention to Newman's realization that, while Christ achieves our redemption through his incarnation, death and resurrection, it is the Holy Spirit who is responsible for the *application* of the atonement to Christians. This corresponds to the Holy Spirit's special role in energising and giving life to creation rather than the Father or the Son, while it "fitting that the Son should be incarnate" rather than the Father or the Spirit. Similarly, it is appropriate that the Son who is begotten of the Father should be the actual agent of creation. So closely related to and involved in the incarnate Son's life and mission, on the other hand, is the Spirit that their roles in Newman are sometimes virtually indistinguishable from each other. Dr Graham is anxious to show that Newman's Athanasian christology does not depreciate in any way the humanity of the incarnate Son, as has often been suggested. Rather, just as Newman emphasises the indwelling of the Holy Spirit as our justification, so he sees the Spirit as ever-present in the humanity of the God-Man. Newman understands perfectly well, for example, that the Spirit can only lead Christ into the desert to be tempted if he is truly human. Dr Graham aptly cites the remarkable words of Newman, "Thou [Christ] are more fully man than the holy Baptist, than St. John, Apostle and Evangelist. Than thy own sweet Mother."

Dr. Graham finds previous Newman scholarship to be deficient in failing to appreciate the importance for Newman of the Ascension as triggering Pentecost and the sending of the Holy Spirit to the Church. He quotes from Newman's *Lectures on Justification*: "...Christ's mission ended when he left the world; He was to come again, but by His Spirit ... The Atonement for sin took place during His own mission, and He was the chief Agent; the application of that Atonement takes place during the mission of His Spirit who accordingly is the chief agent in it." Dr. Graham turns to the *Essay on Development* for evidence that Newman's ecclesiology derives from a pneumatic christology. He acknowledges that that there are "fewer direct references to the Holy Spirit as the divine agent of development ... than one might expect", but he points out that for Newman "the Church is both an 'earthly vessel' subject to the laws, limits and foibles of human nature as well as a graced reality 'quickened by what is more than intellect, by a Divine Spirit.'" Newman, therefore, "understood the Holy Spirit to be the divine agent superintending the doctrinal development of the deposit of the faith committed to the Church."

From Eastertide to Ecclesia: John Henry Newman, the Holy Spirit, and the Church is a valuable addition to Newman scholarship in giving us an enhanced appreciation of the significance of the Holy Spirit in both Newman's christology and ecclesiology.

Ian Ker

INTRODUCTION

In recent memory, the Catholic theologian who has systematically thought through, and written most deeply about, the intersection of ecclesiology and pneumatology is Yves Congar OP. In a reminiscence, he recounted his discussion about the schema on the Church at Vatican II with Orthodox theologians, Nikos Nissiotis and Alexander Schmemann. They told him: "If we were to prepare a treatise on *De Ecclesia*, we would draft a chapter on the Holy Spirit, to which we would add a second chapter on Christian anthropology, and that would be all." Since Vatican II, the doctrine of the Holy Spirit and its integral relationship to the Church has steadily received more attention from Roman Catholic theologians who have benefited in this endeavour by attending closely to the voice of Eastern Christians. This represents a real act of theological *anamnesis* and, in fact, it is not too much to say that the 'forgotten person of the Trinity' has been remembered. Unsurprisingly, the re-emergence of a theology in which the trinitarian foundation of the Church receives its due was not an overnight conciliar phenomenon, but resulted from a confluence of factors preceding the Council. Now it is almost a commonplace to note that many thinkers who prepared the ground for this change learned much from Blessed John Henry Newman.

Some years ago, in a volume devoted to opening up new vistas, and attaining authoritative reassessments of his thought, Avery Dulles SJ said that Newman "is perhaps the most seminal Roman Catholic theologian of modern times" and "nearly all the questions that engaged his interest have an ecclesial dimension" (Ker and Hill 1990, 375). The intersection of the ecclesiological and pneumatological in his thought, as mediated by the Greek Fathers, was identified shortly after the close of the Council by the dean of Newman studies, C.S. Dessain, who attested in a widely cited article that "Newman brought out, strongly, too, the ecclesial nature of the divine gift, which is not a private grace, but establishes a common fellowship. There is only time to notice this in passing, fundamental though it is" (Coulson and Allchin 1967, 109). Since Dessain's observation, several scholars have laboured to deepen our understanding of Newman's idea of the Church and his insightful treatment of theological themes like faith, justification, the indwelling of the Holy Spirit, the laity, infallibility, and development of doctrine. To a lesser extent, some have studied his christology, pneumatology and trinitarian theology, but few have done so systematically with an eye to his theology of the Church. No one, yet, has taken up, and carefully examined, the fundamental pneumatological dimension of Newman's sacramental ecclesiology. This is the aim of my efforts.

My essential argument is that Newman's pneumatic ecclesiology is configured sacramentally to his pneumatic christology. In short, I contend that his ecclesiological understanding rests upon the sacramental analogy between Christ and his Church constituted by the proportionality which exists between two sets of terms: the human nature of Jesus is to the eternal Son what the human dimension of the Church is to the Holy Spirit. The analogy is limited inasmuch as there is a real difference between the hypostatic union of the God-man and the union of believers with the Trinity established by the grace of baptism. The analogy is unlimited insofar as it establishes and makes possible the real participation of believers in the life of the triune God. The essential ecclesiological achievement of Newman is the extent to which he grasps the pre-eminent role of Holy Spirit in making possible and rendering effective both sets of terms in the sacramental analogy. Newman once told Samuel Wilberforce that the sacraments of the Church are "embodied forms of the Spirit of Christ."[1] My book may be summarized by stating that this Spirit-filled description of the sacraments applies as much to Newman's vivified idea of the Church, which mediates and administers these sacred things, as it does to the sacred things themselves.

The intersection of Newman's thought on the Church, the Holy Spirit, the God-man, and the Trinity, therefore, sets the cross-sights through which I perceive and evaluate representative themes in his oeuvre. I treat attendant questions only to the degree to which they reflect Newman's emphasis or clarify my argument. Chapter one describes the historical growth of Newman's ecclesiology from his Evangelical idea of the Church as an invisible union of believers (1816-24) to his gradual acceptance of the visible dimension of the Church (1824-26) to his affirmation of the Church as a sacramental

1 10 March 1839, LD v 39.

communion (post-1826). Chapter two sets forth his trinitarian and incarnational grammar and reviews the state of scholarship concerning his pneumatic christology to conclude that there is a dearth of reflection upon his view of the Holy Spirit in the life of the historical Jesus. Chapter three examines Newman's view of the congruity of divine personhood and temporal office wherein mediation and animation are identified as hypostatic hallmarks of the offices of the eternal Son and Holy Spirit and, then, the implications of this view for his mariology are considered. Chapter four refutes charges that Newman's pneumatic christology is actually an immanent Athanasian christology or is diminished by a deficient view of the humanity of the God-man. The strength of his pneumatic christology is then evinced with reference to events in the life of the God-man from his ontological constitution to his crucifixion. Chapter five discusses Newman's views of the Holy Spirit as the 'leading actor' in the Easter Mystery, the resurrection as the origin of *ecclesia* and the centrality of ascension-pentecost for his 'Body of Christ' ecclesiology. Chapters six and seven test the position that Newman's fundamental ecclesiology rests upon a properly qualified sacramental extension of his pneumatic christology with reference to his *Essay on the Development of Christian Doctrine* (1845) by arguing that he invests his epistemological language with pneumatological and christological significance.

No one familiar with Newman expects to find a tidy, systematic treatise on his view concerning the relationship between pneumatic christology and pneumatic ecclesiology. Usually, he writes in response to pastoral demands rather than out of a preconceived plan driven by academic interests, and conveys his ideas over the broad sweep of a page using an elegant literary style rather than confining his thoughts to the strictures of technical theological terms. Hence, I draw freely upon his early and late work to show how Newman arrives at, maintains, and exploits his pneumatic christology and pneumatic ecclesiology. The *terminus a quo* of the study is the sacramental ecclesiology which Newman came to hold post-1826. Once I verify this fact, the reason for this starting point is apodictic. The *terminus ad quem* of the study is Newman's 1853 sermon, "Order, the Witness and Instrument of Unity, preached in St. Chad's Cathedral on the occasion of the first Diocesan Synod of Birmingham[2] because it contains his most direct

2 OS 183-94.

statement that the office of life-giving is congruous to the person of the Holy Spirit. By extending the study into his early Catholic years, I am also able to draw upon Newman's account of Christ breathing forth of the Holy Spirit from the cross in what is, arguably, his most sustained and penetrating consideration of passion-tide, "The Mental Sufferings of Christ in His Passion".[3]

Finally, the title of this book, *From Eastertide to Ecclesia,* is more than an exercise in theological alliteration. It emphasizes that Newman consciously envisions the Lord and Giver of Life working in concert with, and working within, the God-man, at the most fundamental level, in order to originate, indwell, equip, send, and sustain, the Church in the Easter Mystery. All else in Newman's idea of the Church leads to, and flows away from *this* Mystery. My hope is that by illuminating this dimension of Blessed Newman's ecclesiology those turning to him as a spiritual and theological mentor may more profoundly realize the nature of the Church and render to her – without ignoring human imperfections or the need for purification – the same faithful service for reasons "impressed on our hearts" and "stored in our understandings."

3 Mix. 323-41.

CHAPTER ONE

GROWTH IN NEWMAN'S IDEA OF THE CHURCH

Between the ages of 15 and 25, John Henry Newman's ecclesiology developed significantly from his Evangelical idea of the Church as an invisible union of believers (1816-24) to his gradual acceptance of the visible dimension of the Church (1824-26) to his eventual affirmation of the Church as a sacramental communion (post-1826). Newman's discussion of the idea of the Church during the 1816-24 and 1824-26 phases typically occurred in relation to the issue of baptismal regeneration which occupied a central place in his ecclesiological maturation specifically, and distinguished religious practice and belief in Victorian society generally. Explanation of Newman's post-1826 ecclesiology reflects upon his articulation of the philosophic, poetic and theological sources of his sacramentality, especially, his grounding of this sacramentality in the mystery of the Word made flesh. For, by 1826, he realized distinctly that the ecclesial mediation of redemption required the constitution of the Church to correspond to its mission. Thereafter, developments in his ecclesiology are either based upon, or in accordance with, his burgeoning understanding of the fundamental nature of the Church as incarnational and sacramental.

EVANGELICALISM (1816-24)

The ideas which shaped John Henry Newman's ecclesiology during his Evangelical period began with his conversion in 1816 and waned with his emergent conviction concerning the importance of the visible dimension of the Church in late 1824. The influence of his Evangelicalism upon his ecclesiology comes to light in view in consideration of his conversion, Bishop Beveridge's devotional work, *Private Thoughts*, and Newman's own his essays and sermons. While pinpointing the start of a period in one's life can be difficult, John Henry Newman's recollections of his Evangelical beginnings are precise:

> When I was fifteen (in the autumn of 1816) a great change of thought took place in me. I fell under the influences of a definite Creed, and received into my intellect impressions of dogma, which, through God's mercy, have never been effaced or obscured. Above and beyond the conversations and sermons of the excellent man, long dead, the Rev. Walter Mayers, of Pembroke College, Oxford, who was the human means of this beginning of divine faith in me, was the effect of the books which he put into my hands, all of the school of Calvin.[1]

Previously, the young man's religious formation reflected the "plainness", "power" and "poverty" of his parents' Protestantism which centred largely around the reading of sacred scripture and the Book of Common Prayer (Bouyer, 1960, 2-3). This religiosity was later tempered by a youthful skepticism which Newman recalled in his reading of Paine, Hume and, perhaps, Voltaire. That Newman's childhood and early youth excluded noteworthy Evangelical influences is evident from his parents' dislike of enthusiasm[2] and his account of the history of his religious opinions in the *Apologia*.

Newman's religious conversion at the age of fifteen was occasioned by the collapse of his father's bank and a severe illness which caused him to remain at Ealing school over the summer of 1816. This created an opportunity for "a time of reflection" when, he observed, "the influences of Mr. Mayers" had "room to act upon me." His own estimations are clear that he considered the event to lack the hallmarks of a classical Evangelical conversion. Eleven years after the fact, Newman recorded that in "the matter in question (conversion) my feelings were not *violent*, but a returning to, a renewing of, principles, under the power of the Holy Spirit which I had *already* felt, and in a measure acted on, when young." Some fifty years later, Newman reiterated that he "was sensible that he had ever been wanting in those special experiences, which, like the grip of a secret hand or other prescribed signs of a secret society, are the sure token of a member" and insisted that the "emotional and feverish devotion and tumultuous experiences" of

---

1 Apo. 17. See "Early Journals: Book II," AW 181.

2 AW 175, 176, 179.

Evangelicalism "had never been congenial to him." Newman declined to characterize his conversion as Evangelical because it did not conform to experiences about which he had read. Speaking of himself in this regard, he reflected, "in truth, much as he owed to the evangelical teachings, so it was, he never had been a genuine evangelical ... " Elsewhere he remarked, "I speak of (the process of) conversion with great diffidence, being obliged to adopt the language of books. For my own feelings, as far as I remember, were so different from any account I have ever read, that I dare not go by what *may* be an individual case."[3]

Despite Newman's hesitancy to speak unguardedly of himself or his conversion as "evangelical", several factors suggest that this adjective is not wholly misplaced. After his first conversion, Newman displayed a heightened sensitivity to God's presence in his ordinary affairs. His mentor, Walter Mayers, had counselled him to discern the role of Providence in all things and this solidified Newman's tendency to see the hand of God in the course of his daily round. This tendency was reflected in his later correlation of the "three great illnesses" of his life with significant spiritual events: his initial conversion (1816); his abandonment of "an incipient liberalism" (1827); and his role in the Oxford Movement (1833). While Newman did not experience many typical signs of Evangelical conversion, his sureness about the reality of the spiritual watershed itself approximated the confidence with which many Evangelicals viewed their own conversions. The event bestowed upon Newman, the convert, certitude about fundamental spiritual realities, "as cutting at the root of doubt, providing a chain between God and the soul. (i.e. with every link complete) I know I am right. How do you know it? I know I know. How? I know I know & & ." His effort at personal reformation manifested itself in a scrupulosity which he was later to criticize as the distinguishing feature of Evangelical piety. This habit of constantly glancing inward suggested, not so much an unhealthy introspection, as a youthful concern for holiness which extended to the margins of his existence. This concern for holiness reflected the maxims which Newman adopted as a guide for life from the Evangelical writer, Thomas Scott: "'Holiness rather than peace'" and "'Growth the only evidence of life.'"[4] Further evidence of the Evangelical quality of Newman's post-conversion life is furnished by

3 AW 150, 172, 80, 82, 79 & 166.

4 See LD i 32-4; AW 268; 150; 156-7, 158-9 & 171; LD vi 128-33; Apo. 19.

his involvement with *The British and Foreign Bible Society*, his interest in biblical prophecy and missionary work, his scripturally-rooted spirituality, as well as the emphasis he placed upon Gospel doctrines like the atonement. These facts support his own recollection that he "had been converted by it (the Evangelical teaching) to a spiritual life, and so far his experience bore witness to its truth ...."[5]

While Newman spoke respectfully of the privilege of membership in the established Church and its ordinances which introduced one to God's covenant, he considered those who participated primarily at this level to be nominal Christians. His accent was upon the hidden communion of real Christians whose unmediated entrance into the divine life was accessed by their conscious decision of faith in the atoning sacrifice of Jesus Christ. The 'true Church' existed within the fold of the visible institution whose prime purpose was the provision of a setting within which the individual drama of salvation could be enacted. Unsurprisingly, then, the shape of Newman's idea of the Church in this period was determined by the position he adopted in favour of justification by faith alone and against baptismal regeneration. In this regard, he was like his fellow co-religionists for whom "the denial of the doctrine of baptismal regeneration had come to be the touchstone of Evangelical orthodoxy" (Sheridan 1967, 23).

The first notable instance of Newman broaching the subject of baptismal regeneration occurred in his letter of thanks to Walter Mayers for the gift of *Private Thoughts*, a devotional work by William Beveridge, the Bishop of St. Asaph (1637-1708), an influential divine of Calvinist leanings and High-Church liturgical sensibilities who has been associated with many groups within the Church of England.[6] Indeed, Evangelicals and Tractarians appealed against each other to Beveridge whose ecclesiology was later associated with the Non-Juroring tradition by the Tractarian Newman (Newsome 1966, 176, 179; Elliot-Binns 1953, 129).

Fifty-seven years later, Newman claimed that *Private Thoughts* "exercised a powerful influence" over his devotional life without ever affecting "the formation of my doctrinal opinions". "This work is not mentioned in my *Apologia*, because I am speaking there of the formation of my doctrinal opinions, and I do not think they were influenced by

5 AW 79.

6 LD i 30-1.

it. I had fully and eagerly taken up Calvinism into my religion before it came into my hands. But no book was more dear to me, or exercised a more powerful influence over my devotion and habitual thoughts. In my private memoranda I even wrote in its style."[7] This 1874 recollection about the effect of *Private Thoughts* upon his early doctrinal formation is consistent with the tenor of his 1828 remarks to his sister, Harriett, "As I have already mentioned to you, [*Private Thoughts*] is not always scriptural in its expositions of doctrine; but its pure, and instructive piety outweighs all incidental indiscretions which occur in some of its statements of scriptural truth."[8] This consistency of view supports Newman's belief that he had always understood *Private Thoughts* to be important in his life of piety but uninfluential in the formation of doctrinal positions. However, was his understanding about that belief accurate?

A survey of Newman's reading during his time of conversion affirms the accuracy of his understanding. Newman read Thomas Scott's *Force of Truth* and Phillip Doddridge's *Rise and Progress of Religion in the Soul* on the recommendation of Mayers. He also read William Law's *Serious Call to a Devout and Holy Life*, a work of Romaine's (probably, *The Life, Walk and Triumph of Faith*), Joseph Milner's *Church History*, William Jones' *Catholic Doctrine of the Trinity* and Thomas Newton's *Dissertations on the Prophecies*.[9] Of these authors, Scott and Romaine represented the strongest Calvinist influence upon Newman in his acceptance of doctrines such as the predestination to eternal happiness (final perseverance), the separation of humanity into the regenerate and the reprobate, the total depravity of man's fallen nature, the imputation of Christ's merits to cover sins and the serious necessity of constant repentance. Romaine is specifically mentioned by Newman in connection with the doctrine of final perseverance as being among the first of the authors read; his contact with the more moderate Calvinism transmitted by Scott's works is described by him as dating from his time as a young man.[10] Thus there appears to be little doubt that these authors inculcated in Newman the doctrinal tenets of Calvinist-Evangelicalism prior to his reading of *Private Thoughts*.

7 See AW 154, Apo. 479, n.17.25; LD i 30 n.1.

8 LD ii 87; n.2 of same.

9 Komonchak, 22; AW 79 & Apo. 17-20.

10 Apo. 17, 18 & 479-84, n.17.25-20.7.

The question of how Newman was affected by *Private Thoughts*, however, does not end with his assertion that this work added nothing novel to his Calvinist-Evangelical theology. Circumstantial evidence raises the possibility that *Private Thoughts* tacitly influenced Newman's views on baptismal regeneration, even though positive evidence demonstrates that his 1817 correspondence with Mayers over *Private Thoughts* re-confirmed him in the anti-sacramentalism he held until 1824. That Newman was not converted to Beveridge's moderate sacramentalism in 1817 does not preclude the possibility that *Private Thoughts* remained a latent force until another time of questioning (such as 1824) caused it to exercise an influence.

The circumstantial case begins with suspicion about the categorical nature of Newman's assertion that *Private Thoughts* greatly affected his devotional life but did not influence his formation of doctrine. This statement is out of step with his subtle accounts of human knowing in which the possibility of tacit knowing is given greater due. The practice of piety and the acquisition of doctrine are, after all, inter-related processes which occur within the same feeling, thinking person, not in hermetically-sealed laboratories.[11] Moreover, *Private Thoughts* remained a valued work during the entirety of Newman's Anglican life as his recommendation of it to Harriett in 1828, his gift of it to a servant in 1832, and his circulation of it amongst parishioners and friends as part of his Littlemore 'lending library' in 1840 demonstrate.[12] Thus the place of *Private Thoughts* in Newman's life cannot be relegated to his 'pre-sacramental period' (1816-24) and safely distanced from his embrace of baptismal regeneration or the growth of his sacramental idea of the Church.

The difficulty in dismissing Beveridge as a source of doctrinal influence is manifold. It is raised by the possibility that before 1817 Newman knew of and might have read Bishop Beveridge on baptismal regeneration. In any case, he included Beveridge in a list of authorities to be consulted in his paper, "Scott v. Mant. on Baptism." In 1817, he was both attracted to and perplexed by Beveridge's moderate sacramentalism in a passage from *Private Thoughts* which mentions original sin and baptism. Newman's 1829 hunting in the "old divines for Pusey" on the office of the Holy Spirit revealed his knowledge of Beveridge's

11 US xiii 251-77, GA 222-47 & DA 294.

12 LD i 87; Moz. i 249 & LD vii 250 n.1.

sermons on the topic (Komonchack 1976, 69 n. 62-3).[13] Likewise, in 1836, Newman cited Beveridge in *Tract 76* as part of his illustration of those Anglican divines who held to baptismal regeneration. The passage from Bishop Beveridge, excerpted from sermon xxxv, *On admission into the Church by Baptism,* is one of the lengthiest among the Anglican divines cited. Most suggestive, however, is Newman's rare mention of Beveridge in an 1824 sermon on original sin in the context of his atypical, qualified endorsement of baptismal regeneration.[14]

At the beginning of this 1824 sermon, "on the corruption of human nature," Newman spoke of baptism in sacramental language the likes of which he did not fully adopt until 1826:

> This corruption [original sin] is not the same in those who are baptised and regenerate and those who are not. In those who are not baptised it incurs, as our Church says [Article IX of 39 Articles] God's wrath and damnation – **in those who are [baptised]**, it is still sinful though qualified and (as it were) pleaded for (and (if I may use the word) **sanctified by the principle of grace, by the presence of God the Holy Ghost in the heart** –) it is still sinful. It is still powerful – it is still, alas, in too many cases victorious over the grace of God. It is still such that any one of us may recognize it in himself; recognize it as surely as if he were not regenerate, though (thank God) not so miserably, not so hopelessly – but its presence, though subdued and modified, every one who looks will discern himself. In making some remarks then on this corruption which I propose now to do I shall not be careful to separate between cases of the unregenerate, and the regenerate, and the lapsed – they differ as much as heaven from earth in their character and state – but I am going to speak of that which is one and all of them, though triumphantly and sinful in one, and kept under, pardoned, subdued in the case of the other.

Possibly Newman's atypical characterization of baptism and his less Calvinistic language concerning the 'regenerate' and 'unregenerate' in this passage reflects the modifying influence of John Bird Sumner's *Apostolical Preaching,* which he had read in mid-Aug. 1824 to great effect. There is evidence that Sumner was on his mind as he wrote the sermon.[15] Several pages later, Newman cited Beveridge[16] to illustrate the depth of the damage caused by original sin. There is, admittedly, no 'bridge' establishing a direct connection between Newman's

13 Birmingham Archives, A.9.1; LD ii 169.

14 TFT iii 76: 37-40; JHNS i 302-14.

15 JHNS i 303-4, emphasis added; reference to Sumner at 309.

16 JHNS i 310.

atypical use of sacramental language and his reference to Beveridge. Juxtaposition does not establish causality. Yet, in view of the fact that Newman rarely cited Beveridge in his sermons, his inclusion in this sermon suggests something more than serendipity. Indeed, the reference to Beveridge in the 1824 sermon is from *Private Thoughts*,[17] the same work which caused Newman to wonder about the sacramental efficacy of baptism in 1817. Furthermore, the very passage in *Private Thoughts* which raised the issue about baptismal regeneration in 1817 occurred in a context which, like the 1824 sermon, dealt with original sin. "When children are baptized ... as the guilt of their original sins is washed away ... so that it will never be imputed to them, unless it break forth afterwards into actual transgressions; so they receive also the Spirit of God to prevent all such eruptions ... But that the seeds of grace which were then sown in their hearts, may not be lost, or stifled, but grow up to perfection, great care must be taken that they may be taught, so soon as they are capable to discern between good and evil ...."[18] Finally, the 1824 citation from Beveridge on original sin needs to be considered in the context of Newman's tendency to think about original sin-baptism-infants-salvation as a related cluster.[19] The fact that only one element in the cluster [original sin] directly surfaced in the 1824 Beveridge citation does not conclusively disassociate it from other elements of the cluster [such as baptismal regeneration] as they appeared earlier in the sermon.

Taken together these separate items are suggestive. While these facts do not prove that Beveridge definitely influenced Newman's doctrinal formation, they make a categorical denial that such an influence occurred difficult to accept.

There is one definite way in which *Private Thoughts* influenced Newman's doctrinal formation before 1824. His reading of this book prompted him to ask for and subsequently accept Walter Mayer's interpretation of a problematic passage concerning Beveridge's position on baptismal regeneration. This acceptance confirmed Newman in his Evangelical ecclesiology at a time of perplexity. For the next seven

---

17 *Private Thoughts*, Part I, Article IV, 58.

18 Cited in LD i 30 n.2.

19 For his Anglican view that unbaptized infants merit divine wrath see JHNS i 302 n.1; see Article IX, *The Thirty-Nine Articles of the Church of England*, 357. For his more restrained Catholic view, see LD xxviii 250, 252.

years Newman showed no significant signs of raising this question again and his ecclesiology during that period reflected the idea of a Church set forth by Mayers in his letter of response.

Newman's letter to Mayers[20] was written against the background of controversy in Oxford that year caused by Daniel Wilson, who had "preached before the university a candid sermon on regeneration" – later published as *The Doctrine of Regeneration practically considered: A Sermon* (1817) – which vigorously defended the Evangelical position that baptism was merely a figure of the justifying and saving gift of Christ's atonement. A measure of the depth of this disruption was the refusal of Dr. Thomas Lee, president of Trinity, to print Wilson's sermon at the university press (Reynolds 1975, 89-90). Wilson's sermon was a response to the doctrine of baptismal regeneration which had been advocated by Richard Mant in *Appeal to the Gospel* (1812). Newman's alignment of the views of Beveridge and Mant on baptismal regeneration demonstrated his effort to work through the implications of his newly embraced Evangelicalism. Beveridge's position on the sacrament of baptism as a privileged, though not an exclusive or automatic, instrument of regeneration both attracted and confused Newman: it attracted him insofar as it shed light upon the possibility of salvation for infants; it confused him insofar as it did not neatly square with Evangelical doctrine. A disturbing question arose – might baptism actually convey grace in spite of Evangelical contentions to the contrary?

> There is one passage in the first chapter of the second part, that I do not quite comprehend; it is on the Sacrament of Baptism. I had, before I read it, debated with myself how it could be that baptized infants, dying in their infancy, could be saved, unless the Spirit of God was given them; which seems to contradict the opinion that baptism is not accompanied by the Holy Ghost. Bishop Beveridge's opinion seems to be that the seeds of grace are sown in Baptism, although they often do not spring up; that Baptism is the mean whereby we receive the Holy Spirit, although not the only mean; that infants, when baptized receive the inward and spiritual grace without the requisite repentance and faith. If this be his opinion, the sermon Mr. Milman preached on grace last year was exactly consonant with his sentiments, and he agrees with Dr. Mant.[21]

20 LD i 30-1.

21 LD i 30.

Mayers' response opposed any reading of Beveridge which undercut the Evangelical position that sacraments teach about, but do not convey, salvation. He stressed that baptism indicated the need for regeneration and was an external badge of the entrance into God's covenant much like the sign of circumcision was in the Jewish covenant; similarly, the Lord's Supper signified the saving sacrifice of Calvary in the new covenant; in itself, however, these symbolic rites neither objectively justified nor imparted grace "'*opus operatum*'" as taught by Rome. It was the subjective disposition of the believer approaching God through trust in Christ's atonement which led to a once-and-for-all conversion, the doorway to regeneration. The difficulty of the human mind in grasping the meaning of being born anew in Christ through faith in his saving crucifixion made baptism and the Lord's Supper useful exercises in order to understand these spiritual realities, but they were not vehicles of salvation. That baptism and the Lord's Supper conferred emblematic entrance into God's covenant, not a true renovation of human nature was an Evangelical commonplace. As Mayers stated in his opening and closing remarks, the regenerate Christian was marked by his display of holiness, not by his participation in any sacramental rite.

The ecclesiological analogue, which corresponded to Mayers' understanding of regeneration, was that of a visible Church whose rites and ordinances inform one about that salvation which is realized through an individual expression of faith in the saving death of the crucified Lord. Consequently, Mayers assigns an introductory rather than efficacious role to the visible Church in the historical mediation of grace. "'There is, indeed, a baptismal regeneration, whereby all, that are made partakers of that ordinance, are, according to the scripture language, sanctified, renewed, and made the children of God, and brought within the bond of the covenant: but all this is but after an external manner, as being, in this ordinance, entered members of the visible church. – This external regeneration by water entitles none to eternal life; but as the Spirit moves upon the face of the waters and doth sometimes secretly convey quickening virtue through them.'"[22] Baptism conferred a mere "external regeneration" which simply made one a "member of the visible church". This visible Church was capable of representing salvation mimetically through its rites, but it was incapable of commu-

22 Mayers cites from Bishop Hopkins, *Works* ii 416, 428; see LD i 33.

nicating the gracious reality so figured. In fact, the realm in which salvation is savoured is the invisible Church, the mystical Body of Christ, where the person is born of the Spirit, not by means of the rites enacted by flesh and blood – a point which Mayers makes to Newman by selectively citing Beveridge. "*When a man believes in Christ* the second Adam and so is made a member of his body he is quickened and animated by his Spirit which being the principle of a new life in him he thereby becomes a new creature and therefore is properly said to be born again not of blood nor of the will of the flesh nor of the will of man but God" (Sheridan 1967, 41-2).

Mayers' ecclesiology, therefore, was based upon the Evangelical doctrine that one's proclamation of faith in the atonement is the means of appropriating the work of the cross which bestows entrance into the mystical body of Christ. While Newman's letters do not record any further exchange with Mayers on the issue of baptismal regeneration, his journal entry in the autumn of 1820 makes explicit his agreement with the position advanced by Mayers in 1817:

> I will not *directly* assert that regeneration is not the usual attendant on baptism, if you object to it; but I will put it in this way, and if that tenet does not follow as a consequence, I will not press it. I say then, that it is *absolutely necessary* for *every* one to undergo a *total change* in his heart and affections, *before* he can enter into the kingdom of heaven. This you will agree with me is a scriptural doctrine; the question *then* is, Do we, when children receive this change in baptism? For myself I can answer that I did not; and that, when God afterwards in His mercy created me anew, no one can say it was only *reforming*. I know and am sure that before I was blind, but now I see.[23]

Mayers addressed his former student from their shared position on justification by faith alone and their consequent opposition to baptismal regeneration. In this endeavour, he also assumed Newman's concurrence with the ecclesiological corollary of his sort of Evangelical *solafideism*; the visible and invisible dimensions of the Church were disentangled from, rather than intrinsically related to, each other. Mayers was correct on both accounts. Although Newman's thought on justification underwent subtle refinement from 1822 onwards, this doctrine underpinned his opposition to baptismal regeneration and a spiritualized idea of the Church through the year 1824. Ironically, his attraction to the moderately sacramental *Private Thoughts* resulted in the crucial exchange with Mayers which confirmed him in an

23 AW 165.

anti-sacramental ecclesiology. The lasting ecclesiological effect of this confirmation is visible in a series of essays and sermons written by Newman between 1821-24.

The 1821 synthesis of Newman's Evangelical thought occurs in a nearly ninety page document, "A Collection of Scripture passages setting forth in due order of succession the doctrines of Christianity," which addresses questions of doctrine, describes his conversion and rejects baptismal regeneration in favour of God's gift of justification through faith. The document testifies that John Newman upheld a belief in salvation through the atoning sacrifice of Christ which leads to the bestowal of the gift of the Holy Spirit who infuses life into the soul by various means, but primarily through the reading of sacred scripture. In this document, Newman contends that justification occurs upon the believer's utterance of faith and sanctification follows justification as a separate and subsequent process, which occurs through the gift of the Spirit, who acts by diverse instruments, but particularly by the word of God. There is no mention of a sacramental-ecclesial context in which either the act of justification by faith or the process of sanctification occurs. At most, the visible Church acquaints one with the word of God and its sacraments condition, but do not mediate, one's encounter with God.[24]

Two other essays, also written in 1821, strengthen this judgment that Newman's position on justification entails an anti-sacramental ecclesiology: "Comment on Phil. 2:12-13" and "The nature of holiness." In the first essay, he again affirms his position on justification by faith alone, distinguishes this instantaneous act from the gradual process of regeneration, and identifies reading the Word of God, prayer, fasting, and receiving Holy Communion as normal means of sanctification so long as any efficaciousness is assigned directly to God's action upon the human will rather than to these instruments *in se*. In the second essay, Newman harmonizes the Evangelical doctrine of conversion with the institution of baptism, particularly infant baptism. He expresses his awareness of the holiness of God, the purity of his law and the constancy of human sinfulness, even after justification. The justified sinner requires a process of regeneration by which he is made holy and prepared for his heavenly destiny. That faith justifies is enough for Newman; he does not inquire into how or why this

24 Birmingham Archives, A-9-1.

occurs. Justification is instantaneous; it accords one the privileges of an adopted child of God. Grace is understood, morally, as healing the wounds of sin, as stabilizing and strengthening man's ability to act virtuously, not as an elevation or divinization of human nature. "Baptism" is regarded as "... no more than an 'accidental adjunct' of regeneration; it is not even a common accompaniment, much less an indispensable condition." While the sacrament conveys privileges in the visible Church, Newman's judgment is that it does not impart that grace without which no one can see God (Sheridan 1967, 44-8, 53, 59 n.2, 58-62).[25]

Predictably, Newman's early sermons at St. Clement's in 1824 are not explicitly ecclesiological but evangelical. Several sermons, however, advance positions consonant with his earlier views which have similar ecclesiological implications: (i) the individual believer's faith in the atoning blood of Jesus is the cause of justification; (ii) the spiritual, invisible Church comprises the true communion of the saints; (iii) therefore, the visible Church does not sacramentally mediate divine life. Four sermons in particular illustrate this position, "On reading Scripture", "The Parable of the Talents", "Parable of the ten virgins" and "The Atonement of Christ".

Newman's description of the reading of sacred scripture as the preferential instrument by which the Holy Spirit renews sinners recurs in his 1824 sermon, "On reading Scripture". His account of the work of the Holy Spirit, reading scripture and sanctification depicts a private, unmediated activity between the believer and God. Though a minister committed to preaching the word of God, Newman omits any reference to the community at prayer as a Spirit-filled medium through which God in his word is encountered:

> Lastly, above all we must read in the spirit of *prayer* – prayer for divine grace – Without the grace of God, we cannot read with faith, or humility, or simplicity, or profitable self-application – Our hearts are of themselves full of prejudice, unbelief, worldliness, pride, selfishness – and it is the Holy Ghost alone [sic] can make them anew. – Now the word is His principal instrument in this renewal – if then there be a time when we should especially pray for His healing grace, it is when we are taking the medicine. – We must ask God for two things – first to prepare our minds and secondly to bless us while reading – on the one hand to open our hearts to receive the seed, and on the other to prosper the seed that it may work

25 Birmingham Archives, A-9-1.

> effectually within us. – There is no rule so important as this – it may be said to include all others. – The Bible is meant to give light and holiness – to instruct and improve – to convince and persuade – to edify head and heart – to afford principles and motives ... The Holy Spirit is the only author of regeneration and holiness – As therefore you would enter into life, lift up your hearts to God when you begin to read, and while reading, and when you finish – .

The emphasis upon encountering God through the prayerful, private reading of sacred scripture confirms the view of Newman's idea of the 'true' Church as a 'spiritualized' Church. The Holy Spirit is clearly presented as working through the individual's private reading of sacred scripture rather than through any sacramental agency of the Church.[26]

In "Parable of the Talents," Newman is on the verge of recognizing a mediatorial dimension to the Church when he states that "the Church of Christ is a visible public body and that the religion of Christ is social." At no point, however, does he exploit the latent theological implication that the visible-social constitution of the Church suggests that the historical mediation of Christ's merits requires a corporal-societal mean. On the contrary, he stresses individual responsibility before God and concludes the sermon by emphasizing personal faith in Christ's "love, His power, His meritorious death and the influences of His Spirit ...." Omission of this phrase later suggests that his original Evangelical conclusion did not sit well with his sacramental ecclesiology when he re-preached the sermon on 11 Sept. 1831 and 12 July 1835.[27] The presence of language capable of supporting a sacramental ecclesiology indicates that Newman's idea of the Church, while outwardly Evangelical, was on the verge of transition.

Newman's allegorical interpretation of the "Parable of the ten virgins" also witnesses to his spiritualized idea of the Church. This is apparent in his description of religion as an internal affair of the heart which is not, at the end of the day, connected to external manifestations of good works as reasonable signs of a life of faith. The priority of the internal over the external, as well as the dependence of the latter upon the former, is clear in his description of "good works [as] the *flame*" which feeds upon "the oil of faith and holiness" or the "preparation of heart". Thus, the wise virgins represent the few in the church who keep their vows to God and the foolish virgins represent those

26 JHNS ii 3-10; citation, 7.

27 JHNS ii 324-41; citations, 238 & 240-1n.8.

who, for sundry reasons, do not remain steadfast. The righteous fuel, the "oil of faith and holiness", burns in the lamps of the wise virgins until the bridegroom arrives, while the lamps of the foolish virgins have long since been exhausted because of a dissipation of oil or a failure in "the preparation of heart".[28]

Until this point, Newman's interpretation of the parable seems to integrate the internal and external aspects of religion. His hermeneutic requires that the flame of good works live upon the oil of a prepared heart; it does not burn unless sustained by internal, invisible faith and holiness. This internal-external integration also seems operative in his depiction of "the Christian" as someone who possesses "the oil of faith and love, of holiness and comfort, shed on his heart by the inspiration of God's Holy Spirit", someone who might be "a good neighbour, a kind father, a faithful servant, an obedient subject, an useful member of society, nay a blessing to his country and mankind". Nonetheless, Newman's interpretation of the parable comes undone precisely at the point where he evaluates the situation of those who are visibly, although perhaps only ordinarily, faithful to their daily round. He so suspects that these persons lack sufficient oil to keep their lamps aflame that he places them among the foolish virgins.

> And thus we have arrived <come> at a *third* <another> class of individuals <men> who think, if they do but lead decent, quiet lives, go constantly to church and receive the sacrament at *certain* times, that *then* indeed they are in a state of salvation. And doubtless such individuals <persons> are in a much <far> better state than open swearers, and drunkards – But, still we may be active and useful men, and withal regular attendants on divine worship <service> and holy communion 'from our youth up,' and yet 'lack one thing' – and that one thing (in the words of the parable is *oil*. – we may have no oil in our lamps – religion may not be seated *in our hearts* ...[29]

While one may readily agree with Newman's Gospel judgment that external observances are not irrefutable signs of a total commitment of one's life to Christ, his suspicion of this class of persons rests heavily upon his presumption that their good works are suspect, that the flame of their lives does not really attest to the presence of enough oil in their lamps. He offers no reason for placing them among the foolish virgins aside from his doubt about the evidence furnished by the ordinary goodness of their lives. This contrasts sharply with his Catholic

28 JHNS ii 225.

29 JHNS ii 225.

mind about an assessment of the faithful performance of the ordinary duties of life relevant to holiness. "It is the saying of holy men that, if we wish to be perfect, we have nothing more to do than to perform the ordinary duties of the day well. A short road to perfection – short, not because easy, but because pertinent and intelligible. There are no short ways to perfection, but there are sure ones .... He, then, is perfect who does the work of the day perfectly, and we need not go beyond this to seek for perfection. You need not go out of the *round* of the day."[30]

Newman's distrust of external works derives from his Evangelical desire to preserve God's gift of grace (through justification by faith) from any diminution by an attribution of merit to something external to that gift. Works and gestures may speak about Christ but they neither sacramentally mediate His presence, nor even signify that presence with assurance.[31] The ecclesiological analogue to this doctrinal position is the tidy division of Christians into the separate camps of the wise virgins who participate in the invisible Church and the foolish virgins who participate merely in the visible Church. While the division of believers into the wise and foolish virgins is a Gospel truth, Newman's ready classification of members of the Church according to a religion of the heart is the manifestation of his Evangelical theology which disconnects rather than integrates the internal-external dimensions of Christianity.

The emphasis upon the private, unmediated, quality of justification by faith alone which inserts one into the invisible Body of Christ that characterizes the "Parable of the ten virgins" is also present in "The Atonement of Christ." Here Newman recounts how the human desire for expiation of guilt and sin in the Jewish covenant resulted both in animal sacrifices which "shadowed out and typified" the perfect sacrifice offered by the crucifixion of the Son of God and prophecies which prefigured "that one equal to God should come on earth to redeem mankind – and that he should redeem them by becoming a sin offering for them, and suffering in their room." He reflects upon how the glorious gift of the atonement, effected by the death of the only Son of God, both speaks to "the malignity of sin" and assures one of forgiveness by bridging "that wide and fearful chasm <gulf> which sin had caused between man and His Maker". Newman, then, concludes

30 PVD 328.

31 See JHNS ii 221, 222.

with a recommendation of how one is to access this treasury of God's mercy.

> – **Believe** on the Lord Jesus, and thou shalt be saved <Acts 16> – ... **Your** case is not peculiar – thousands now rejoicing in glory have been in **your** situation – they feared there was no help for them – but in time were led to **trust** in Christ and so had peace. Only have **faith** in Him, and **you** are of that little flock to whom it is the Father's good pleasure to give the Kingdom. Only have **faith**, and **you** are the child of God in Christ Jesus <Gal 3> being sanctified by the power of the Holy Ghost – Only have **faith** and **you** are the one of those for whom the Saviour interceded when he said, 'neither pray I for these alone, but for them also which shall *believe* on Me through their word' <John 17> – He prayed for **you** – He had *you* in His mind that last sad trying night – He thought of **you** just before His passion – And now He is equally gracious, and more powerful – He has overcome sin and death <Hos 12 1 Cor 15 [Hos 13:14 cited in 1 Cor. 15:55]>.[32]

In this passage, Newman implores his hearers to make a concrete act of faith in Christ so that they – like past Christians – may secure divine peace, entrance into God's Kingdom, adoption as His children and sanctification by His Spirit. In order to appropriate this treasury of God's mercy, Newman urges his congregants to proclaim their faith in the atonement. The fact that this passage – indeed, that the entire sermon – is bereft of any mention of the visible Church having some place in the mediation of this salvation is telling. Again, salvation comes through the naked declaration of faith by the believer. Moreover, the believer's proclamation of faith is presented by Newman as a relatively unmediated act, an utterance made by someone standing alone in the presence of God which, only subsequently, involves a communal dimension, that is, an entrance into the spiritual fellowship depicted as a "little flock". Thus the subsequent and related gift of the Spirit is also depicted as a consequence of this private event of faith involving the individual and God. This is exemplified by his decision to omit reference to an attribution of sacred privileges to the visible Church by virtue of Christ's prayer for those will believe in Him throughout history on the strength of the apostolic witness cited in John 17:20 – "'neither pray I for these alone, but for them also which shall *believe* on Me through their word.'" But, in this sermon, Newman's doctrine of *solafideism* has committed him to a spiritualized interpretation of the

32 JHNS i 315-21, 316, 319, 320, 321 (bolded emphasis added).

event of faith that occurs without reference to the historical mediation of the apostolic witness by the visible Church.

Newman's ecclesiology between 1817-24 presents the reception of the gift of the Holy Spirit as an event which follows directly upon the believer's private proclamation of faith in the Crucified One and is therefore, relatively unmediated and disconnected from the visible, corporate Church and its sacraments. Preaching and reading the word of God dispose the heart to receive salvation and, therefore, assume priority over sacraments which represent but do not communicate that salvation. Those who accept the Crucified One as their Saviour form the true, invisible Church and are known to be regenerate by their saintly lives. Conversely, those who merely participate in the external activities of the Church form the outer husk of the Body of Christ, a visible society which is distinguishable from the mystical kernel and which will be separated from it on the winnowing day of judgment.

DISCOVERY OF THE VISIBLE CHURCH (1824-26)

Newman's rejection of an efficacious role for the external dimension of the Church in the historical mediation of the mystery of salvation began to give way by the end of 1824. While his movement towards acceptance of a visible ecclesiology was an uneven process, his full embrace of baptismal regeneration in 1826 indicated that a fundamental ecclesiological shift had occurred. Although Newman's sacramental understanding of the Church developed dramatically after this time – especially under patristic influences from1828 onwards – acceptance of baptismal regeneration inaugurated his sacramental ecclesiology.

The Evangelical minster who took the service for the first time at St. Clement's on 4 July 1824 attributed sacramental power neither to ordination nor baptism. Rather Newman perceived his office as a pastorate of souls involving self-dedication to God.

"Can I forget, – I never can forget, – the day when in my youth I first bound myself to the ministry of God in that old church of St. Frideswide, the patroness of Oxford? nor how I wept most abundant, and most sweet tears, when I thought what I then had become; though I looked on ordination as no sacramental rite, nor even to baptism ascribed any supernatural virtue?"[33] His parochial schedule witnesses

33 Diff. i 81.

to his conscientious exercise of this office by frequent visitation of his charge, especially, the sick. Newman provided consolation to the desolate, called strays to conversion, read sacred scripture aloud to the sick, prepared parishioners for death and, sometimes, left pious tracts and Evangelical books the likes of Philip Doddridge's *Rise and Progress of Religion in the Soul* (1745) in his wake. Close contact with his parishioners was, at length, to convince Newman that his Calvinist form of Evangelical theology did not square with his daily experience of God's grace in the lives of ordinary folk who were neither wholly regenerate nor reprobate.[34]

The more immediate impulse to change came, however, from another direction. With the absence of other Oriel fellows during the Long Vacation of 1824, Newman came under the influence of senior fellow, Edward Hawkins, whose criticism of the ecclesiology in his first written sermon signalled the onset of its demise:

> His first Sermon, on 'Man goeth forth to his work and to his labour until evening', implied in its tone a denial of baptismal regeneration; and Mr. Hawkins, to whom he showed it, came down upon it at once upon this score. The sermon divided the Christian world into two classes, the one all darkness, the other all light, whereas said Mr. Hawkins, it is impossible for us in fact to draw such a line of demarcation across any body of men, large or small, because [difference in] religious and moral excellence is a matter of degree. Men are not either saints or sinners; but they are not so good as they should be, and better than they might be, – more or less converted to God, as it may happen. Preachers should follow the example of St. Paul; *he* did not divide his brethren into two, the converted and unconverted, but he addressed them all as 'in Christ', 'sanctified in Him,' as having had 'the Holy Ghost in their hearts;' and this, while he was rebuking them for the irregularities and scandals which had occurred among them. Criticism such as this, which of course he did not deliver once for all, but as occasions offered, and which, when Newman dissented, he maintained and enforced, had a great though a gradual effect upon the latter, when carefully studied in the work from which it was derived, and which Hawkins gave him; this was Sumner's 'Apostolical Preaching'. This book was successful in the event beyond any thing [sic] else, in routing out evangelical doctrines from Mr. Newman's Creed.[35]

Hawkin's criticism unsettled Newman's confidence in the type of Evangelicalism he had adopted and left him praying, "May I get light,

34 See LD i 196, 199, 181, 188, 189,191 & AW 206, 79.

35 AW 77.

as I proceed."[36] His concern over the issue of baptismal regeneration – with all its ecclesiological implications – was palpable during August. In mid-August, Hawkins gave him John Bird Sumner's, *Apostolical Preaching*, the immediate reading of which not only intensified his angst, but precipitated change.[37] Sumner's *Apostolical Preaching* (1815) charted a course between the Charybdis of Calvinism and the Scylla of sacramental realism. He rejected the latter's "fancied security and dependence upon baptismal privileges" and castigated the former saying: "It is indeed a sufficient confutation of the doctrine of special grace that it absolutely nullifies the sacrament of baptism. It reduces it to an empty rite, an external mark of admission into the visible church, attended with no real grace, and therefore conveying no real benefit, nor advancing a person one step towards salvation." He advanced a middle position in which emphasis upon the personal ratification of one's baptism was modified by esteem for the vows of believing sponsors pledged upon an infant's behalf (Sumner 1839, 2, 176, 256-7, 254-5). Sumner's Evangelical ecclesiology endowed with purpose and treated positively some aspects of the visible dimension of the Church. As a consequence, he warned against divisions caused in a congregation by "the indiscriminate severity with which those are sometimes arraigned, who do not answer to the preacher's idea of regenerate, nor any more frequent and specious error than the notion that enough cannot be given to Christ or to grace, unless the corruption of human nature be expressed in the strongest terms."[38] In place of the exclusivist Calvinist categorization of regenerate or reprobate, Sumner distinguished inclusively amongst all those who "have personally ratified the covenant of their baptism" by his admittance of degrees of progress "in the road which Christ has set before them." Difference amongst believers is "accidental" while their "resemblance ... is essential, that all alike profess 'one Lord, one faith, one baptism [*Eph* 4:5]'" (Sumner 1839, 139, 132-3, 22).

Newman assimilated these ecclesiological aspects of Sumner's work. In spring and summer journal entries of 1825, he described baptismal regeneration in an anti-Calvinistic manner as an instrument which brings persons "into the kingdom of grace, where the Spirit will

36 AW 201.

37 AW 201-2; LD i 185 n.2; Apo. 21.

38 LD i 203 n.2.

constantly meet them."[39] Although he did not quite ascribe sacramental efficacy to the baptismal rite, he endowed it with the meaningful function of facilitating access to the Spirit. His acceptance of this positive role for baptism is attributable to Sumner as well as his parochial experience of "many, who in most important points were inconsistent, but whom yet I could not say were altogether without grace."[40] Newman thus modified his positions so as to view more favourably both the rite of baptism in particular and the visible Church in general: baptism could serve, at least, as an ante-chamber to the reception of the Holy Spirit, and the visible Church considered, *in toto*, was more related to than separate from the invisible realm of Christ's grace.

Growing confidence in the visible Church as a means of grace, and particular interest in baptism as an ecclesial instrument, also surfaced in his sermons. In his 1825 April sermon, "Personal Interest in Christ," baptism remained for Newman a "sign and a pledge" rather than a means of justification. Nevertheless, he favourably depicted baptism as "the outward rite" by which "we are made one with the body of Christ" and promoted the practice of infant baptism as well as the role of sponsors in securing "the blessings of baptism" until the age of reason. The communal responsibility to bring the child to the font, to pledge on behalf of the child and, subsequently, to form the child in a manner conducive to a personal declaration of faith was, likewise, underscored by Newman in his May sermon, "John and Christ's Baptism Compared"(Komonchack 1976, 155, 156).

By late spring of 1825, under the twin influences of parochial experience and *Sumner's Apostolical Preaching*, Newman had moved away from a Calvinistic Evangelicalism which denigrated baptism and discriminated between the 'really regenerated' in the true, invisible Church and the 'nominally baptized' Christians in the visible Church. Nascent confidence in a visible ecclesiology had not yet fully led him to ascribe an objective sacramental character to either baptism or the Church. He continued to insist upon a subjective change of heart leading to a personal declaration of faith in the atonement as the means of regeneration.

Five months later, however, Newman's autumn and winter sermons reveal his "fullest statement of his church-principles ... ever attempted

39 AW 206.

40 AW 206.

[to date]". This is particularly so with two sermons, "Our Admittance into the Church our Title to the Holy Spirit" and "The Use of the Visible Church." These two sermons constituted part of a wider series of Sunday afternoon sermons delivered between 11 September 1825 and 22 January 1826 on topics such as law, church and education (Komonchack 1976, 209, 208-16).[41]

In Nov. 1825, Newman preached the sermon, "Our Admittance into the Church our Title to the Holy Spirit," based upon *Hebrews* 8: 8-10, which includes this citation of *Jeremiah* 31:33 indicated by the bold type. "The days are coming, says the Lord, when I will make a new covenant with the house of Israel and the house of Judah. It will not be like the covenant I made with their fathers the day I took them by the hand to lead them forth from the land of Egypt; for they broke my covenant and I had to show myself their master, says the Lord. **But this is the covenant which I will make with the house of Israel after those days, says the Lord. I will place my law within them, and write it upon their hearts; I will be their God, and they shall be my people.**" This scripture reference situates the activity of God's Spirit within a covenantal context. By choice of title, Newman indicated his understanding that this mention of God's activity in *Jeremiah* foretold the action of the Holy Spirit in the Church of the new covenant. The explicit aim of the sermon is to discover "*how* we become entitled to this great gift of Christ, viz., the promise of the Holy Ghost, so that, in the words of the text, He may be to us a God and we to Him a people." Although the sermon directs its efforts towards the individual's entitlement, its ecclesiological significance lies in the fact that the gift of the Spirit is now viewed as being given first and foremostly to the Church as a whole and distributed by means of baptism. As Newman plainly states, "the Holy Spirit is given *generally* to all the visible church, i.e., to all who are called Christians and therefore the covenant spoken of in the text and the promise of grace is upon all who are by baptism admitted into the Christian body." The Calvinist divide between reprobate and regenerate is removed by the common baptismal "beginning" which admits of a difference of "degree" rather than of kind, in regards to reception of the "gift" of "the Holy Ghost" in Christ's kingdom. "Yet all these characters the weak, the inconsistent, the partially ignorant, even the proud, the Apostle acknowledges as

41 Birmingham Archives B.3.4, General Theology.

under grace – not, indeed, as if grace had done its perfect work with them, or all had a good hope of salvation; but because there had been a *beginning*, because they were within Christ's kingdom and thus there was a hope of them, because they had in some degree partaken of His illumination, because a gift had been committed to them, even that of the Holy Ghost." Further on, he speaks very directly of the sacrament of baptism in dynamic, efficacious terms:

> [T]he ordinary and prescribed way of becoming entitled to His Spirit is by admittance into His church – and as all are invited into it, the call is as free and general as if no such ordinance of baptism were prescribed. – All are invited to Christ through baptism as the *means* of His grace. – But that sacrament gives more than a title to grace – it is the means of justification, of adoption, it conveys pardon, it gives us a right to rejoice in God, to look upon Him as our reconciled Father in Christ, in the words of the text, to have Him for our God and to be His people, to consult Him in all our sufferings, to hold communion with Him all our life long, and to console ourselves with the hope of seeing Him in His heavenly kingdom.

In spite of his apparently strong endorsement of sacramental realism, Newman's inconsistent identification of what is meant by 'regeneration' and his lack of clarity as to whether ontological priority is assigned to sacramental change instead of change of heart mean that his position on the nature of the change effected by baptism is still fluid. Prior to speaking robustly about baptism's efficacy, Newman temporizes the sacramental position by his denial that "all Christians, however, wickedly they live, are approved by God and regenerate in spirit." Although his point – that regeneration marks a spiritual beginning rather than an end – is absolutely reconcilable with sacramental theology, other aspects of Newman's phraseology cast doubt upon his affirmation of the universal, objective efficacy of the sacrament. His language about the need for a "birth" beyond baptism and insistence that "the only evidence of grace is a change of heart" signifies the remnants of his Calvinist ecclesiology and softens the sacramental realism he enunciates so vigorously. Still the sermon gives substantive evidence of a growing confidence in the visible Church. Newman attributes the promise of the Spirit to the visible Church and not, as previously, to an individual in a relatively unmediated encounter. Moreover, he endows baptism with a qualified role in the mediation of grace. Although this role falls short of a genuine sacramental efficacy, it indicates his developing thought that baptism somehow serves as more than simply an ante-chamber to the kingdom of the Spirit (Komonchack 1976, 210-13).[42]

Increased appreciation of the external dimension of the Christian Church is manifested by Newman in his early December sermon, "On The Use of the Visible Church." In its presentation of the broad, educative task of the entire Church to preserve, transmit and clarify the Gospel through its life this sermon contrasts starkly with his earlier characterization of one's appropriation of salvation by a relatively unmediated act of faith. The sermon underscores the importance of the personal study of sacred scripture which is "the storehouse of all truth and spiritual knowledge" but balances and places it in context by insisting upon the important principle learned from Edward Hawkins:[43] "the Bible is not our first *teacher* in the truth – the church is to teach us – we are to learn from the ministers of God, from the public prayers and services from the creeds, and still earlier from our parents, from our friends, from our guardians, masters and governors – We are taught indeed *from* the Bible, but not at first *by* the Bible ... The church is to explain and teach the truth, and the inspired word is to prove it"(Komonchack 1976, 221).[44] Newman recalled in the *Apologia* that he had heard Hawkins' sermon as an undergraduate (23 May 1818), although comprehension of its meaning only occurred later "when I read it and studied it as his gift" at which time "it made a most serious impression upon me."[45] Hawkin's belief that the Church was God's designated interpreter of the revealed truth in sacred scripture became a mainstay of Newman's theology.[46] "On the Use of the Visible Church" is, perhaps, the earliest of his writing in which appears this pivotal position concerning the interpretation of the Bible in the Church. This might account for his speaking of this sermon as one of the first to demonstrate his acquisition of High Church principles.[47] This High Church position still left Newman a fair distance from his eventual 1845 understanding of the Church as the interpreter of

42 Sermon 118: 3, 3-4, 8-9, 14-15, 11, & 18.

43 See Edward Hawkins, *A Dissertation upon the Use and Importance of Unauthoritative Tradition* (1818).

44 Sermon 121:7-8.

45 Apo. 22.

46 See VM i 309-12; Apo. 219-20, Dev 1845: 124-9, Dev 1878: 88-9; TP ii 97 #4.

47 See a post-1859 note on the cover of sermon 157, "On the One Catholic and Apostolic Church,"referring to sermon 121 (Komonchak 1976, 216 n.110).

sacred scripture and the judge of what constituted the content and boundaries of revelation. This eventual extension emerged in his discussion of development of doctrine and was a consequence of his conclusion that a "revelation is not given if there be no authority to decide what it is that is given."[48]

The sermon also shows that Newman's intellectual conversion was a slow process in which long-held beliefs were only displaced gradually. The tenuousness of this intellectual development is demonstrated by the sermon's inclusion of a passage marked by language more typical of Newman's Calvinist ecclesiology: "the visible church is made up of those who profess faith, the invisible of all who have it" and he says that "the invisible church is unseen, because the baptism of the Spirit is secret and without our knowing when and where it descends and because Christ our Governor is unseen also."[49] Newman still had not yet successfully integrated his emergent views on the visible Church and the sacrament of baptism into his core ecclesiology.

In the new year of 1826, the position of tutor at Oriel College became available and Newman decided to fill the vacancy. By early April, he had left his vice-principalship at St. Alban Hall, preached his last sermon as curate of St. Clement's and begun his new work at Oriel. His birthday entry for his journal reports that during "the last year I have become more intimate with Whately. I think him an excellent man. I quite love him."[50] In the *Apologia*, Newman recalled how Whately "emphatically, opened my mind, and taught me to think and to use my reason." The senior fellow's influence was directly felt in matters ecclesiological:

> What he did form in point of religious opinion, was, first, to teach me the existence of the Church, as a substantive body or corporation; next to fix in me those anti-Erastian views of Church polity, which were one of the most prominent features of the Tractarian movement .... In the year 1826, in the course of a walk, he said much to me about a work then just published, called 'Letters on the Church by an Episcopalian'. He said it would make my blood boil. It was certainly a most powerful composition ... It was ascribed at once to Whately; I gave eager expression to the contrary opinion; but I found the belief of Oxford in the affirmative to be too strong for me;

48 Dev. 1845: 126-7; Dev. 1878: 89.

49 Sermon 121:1-3 cited in Komonchak, 217.

50 AW 208-9.

rightly or wrongly I yielded to the general voice; and I never heard, then or since, of any disclaimer of authorship on the part of Dr. Whately.[51]

Newman always assumed Whately's authorship of *Letters on the Church by an Episcopalian* although the author never confirmed it personally.[52] The title, *Letters on the Church by an Episcopalian*, derived from Whately's use of a series of letters written by a Scotch Episcopalian to a member of the Church of England as the framework upon which to hang his argument. In the text, Whately argued that the New Covenant Church, unlike the Old Covenant Israelite theocracy, existed as a community separate from the state equipped with its own laws, customs, authority, governors and purpose. His denouncement of encroachment by either Church or State on each other's territory in his defence of their respective independence and co-existence gave his work an unmistakeably anti-Erastian character. In short, Whately upheld the apostolic authority to govern and teach, expressly attacked the State-Church alliance as envisioned by Bishop William Warburton of Gloucester (1759-79) in *The Alliance between Church and State* (1736), and he advocated dis-establishment.

The influence of *Letters of the Church* upon Newman was almost immediate. Whately's work is among those mentioned as "new publications" in a February 1826 issue of *The Christian Observer* (Komonchack 1976, 237 n.1). A sign that Newman had quickly read and appropriated its argumentation is furnished by his pencil notation **"vid. Letters on the Church"** on the left hand page of his March 1826 sermon "on the temporal sanctions of the Jewish Law." Vincent Blehl's editorial suggestion that this is a "later notation" which refers "to Newman's 'Letters to the Editor of the *Record* on Church Reform" (1833) is untenable.[53] Newman's declaration of the influence of *Letters of the Church* upon his developing ecclesiological thought,[54] the proximity of his March notation to the February publication date of *Letters on the Church* and his paraphrasing of *Letters on the Church* in his March and April sermons furnish conclusive proof that his notation is a direct reference to Whately's work.

51 Apo. 24-5.

52 See Diff. i 203-5, DA 360-1; LD xxiv 219 n.1.

53 JHNS ii 422 n.6.

54 Apo. 24.

The influence of Whately's *Letters* is especially evident in two sermons: "[O]n the temporal sanctions of Jewish law" and "General Observations on the Whole Subject. Conclusion". Each sermon draws upon the important distinction made in *Letters on the Church* between the Church/State relationship in the Old and New Covenants in order to paraphrase its argument that the future punishment of offenses committed in the New Covenant can hardly be spoken of as less severe than present punishment of offenses in the Old Covenant.[55] The immediate effect of Whately's *Letters on the Church by an Episcopalian* was to galvanize Newman's emergent belief in the purposefulness and necessity of the visible Church in God's design. Later the same work would support the Tractarian Newman's anti-Erastianism. While Whately's work was still fresh in his mind, Newman returned to the topic of infant baptism during one of his last turns as a curate of St. Clements. Conclusions reached in this important sermon, "on infant baptism,"[56] repeat those expounded five months earlier in "Our Admittance into the Church, our Title to the Holy Spirit" as regards the necessity of infant baptism, the indispensability of adult sponsors and religious education in the ecclesial task of pre-disposing children towards making future acts of faith, use of vigorous, quasi-efficacious language about baptism "conveying" salvation and granting membership in the Kingdom and remnants of an Evangelical language of the heart.[57] There is, however, a crucial difference. While the former sermon stopped short of endorsing baptism as imparting regeneration, the latter, though reluctant to use the term 'regeneration', made absolute the connection between salvation, the sanctifying presence of the Holy Spirit and baptism.

Reluctance to identify regeneration with baptism had previously devolved from Newman's denigration of the visible Church and its ordinances, in service of the theological principle of justification by faith alone, which made the gift of the Holy Spirit consequent upon one's acceptance of Christ crucified as Lord and Saviour. The reason for Newman's reluctance is now quite different. He identifies baptism with justification, but hesitates to equate the totality of regeneration

55 According to Komonchak (1976, 259 n.4, 261), Newman paraphrases Whately's *Letters on the Church* (15-16) at JHNS ii 416-23, especially, 422-3 & sermon 150: 16-17.

56 JHNS i 172-8.

57 JHNS i 177, 175, 177.

wholly with the act of baptism since he sees regeneration as a process of sanctification which truly begins at baptism ending only in heaven (Sheridan 1967, 119-120). The indispensable role of baptism as a sacrament of the visible Church in service of the related missions of the Son and Spirit in the economy of salvation is very clear in his exegetical remarks.

> I take a remarkable text from St. Peter, 'baptism (he says) doth ... *save* us' <1 Peter 3> – What is meant by the word *'save'* us in this passage? for it is a very strong word – Now the usual meaning of 'to save' in the New Testament is put in a state of salvation, a state of acceptance with God, of holiness, of peace – It sometimes indeed means a state of *glory* in heaven, sometimes a state of *sanctification* on earth – but this is no difference of meaning – for to be glorified is merely the fulfilment and completion of being sanctified – they are parts of the same course, the same divine life which is begun below, continued in perfection above – both may be called [[as]] *state of salvation*. Thus we are said at one time to be saved *through Christ* <Rom 5> – as being put into this state of salvation for His sake and through His merits – at another, saved *by grace* <Eph 2> – i.e. put into this state without merit of *our own* – again saved *through faith* <Eph 2> – because by faith we stand, continue in this state – again saved [[*in*]] *hope* <Rom 8>, i.e. the present state of salvation is a state of hope not of enjoyment, our rest being future – lastly saved by the renewing of the Holy Ghost because the Spirit fits us to understand and enjoy salvation. In all these passages 'saved' has substantially the same meaning – When St. Peter says, 'baptism doth save us', – I do not see that he can mean otherwise than that baptism doth *bring* us into that state of salvation, and thus grace *caused* our salvation, Christ effected it, baptism conveys it, and the Spirit applies it, faith evidences it, and hope is the character of it.[58]

This remarkable passage so closely aligns the missions of the Son and Spirit in the Christian dispensation as to anticipate Newman's more explicit address of this relation in his *Lectures on Justification*. Hereafter, Newman can no longer be called an Evangelical for he understands baptism to be a sacrament of the visible Church which efficaciously "conveys" God's offer of salvation "effected" by the Son and "applie[d]" by the Holy Spirit. His idea of the sacramental Church has commenced.

58 JHNS i 174-5; see 1 *Pt* 3: 20-1.

THE SACRAMENTAL-INCARNATIONAL CHURCH (POST-1826)

By 1826 Newman recognized that the ecclesial mediation of redemption requires the constitution of the Church to correspond to its mission; therefore, post-1826 developments in Newman's ecclesiology are either based upon, or in accordance with, his burgeoning understanding of the fundamental constitution of the Church as sacramental and incarnational. Two questions arise at this point: what are the sources of Newman's sacramental perception of reality which precede and accompany this aspect of his ecclesiological growth? and, how does he theologically ground his idea of the sacramental Church in his understanding of the incarnation?

As a child, Newman possessed the prerequisite for developing a vivid sacramental awareness of the world – a lively imagination which sensed that reality was more than what met the eye. In the *Apologia*, he recounts the workings of his mind.

"I used to wish the Arabian Tales were true: my imagination ran on unknown influences, on magical powers, and talismans .... I thought life might be a dream, or I an Angel, and all this world a deception, my fellow-angels by a playful device concealing themselves from me, and deceiving me with the semblance of a material world."[59]

This childish solipsism was less a statement of disbelief in the material than an affirmation of belief in the immaterial. The memory suggests that Newman was pre-disposed to an interpretation of existence that went beyond that immediately established by the senses. In his twenties, he read two Anglican authors who transformed his affinity for a symbolic view of the world into a truly sacramental vision: Joseph Butler and John Keble.

Newman read *The Analogy of Religion*[60] by Oriel alumnus, Bishop Joseph Butler (1692-1752) around 1823. He characterized this encounter as "an era" in the maturation of his religious opinions. Although primarily a work of apologetics and moral philosophy, *The Analogy of Religion* presented the visible Church as a providential instrument both in the acquisition of natural virtue and in the supernatural work of the Trinity in "the recovery and salvation of mankind".

59 Apo. 15-16.

60 Joseph Butler, *The Analogy of Religion* (1736).

Butler's approach helped Newman to realize that the nexus of the visible and invisible was their common, divine authorship. He was impressed by "the very idea of an analogy between the separate works of God [which] leads to the conclusion that the system which is of less importance is economically or sacramentally connected with the more momentous system."[61] As the constitution or scheme of the natural world displayed God's providence through a series of related, though mysterious events, in which the fulfilment of one event opened the way for another, in which one event was the means to another, so to with the constitution and scheme of the supernatural world.

Newman relied upon this analogous reasoning in an 1825 sermon, "probable reasons for the partial extension of Christianity," to explain the timing and partiality of the Christian dispensation:

> Now in considering why the Christian revelation was so tardily made and why it is even now so little known to the world at large, we must recollect in the first place that there are *numberless* particulars in the present disposition of things which we cannot account for; and therefore we have no reason to be surprised should *this* arrangement for God's providence prove to be one of them. – There are many contrivances in nature, many productions, many animals ... of which we do not see the use – Indeed we know *little* of the counsels of God ... Is it wonderful then that in the workmanship of the infinite Architect of nature, there should be very many things which short-sighted creatures, as we are cannot comprehend?

Elsewhere, in the same sermon, he commented:

> [T]he gradual revelation of the gospel affords us a more striking proof of what the Apostle calls (πολυποὶκιλος) the *manifold* wisdom of God <Eph.3> who in diverse manners carried on His work from age to age in the Jewish church making preparations for the introduction of the gospel, providing the means, predicting the event, strengthening the evidence, till in the fullness of time Christ appeared. – This gradual revelation is analogous to the growth of living things in the natural world. God might create animals and herbs in an instant – But He has provided that the tree should rise slowly and spread from a slender twig or a small seed, watered by the dew and cherished by the sun – Is there not more to admire in these contrivances than if by the operation of His almighty word all things were at once perfect and at their full growth? – The case is similar as regards the revelation of the gospel ... Had God introduced the gospel suddenly, His work would have been as the lightening flash – we should not have discerned whence it came or wither it went – In condescension then to our

61 Apo. 22, *Analogy* 130-4; Apo. 21.

weakness, He has wrought slowly and gradually, and that we might trace the movements of the divine hand.[62]

Similar use of Butlerian sacramental logic is also found in Newman's 1825 explanation of a miracle as "a deviation from the subordinate [natural] for the sake of the superior [supernatural] system ... For we must view the system of Providence as a whole; which is not more imperfect because of the mutual action of its parts, than a machine, the separate wheels of which effect each other's movements."[63] Three years later, in his sermon, "On the Christian scheme of mediation as connected with the natural and Jewish systems," he again used Butlerian logic to show the similarity of mediation in the orders of nature and grace:

> Today I wish to point out to your notice that this mediatorial plan of salvation revealed to us in Scripture, is quite parallel to the methods which providence has adopted in imparting His blessings both in the ordinary course of this world's affairs – and in His extraordinary dealings with the patriarchs and the Jewish people. – that, in blessing us spiritually through means of His Son He has chosen a mode of acting, not in itself new and unusual, and displayed for the first time in the Christian system, but one which He has made use of every where [sic] and in every age for the preservation and benefit of the human race.

Newman's distinct contribution, however, lay in his attribution of the principle of mediation directly to the agency of the pneumatic Church in respect of redemption:

> And since God ordinarily conducts the course of this world and brings about His purposes by the means or mediation of others, it is not surprising that this plan of mediation is discoverable in other parts of the Christian system ... the Christian Church itself is one most important mediator between God and the world – being intended to be the means of proclaiming and impressing truth on men's hearts and converting them from sin to holiness. – It receives the gifts of the Holy Spirit from God, and by the sacraments and ordinances, by prayers by preaching, by establishments for education, it conveys them to the world at large <And so priests>.[64]

Adaptation of Butlerian sacramental reasoning for an ecclesiological purpose remained part of Newman's theological method. Most noticeably, it buttressed Newman's 1845 argument in his *Essay on the*

62 JHNS ii 344, 346.

63 Mir. 17-18 referencing *Analogy* I iii, "On the Moral Government of God".

64 JHNS i 213 & 214.

Development of Christian Doctrine on behalf of the reasonableness of expecting developments of doctrine in revealed religion and an infallible interpreter of that revelation and its developments. Newman argued that, while the facts of revelation were singular and unrepeatable, the principle of preservation applied analogously to the orders of nature and grace. God, who had made provisions to preserve the natural order, could reasonably be expected to do the same in the supernatural order.[65] Thus the Butlerian version of *analogia entis* which had been pressed into service against deism in the eighteenth century underwrote Newman's nineteenth century *a priori* explanation of the necessity of an infallible ecclesial authority at the service of revealed religion.

The appearance of John Keble's *The Christian Year* in 1827 likewise made a lasting impression on Newman by deepening his appreciation of the sacramental capacity of creation. He recalled his indebtedness to this work with verve. "It is not necessary, and scarcely becoming, to praise a book which has already become one of the classics of the language ... Keble struck an original note and woke up in the hearts of thousands a new music, the music of a school, long unknown in England. Nor can I pretend to analyze, in my own instance, the effect of religious teaching so deep, so pure, so beautiful. I have never till now tried to do so."[66] Distinct both from contemporary pantheism which confused the orders of nature and grace, and subjectivism which reduced the truth and beauty of creation to personal experience, Keble's poetry stressed the objective character of nature which symbolically conveyed real meaning about its divine Author (Härdelin 1965, 61-5). This sacramental understanding of nature – set against the unveiling of soteriological themes in and through the rhythm of the liturgical calendar – further opened Newman to the capacity of nature to serve grace. He stated:

> I think I am not wrong in saying, that the two main intellectual truths which [*The Christian Year*] brought home to me, were the same two,[67] which I had learned from Butler, though recast in the creative mind of the my new master. The first of these was what may be called, in a large sense of the word, the Sacramental system; that is the doctrine that material

65 *Analogy* 135, 153, 154, 170-1 & 219 is cited in Dev. 1845: 50-1, 102, 110-11, 113-14, 122-24; Dev. 1878: 47-8, 64, 71-2, 74-5, 83-5.

66 Apo. 29.

67 Probability as a guide in religious life was the second "intellectual" truth.

phenomena are both types and the instruments of real things unseen – a doctrine, which embraces in its fullness, not only what Anglicans, as well as Catholics, believe about Sacraments properly so called; but also the article of 'the Communion of the Saints;' and likewise the Mysteries of the faith.

The stirring of Newman's sacramental imagination by Butler and Keble found fuller exercise in his encounter of the Alexandrian Fathers during his researching and writing of *Arians of the Fourth Century* between 1831-33. As he recalled in the *Apologia*:

> The broad philosophy of Clement and Origen carried me away; the philosophy, not the theological doctrine ... Some portions of their teaching, magnificent in themselves, came to my inward ears, as if the response to ideas, which, with little external to encourage them, I had cherished so long. These were based on the mystical or sacramental principle, and spoke of the various Economies or Dispensations of the Eternal. I understood these passages to mean that the exterior world, physical and historical, was but the manifestation to our senses of realities greater than itself. Nature was a parable: Scripture was an allegory: pagan literature, philosophy, and mythology, properly understood, were but a preparation for the Gospel .... Holy Church in her sacraments and her hierarchical appointments, will remain, even to the end of the world, after all but a symbol of those heavenly facts which fill eternity. Her mysteries are but the expressions in human language of truths to which the human mind is unequal. It is evident how much there was in all this in correspondence with the thoughts which had attracted me when I was young, and with the doctrine I have already associated with the Analogy and the Christian Year.[68]

Economy was a pliant term that Newman learned from the Alexandrian Fathers in order to specify the prudent reserve by which the presentation of truth is accommodated to the circumstance of the hearers. This principle of reserve, and its resultant method of economy, operates variously in all dimensions of the orders of nature and grace from the incremental process of children learning to read to the diverse dispensations by which God has condescended to reveal Himself to humanity (Selby 1971).[69] By virtue of this Alexandrian instruction, Newman understood "symbol" philosophically not only to refer to something else, but actually to participate in and make present that which is symbolized. Hence his comment, that "Holy Church in her sacraments and her hierarchical appointments ... [is] but a symbol of those heavenly facts which fill eternity", indicated that the Church

68 Apo. 29, 36-7.

69 See Ari. 64-88.

was so constituted as to mediate, not simply speak about, salvation. This philosophical understanding was manifested in sermons such as "The Communion of the Saints" where the visible-invisible structure of the Church was presented as the vessel of the Holy Spirit through which one is granted participation in divine life. "But seeing that the Holy Ghost is our life, so that to gain life we must approach Him, in mercy to us, His place of abode, the Church of the Living God, is not so utterly veiled from our eyes as He is; but He has given us certain outward signs, as tokens for knowing, and means for entering that living Shrine in which He dwells. He dwells in the hearts of His Saints, in that temple of living stones, on earth and in heaven, which is ever showing the glory of his kingdom ... He has given us something outward as a guide to something inward, something visible as a guide to what is spiritual."[70]

Contact with Butler, Keble, Origen, and Clement aided in the formation of Newman's inherent sacramental sensibility, that is, his understanding that the visible mediated and was at the service of the invisible because the Author of Nature was the Author of Grace. Under their influence, he came to view the mediation of the economy of salvation and, occasionally, even the role of the Church itself, according to this logic of the *analogia entis*. This is not to deny that Butler, Keble or the Alexandrians understood their own thought on sacramentality to be derived from the Word made flesh, but to affirm that this specific theological aspect of their work is not what attracted Newman: "The broad philosophy of Clement and Origen carried me away; the philosophy, not the theological doctrine ...."[71] While these philosophic-poetic sources imaginatively opened Newman's mind to the structure of reality, they did not directly furnish the theological ground of his understanding of the sacramental, mediatorial Church. This he specified as the Word made flesh.

That Newman theologically grounds his vision of the Church in his sacramental understanding of the Word made flesh is, by now, a commonplace in Newman studies. Scholars have extensively uncovered his understanding of the Church as a living communion, a sort of ecclesial extension of the incarnation across time and space (Ker 1993, 60-70; Dessain 1977, 99-121; Miller 1987, 130-41).

70 PS iv 172-3.

71 Apo. 36.

The clearest, extended case of Newman theologically grounding his ecclesiology in the fact of the incarnation occurs in his *Essay on Development*. There revelation of the God-man is presented as both perfectly exemplifying and unimaginably surpassing the *analogia entis*:

> Any how [sic], Analogy is in some sort violated by the fact of a revelation, and the question before us only relates to the extent of that violation .... I will hazard a distinction here between the facts of revelation and its principles; – the argument from Analogy[72] is more concerned with its principles than with its facts. The revealed facts are special and singular, from the nature of the case: but it is otherwise with the revealed principles; they are common to all the works of God: and if the Author of Nature be the Author of Grace, it may be expected that, while the two systems of facts are distinct and independent, the principles displayed in them will be the same, and form a connecting link between them. In this identity of principle lies the Analogy of Natural and Revealed Religion, in Butler's sense of the word. The doctrine of the Incarnation is a fact, and cannot be paralleled by anything in nature; the doctrine of Mediation is a principle, and is abundantly exemplified in its provisions.[73]

Elsewhere, Newman makes his derivation of the sacramental Church from the fact of the incarnation more explicit. In the first instance, he straightforwardly says the "Incarnation is "the antecedent of the doctrine of Mediation, and the archetype both of the Sacramental principle and of the merits of the Saints."[74] In the second instance, he describes the incarnation as "the announcement of a divine gift conveyed in a material and visible medium" which unites "heaven and earth" and "establishes in the very idea of Christianity the *sacramental* principle as its characteristic."[75] In each instance, Newman forcefully indicates that Christianity is an ecclesial reality which involves the mediation of grace by nature and that the source of this sacramentality is the incarnate Word. In each instance, Newman vigorously employs the *analogia fidei* to indicate that the constitution and principles derived from the incarnate Word equip the Church to bear and mediate the "divine gift" of redemption and revelation in human history. These passages make it abundantly clear that Newman's identification of the incarnation as the source of his idea of the sacramental Church cannot be underestimated.

---

72 Dev. 1845: 122 n.1;Dev. 1878: 84 n.2 cite *Analogy* II iii.

73 Dev. 1845: 122-3, Dev. 1878: 84-5.

74 Dev. 1845: 154; Dev. 1878: 93-4.

75 Dev. 1878: 325.

CHAPTER TWO

TRINITARIAN & INCARNATIONAL GRAMMAR

Proper appreciation of Newman's pneumatic ecclesiology requires a prior understanding of his view of the office of the Holy Spirit in the life of Christ. For his pneumatic ecclesiology is premised upon the sacramental analogy wherein the same Holy Spirit who operates in the life of the God-man indwells, sanctifies, divinizes and makes believers into the body of Christ. In turn, knowledge of his pneumatic christology presupposes an understanding of his view of the Trinity and the incarnation. Providing this knowledge is accomplished in three basic steps. Initially, Newman's view of the tri-unity of God is addressed with specific attention to his position on the unity, distinctness and complementarity of divine acts *ad intra* and *ad extra*. Next, his equation of the economy of redemption with the one, full, personal mystery of the God-man is articulated, since it is within this horizon that he makes his most sustained comments concerning the Spirit of Christ. Finally, the state of scholarship concerning Newman's pneumatic christology is reviewed and its received interpretation, in terms of the atoning Christ and justifying Spirit, is evaluated. These steps clear the way for future discussion of his pneumatic christology and his pneumatic ecclesiology.

TRINITARIAN GRAMMAR

As a way into Newman's trinitarian theology, it is helpful to consider his sermon, "The Mystery of the Holy Trinity."[1] In the sermon Newman

1 PS vi 24: 343-61. The sermon text is Matthew 28:19.

sets forth his perception of the unity of God, as constituted through the mutual relations of the Father, Son and Holy Spirit, in order to suggest how this trinitarian life is present in the economy of salvation with reference to Christ's apostolic injunction to teach and baptize all nations. By stressing that one's appropriation of the faith is as much a matter of worship as intellectual assent, affirming the *Filioque* and emphazising the oneness of God, he explicates the Christian "war-song of faith", the Athanasian Creed.[2] By stressing the trinitarian relations of origin, he reveals the influence of his Alexandrian mentors. From the first, however, Newman uncompromisingly insists upon the "great Truth that there is one God". "Thus we must ever commence in all our teaching concerning the Holy Trinity; we must not begin by saying that there are Three, and then afterwards go on to say that there is One, lest we give false notions of the nature of that One; but we must begin by laying down the great Truth that there is One God in a simple and strict sense, and then go on to speak of Three, which is the way in which the mystery was progressively revealed in Scripture."[3] Yet, he is equally insistent that the unity of God exists through the mutual relations of the divine persons, a doctrine that he approaches by way of the sacred names used in Christ's injunction to evangelize and baptize all nations.[4] "Yet when Christ would name the Name of God, He does but say, 'in the Name of the Father, and of the Son, and of the Holy Ghost' .... What can be meant by saying, in the Name, not of God, but of the Three? ... the Three Sacred Names introduced have a meaning relatively to each other ...."[5] He proceeds to insist that these distinct relations are of the essence of the Mystery itself.

> [S]o may we suppose that though God is a Spirit and One, yet He may be also a Trinity: not as if that Trinity were a name only, or stood for three manifestations, or qualities, or attributes, or relations, – **such mere ideas or conceptions** as we may come to form when contemplating God – ... the Eternal Three are worshipped by the Catholic Church as distinct, yet One; – the Most High God being wholly the Father, and wholly the Son, and wholly the Holy Ghost; yet the Three Persons being distinct from each other, not merely in name, or by human abstraction, but in very truth, as

2 PS vi 24: 353 (assent); PS vi 5: 64 & OS 186 (*Filioque*); PS vi 24: 348-52 (Divine Unity); PS vi 24: 353; GA 133 (Athanasian Creed)

3 PS vi 24: 349.

4 TT 149; see ST 1 q.40 a.2.

5 PS vi 24: 344-5.

truly as a fountain is distinct from the stream which flows from it, or the root of a tree from its branches.[6]

Now Newman's qualifying clause "such mere ideas or conceptions … " makes it transparent that his potentially confusing use of 'relation' here does not correspond to that of traditional trinitarian discourse, but is simply a synonym for a concept on the cognitional level of understanding as opposed to a trinitarian person on the ontological level of being. In his resolve to uphold the orthodox understanding of the mystery of God, Newman maintains this truth: that which makes the Father, Son, and Spirit one is precisely that which makes them three and, again, that which makes the Father, Son and Spirit three is precisely that which makes them one – Divine essence and divine personhood are coincident not opposite. Leaning upon the authority of Denis Pétau as "the most learned expositor of the doctrine of the Fathers", Newman judges tri-unity to mean, "It is a Three or Triad, Each of whom is intrinsically and everlastingly distinct from Each … yet Each is One and the Same individual Divine Essence."[7]

Years later, within the same carefully delineated understanding of the tri-unity of God,[8] Newman further elucidates aspects of the Divine Mystery in terms of the "great Catholic truth" of the *principatus* of the Father, a truth which he considers too important to be left by the wayside notwithstanding his cognizance of its "capability" for Sabellian or Arian "perversion". "Catholic theologians met this difficulty, both before and after the Nicene Council, by insisting on the unity of origin, which they taught as existing in the Divine Triad, the Son and Spirit having a communicated divinity from the Father, and a personal unity with Him; the Three Persons being internal to the Divine Essence …. It was for the same reason that the Father was called God absolutely, while the Second and Third Persons were designated by Their personal names of 'the Son,' or 'the Word' and 'the Holy Ghost;' viz. because they are to be regarded, not as separated from, but as inherent in the Father."[9]

---

6 PS vi 24: 352; emphasis added.

7 See Ath. ii 319 depending upon St. Gregory of Nazianzen, *Orations*, 40, 41; citation at Ath. ii 316 from Pétau, *de Trinitate* iii II 7.

8 TT 172.

9 TT 167, 168.

Newman acknowledges that this manner of speaking about the Son and Spirit's equality ascribes "a sort of subordination to the Son and the Spirit, which, scriptural though it was, became a handle to Semi-Arianism." Thus he warns against Bishop Bull's use of the term "subordination" because "however grammatically exact, in its effect it is misleading."[10] Nonetheless, Newman believes that there is a correct manner of referring to the subordination of the Son. This belief is signalled by his rare, enduring criticism of his beloved Athanasian Creed on the ground that its less scriptural phraseology does not articulate an orthodox understanding of subordination as well as the Nicene Creed.[11] Newman's own orthodox understanding of a "sort of subordination" is clarified by his stated preference for "St. Hilary's felicitous paradox, that 'The Father is greater without the Son being the lesser'" and his consequent suggestion, "instead of 'subordinatio Filii,' let us speak of the 'Principatus Patris.'"[12] Newman specifies that this 'greatness' of the Father consists in his dignity as the unoriginate Origin which in no way involves a diminution of the divinity of the Son and Spirit. The Son and Spirit are 'subordinate' then, only in the limited, comparative sense that by being 'the only-begotten' and 'the breathed forth', they are 'not first' in "priority and precedence in the order of our ideas" about the Godhead.

> In this enunciation of the August mystery [of the *principatus*] they [Catholic theologians] were supported by the usage of Scripture, and by the nature of the case; since the very notion of a Father carries with it a claim to priority and precedence in the order of our ideas, even when **in no other respect** he had any superiority over those on whom he has this claim. There is one God then, they would say, 'not only because the Three Persons are in one *usia*, or substance (though this reason is good too), but because the Second and Third stand to the First in the relation of derivation, and therefore are included in their Origin as soon as named; so that, in confessing One Father or Origin, we are not omitting, but including, those Persons whom the very name of One Father or Origin necessarily implies.'[13]

By advocating this "sort of subordination" – understood precisely as an expression of the doctrine of the *principatus* – Newman means

10 On the 'subordination of the Son' see JHNS i 329-43, esp. 329 n.1. Other references at TT 172, 172-4, 174.

11 See LD ii 185 & LD xxvi 37.

12 TT 174 citing St. Hilary, *de Trinitate* ix 56.

13 TT 169. Bolded emphasis is added.

no more than what William Hill wrote regarding the Cappadocian contribution to trinitarian theology. "The Cappadocians continue to teach, it is true, that the *Logos* and Spirit are God in virtue of their origin from the Father as the *fons divinitatis*. But this sort of thinking no longer presents itself as a residue of Monarchial Trinitarianism. Since Athanasius, it is acknowledged that Son and Spirit are divine not in virtue of a hierarchical order to the Father but by a numerical identity of essence (*ousia*)" (1992, 47; Strange 1981, 22).

While Newman's position is sound in terms of its orthodoxy, the same cannot be said of the methodology he employs in arriving at his conclusion. The manner in which he assembles the patristic witness in support of his reading of the doctrine of the *prinicipatus*, as "taught in the Church after the Nicene Council as well as before it", is open to question. The difficulty is that he does not sufficiently specify the content and/or context of the trinitarian witness of the ante-Nicene Fathers whom he cites, discriminate among their individual voices and differentiate, when necessary, among those elements in their collective witness which might be discordant with the fourth and fifth century Fathers whom he lists. Although he records his dependence upon reliable authorities,[14] in the coming to judgment there is no evidence that he uses these authorities to engage in this type of specification, discrimination and differentiation. Newman's harmonization of ante-Nicene and post-Nicene interpretations of the *principatus* does not represent the culmination of his historical investigation. In fact, he harmonizes in a manner which omits intervening methodological steps. Newman chooses to assess the authenticity of the earlier doctrine of the *principatus* in light of its later development[15] thereby concluding in an *a priori* manner that there is definite continuity on essentials without really establishing this continuity in an *a posteriori* manner (Lash 1976, 80-113).

Regardless of questions surrounding his historical method, it remains that Newman sees the Divine Mystery in light of the received doctrine of the *principatus* as worked out in the terms of a trinitarian theology of relations of origin. Consequently, he recognizes the oneness and threeness of the Divine Mystery in a way that gives utmost

---

14 Citation at TT 167; 172-76.

15 Newman proceeds this way in Dev. 1845: 152-3, 240-2, 269, 281, 316-17; Dev. 1878: 105-6, 245-7, 272-3, 284, 320-1.

play to the distinctness of the divine persons who constitute the unity of the Godhead especially through their mutual indwelling; that is, their coinherence or *circumincessio*. So important, in fact, is the doctrine of "Divine *Circumincessio*" to Newman's view of the Trinity that in his *Essay on Development* he characterizes it as "the most distinctive portion of Catholic doctrine" regarding this sacred subject.[16] Again, in his *Select Treatises on St. Athanasius*, he says, "[t]his doctrine is not the deepest part of the whole, but **it is the whole**, other statements being in fact this in other shapes. Each of the Three who speak to us from heaven is simply, and in the full sense of the word, God, yet there is but one God; this truth, as a statement, is enunciated most intelligibly when we say the Father, Son, and Holy Ghost, being one and the same Spirit and Being, are in each other ...."[17] A stronger statement of his view about the necessity of embracing the doctrine of *circumincessio* in order to enter fully into the meaning of the mystery of the Trinity is hard to conceive.

TRIUNE GOD IN HISTORY

Now Newman's insistence upon the triune nature of God *in se*, in the above sermon, is complemented elsewhere by the attention he devotes to the Trinity in creation and redemption.

> [A]lthough Scripture tells us not a little concerning those Divine Persons, as They are in Themselves, it tells us much more about Them, as They are to us, in those ministrative offices towards creation, towards the Universe and towards mankind, which from the first They have exercised in contrariety to our higher conceptions of Them. Nor without reason; for it is by means of Their voluntary graciousness that man primarily has any knowledge of Them at all; since, except for that *condescension*, to use St. Athanasius's word, man would not have existed, man would not have been redeemed or illuminated. It is reserved for the close of that series of Dispensations which has innovated upon Eternity, for God to manifest Himself as in Eternity He was and ever has been ... what He is in Himself; and, in particular as regards the Son and the Spirit, we know them mainly in Their economical aspect, as our Mediator and our Paraclete.[18]

Without diminution of its eternal nature, Newman understands the Trinity to be immersed in creation and history through the temporal

16 Dev. 1845: 16; Dev. 1878: 19.

17 Ath. ii 72; emphasis added.

18 TT 192-3.

missions of the "Son and Spirit" which he states "took place, not from the era of redemption merely, but, as I have remarked from the beginning of all things ...." The presence of the triune God in creation and history occurs through what Newman, in imitation of the Fathers, called "this synkatabasis, or economy of condescension".[19] Thinking through the implications of what is involved in this economy of condescension leads Newman to insist upon a continuity between the distinctness of each divine person in the inner life of the Trinity, and the proper role of that person in the economy of salvation. Accordingly, he argues that the eternal Word became flesh precisely because this mission was fitting to his nature as eternal Son in a way that it was not fitting to the Father *qua* Father or the Spirit *qua* Spirit.

> [O]ur Lord's Sonship is not only the guarantee to us of His Godhead, but also the antecedent of His incarnation. As the Son was God, so on the other hand was the Son suitably made man; it belonged to Him to have the Father's perfections, it became Him to assume a servant's form. We must beware of supposing that the Persons of the Ever-blessed and All-holy Trinity differ from each other only in this, that the Father is not the Son, and the Son is not the Father. They differ in this besides, that the Father *is* the Father, and the Son *is* the Son. While They are one in substance, Each has distinct characteristics which the Other has not. Surely those sacred Names have a meaning in them, and must not be passed lightly over.

The consistency of this important theological position in Newman's thought is underscored by its presence in this 1836 sermon, "Christ, the Son of God made Man and its re-presentation in one of his essays of 1872.[20]

The significance of Newman's correlation of the distinctness of divine persons *ad intra* with the 'fittingness' of their missions *ad extra* is illumined further by his conviction that the doctrine of *circumincessio* is, at some level, "the whole" of trinitarian doctrine.[21] In this light, his correlation affirms that the economic Trinity is the immanent Trinity without thereby reducing the immanent Trinity to the economic Trinity. Trinitarian acts *ad extra* are understood wholly to

19 TT 196 n.1 & TT 193. Newman likewise speaks specifically of the temporal mission of the Spirit as a condescension. See PS ii 12: 132; PS ii 19: 217-8 & SN 306. His archaic spelling of *Syncatabasis* has been modified to meet current usage and now reads as *synkatabasis*.

20 PS vi 5: 58 is cited by Newman at TT 185-6 to support use of the *principatus* despite its abuse by heretics.

21 Ath. ii 72.

be acts of the self-same God; that is, perichoretic acts which are coincidently one, relationally distinct and complementary. This insight corresponds to patristic, medieval (Ott 1974, 68-72; Augustine, *De Trinitate* v 14, 15 & Anslem, *De Processione Spiritus Sancti*, chpt. I) and conciliar teaching (Tanner i 1990, 230, 570, 571) according to which every *ad extra* act of the triune God engages the oneness of the Divine Nature, and respects the distinctness of the divine persons who constitute the trinitarian communion, so that oneness and distinctness are comprehended as complementary realities. Newman's awareness of the unity, distinctness and complementarity of trinitarian acts *ad extra*, relative to divine personhood *in se*, provides a means by which to clarify his pneumatic christology. One can analyze his understanding of the Holy Spirit in the life of Christ by referring to his view of the uniqueness of divine personhood and placing it over and against his view of the indivisible, distinct and complementary nature of the economic missions.

INCARNATIONAL GRAMMAR

Just as the exploration of Newman's pneumatic christology requires prior knowledge of his trinitarian grammar, so too, it demands knowledge of his view of the incarnation. For Newman invariably comments upon the office of the Holy Spirit relative to Christ in the context of his theology of the incarnate Word. To this end, his idea of the one, full, personal, mystery of the God-man is set against his opposition to reductionist tendencies within liberalism (Chadwick 1975, 21-47) and Evangelicalism to establish the horizon within which his pneumatic christology can be clarified.

Now Newman identifies the fullness of salvation with the one Word incarnate. In many sermons, he equates "the wonderful economy of grace" with the incarnation.[22] Likewise, in his *Essay on the Development of Christian Doctrine*, he speaks alternately of the incarnation as the "central aspect of Christianity" and "the central truth of the gospel" as well as firmly specifying the incarnation as the sacramental source of the Church.[23] Admittedly, he qualifies his equation in the 1878 edition by asserting that the approach is taken "for the convenience of

22 PS v 7: 87; see PS ii 3: 38-40 & PS vi 6: 79-80.

23 Dev. 1878: 36, Dev. 1878: 54; Dev. 1878: 324; Dev. 1845: 154-5, Dev. 1878: 324-6.

arrangement" and, in the 1845 edition, by refusing to describe the incarnation as the "leading idea" of Christianity.[24] These qualifications derive from his concern to safeguard the plentitude and transcendence of the Divine Mystery. Elsewhere he speaks of God's "illimitable being and existence" and, consequently, of his divine revelation as "independent and real, of depth unfathomable, and illimitable in its extent" and states that "There is some chance of our analyzing Nature, [but] none of our comprehending God." [25] In this respect, his approach approximates the apophaticism of the eastern Fathers who used antinomy in order to speak of the unspeakable (Dulles 1996, 1-9; Chirovsky 1988, 71-87; Hopko 1992, 153). Newman's solicitude for the Trinity's impenetrability is surpassed only by his sensitivity to the mystery of the Incarnate Word.

> In truth, it is a more overwhelming mystery even than that which is involved in the doctrine of the Trinity. I say, more overwhelming, not greater – for we cannot measure the more and the less in subjects utterly incomprehensible and divine; but with more in it to perplex and subdue our minds. When the mystery of the Trinity is set before us, we see indeed that it is quite beyond our reason; but, at the same time, it is no wonder that human language should be unable to convey, and human intellect to receive, truths relating to the incommunicable and infinite essence of Almighty God. But the mystery of the Incarnation relates, in part, to subjects more level with our reason; it lies not only in the manner how God and man is one in Christ, but in the very fact that so it is ... the mystery lies as much in what we think we know, as in what we do not know.[26]

Awe for the Sacred Mystery leads Newman to criticize both the liberal treatment of the God-man as a moral exemplar, with its resultant reduction of Christianity to a system of ethics, and the Evangelical treatment of the atonement as an instrument for conversion rather than a "sacred doctrine ... to be lived upon."[27] He thinks that each mishandles the precious gift of the incarnation by preferring its own narrowness to the fullness of the mystery of God become man.

Caution about the activity of reason in matters revelatory pervades Newman's life and emerges from his realization of the gulf between

---

24 Dev. 1878: 324; Dev. 1845: 34-5, citation 34; Dev. 1878: 35.

25 Ess. i 38, 41, 39.

26 PS iii 12: 156-7.

27 PS vi 7: 90; see Ess. i 30-101, Apo. 254-62, Campaign 393-400, KC 206, LD v 45.

the greatness of the Mystery approached and the smallness of those who come near. Although effusive in his recognition of "freedom of thought" as "one of our greatest natural gifts", Newman judges that its unfettered operation, especially in the realm of religion, inexorably leads to "suicidal excesses." Caution and reserve, however, does not mean silence. The mystery of the Word made flesh means that the divine has been sacramentally mediated by nature. As a result, there exists the grammar of sacramentality, the mysterious possibility of the finite bearing the infinite.[28] On this basis, Newman arrives at a balanced judgment about the constrained, yet real, capacity of cognition and language to grasp and express insights relating to God which coincides with his conviction about the inexhaustibility of the Divine Mystery. He assigns a positive role to reason in the understanding and accepting of revelation in terms of one's unavoidable assessment of testimony, calculation of probabilities and interpretation of meaning. However, he opposes the exaltation of reason into "the standard and measure of the doctrines revealed" for this mutilates religious truth, which then is "hewn and chiselled into an intelligible human system"; whereas, the mystery of revelation really "is like the dim view of a country seen in the twilight, with forms half extricated from the darkness, with broken lines, and isolated masses."[29]

Newman values all that reason offers in the navigation of life. Upon his elevation to cardinal and reception of the *biglietto* in 1878, he stated, "there is much in the liberalistic theory which is good and true; for example, not to say more, the precepts of justice, truthfulness, sobriety, self-command, benevolence ... and the natural laws of society."[30] He contends, however, that liberalism stumbles precisely in its attempt to make a set of abstract precepts the heuristic by which the incarnate Word is to be understood rather than reversing the procedure in order to understand how those precepts are perfectly fulfilled in Him. Almost fifty years earlier, he had addressed this issue by contrasting the impersonal principles of goodness presented by natural religion and the personal Divine Agent presented by revealed religion.

> The life of Christ brings together and concentrates truths concerning the chief good and the laws of our being, which wander idle and forlorn over

---

28 PS ii 3: 26, 28; Mix. 294; Apo. 220; Dev. 1878: 325, 85; Dev. 123; US xv 331-2.

29 Ess. i 31, 48, 42.

30 Campaign 398.

> the surface of the moral world, and often appear to diverge from each other. It collects the scattered rays of light, which, in the first days of creation, were poured over the whole face of nature ... Our Saviour has in Scripture all those abstract titles of moral excellence bestowed upon Him which philosophers have invented. He is the Word, the Light, the Life, the Truth, Wisdom, the Divine Glory. St. John announces in the text, 'The Life was manifested, and we *have seen* It' [*1 Jn* 1: 2].[31]

This text is important for understanding Newman because it embodies his recognition that the incarnate Christ embodies the realization of authentic humanity. This recognition underpins his life-long opposition to that more paltry humanism which collapses theology into anthropology, substitutes ethics for worship of the Living God, equates knowledge with virtue and separates virtue from Christian discipleship ending up in what he once derisively called, "The Religion of the Day":[32] alternatively, Newman proposes that human fulfilment lies not in the achievement of a set of abstract ideals, but in immersion into the deified humanity of Christ, so that one might meet him, feel his touch, hear his voice, feed upon his life, be restored by his embrace and prepared for life eternal.

> A thick black veil is spread between this world and the next. We mortal men range up and down it, to and fro, and see nothing. There is no access through it into the next world. In the Gospel this veil is not removed; it remains, but every now and then marvellous disclosures are made to us of what is behind it. At times we seem to catch a glance of a Form which we shall hereafter see face to face. We approach, and in spite of the darkness, our hands, or our head, or our brow, or our lips become, as it were, sensible of the contact of something more than earthly. We know not where we are, but we have been bathing in water, and a voice tells us that it is blood. Or we have a mark signed upon our foreheads, and it spake of Calvary. Or we recollect a hand laid upon our heads, and surely it had the print of nails in it, and resembled Him who with a touch gave sight to the blind, and raised the dead. Or we have been eating and drinking; and it was not a dream surely, that One fed us from His wounded side, and renewed our nature by the heavenly meat He gave. Thus in many ways He, who is to Judge us, prepares us to be judged, – He, who is to glorify us, prepares us to be glorified, that He may not take us unawares; but that when the voice of the Archangel sounds, and we are called to meet the Bridegroom, we may be ready.[33]

31 US ii 25-6.

32 PS i 24: 309-24; see Ess. i 57, 93, 95, PS iv 20: 295-306, DA 261-82.

33 PS v 10-11.

In the early decades of the 19th century, English Evangelicalism evinced the tendency of western Christianity to highlight a theology of cross at the expense of other aspects of the Divine Mystery. From the 11th century onwards most western thought concerning the economy of redemption was heavily influenced by the satisfaction theory of Anselm of Canterbury (1033-1109), as expressed in his principal work on the atonement, *Cur deus homo* (1097-98). This work rejected interpretations of Christ's death as a ransom from the devil, and shifted the lens through which redemption was seen, from the patristic view of the incarnation as the pathway to human divinization, to "an emphasis upon a supererogatory satisfaction for human sin" made by the vicarious death of Jesus. Anselm creatively expressed these insights in the civil and ecclesiastical categories of medieval jurisprudence (NDT 1987, 842; Meyendorff 1979, 32).

The Anselmic enterprise set the agenda such that a theology of the cross often overshadowed the mysteries of resurrection, ascension and pentecost in western thought until the mid-20th century (Davis, Kendall, O'Collins 2001, 7). Although sensitivity to fullness of the Divine Mystery, as revealed in Jesus Christ, was not unheard of in the annals of Anglicanism (Allchin 1980, 48-62), Anne Hunt suggests it was unusual in post-Anselmic western theology, atypical of 19th century, and even much of 20th century theology (1997). Thus Newman's recovery of a patristic view of the economy of grace, as disclosed in the entirety of the mystery of the incarnation, differed from that of many English contemporaries who focussed upon the atonement to the practical exclusion of other aspects of God's salvific action in Christ Jesus (Newsome 1964, 32-53).[34] He characteristically wrote vigorously about the oneness of the mystery of the incarnation. In his essay, "The Theology of the Seven Epistles of St. Ignatius," he underlined how Ignatius of Antioch (c.35-107) situated "life and salvation" squarely within the fullness of Christ's life decrying those divided the one mystery of crib, cross, empty tomb and descent of the dove:

> It would seem then to be certain, that Ignatius considers our life and salvation to lie, not in the Atonement by itself, but in the Incarnation; but neither in the Incarnation nor Atonement as past events, but, as present facts, in an existing mode, in which our Saviour comes to us; or, so to speak, more plainly, in our Saviour Himself, who is God in our flesh, and not only so,

34 See Mix. 346.

> but in flesh which has been offered upon the Cross in sacrifice, which has died and has risen. The being made man, the being crucified in atonement, the being raised again, are the three past events to which the Eternal Son has vouchsafed to become to us What He is, a Saviour; and those who omit the Resurrection in their view of the divine economy, are as really defective in faith as if they omitted the Crucifixion. On the Cross He paid the debt of the world, but as He could not have been crucified without first taking flesh, so again He could not, as it would seem, apply His atonement without first rising again. Accordingly, St. Ignatius speaks of our being saved and living not simply in the Atonement, but ... in the flesh and blood of the risen Lord, first sacrificed for us, then communicated to us.[35]

The passage makes clear that Newman associates the economy of salvation with the person of Christ, who – by virtue of the hypostatic union – is the sacrament of the Father *pro nobis*. Similarly, in his *Select Treatises of St. Athanasius* he writes, "S. Leo speaks of the whole of redemption, i.e. incarnation, atonement, regeneration, justification, &c., as one sacrament, not drawing the line distinctly between the several agents, elements, or stages in it, but considering it to lie in the intercommunion of Christ's person and ours." This citation contains characteristic features of Newman's neo-patristic christology: the atonement is viewed relative to the prior and subsequent events of the incarnation and Easter mysteries which indicates the indivisible, historical nature of salvation in Christ; the mission of the incarnate Word surpasses (not to say eclipses) the gift of forgiveness by opening up the possibility of deification; and, therefore, redemption entails the communication of an intimate, sacramental union with the Son of God eternally mediated by his divinized humanity.[36]

Newman's preaching on the incarnation transcends Evangelical strictures without diluting its faith-filled proclamation of Christ's atoning sacrifice. The extensive scope of his incarnational theology is further illustrated by his Scotist belief that the incarnation would have occurred even if the Fall had not happened and his correlative claim that Divine Love chose to redeem us by way of the cross when divine *dabar* alone would have sufficed.[37] He criticizes Evangelicals for diminishing Christ's "actual sojourn on earth, in His gestures, words,

---

35 Ess. i 247-8; see Jfc.174.

36 Ath. ii 190; see also, US ii 27-8, SD 61 & Jfc. 193-4 (person of Christ); Ath. ii 88-90, PS v 7: 93, PS ii 3: 32 n.2 (divinization), PS ii 13: 145, PS vi 5: 63-4 (redemption), PS i 13: 176 (sacramental union).

37 See Mix. 305, PS ii 3: 30, Ath ii 187-8, PVD 421.

and deeds" by an "irreverent and unreal way" of focussing on "vague statements about his love, His willingness to receive the sinner, His imparting repentance and spiritual aid".[38] Conversely, he safeguards the oneness of "His Person, work and will" because this recognizes that God has come "in the form and history of man". Contemplation of the atoning and sanctifying work of Christ separated out from his presence, "as manifested in the Gospels", only leads to a gloomy disposition instead of "lighting up the image of the Incarnate Son in our hearts".[39]

Appraisal of Newman's theology clearly demands that one attend closely to his equation of the economy of redemption with the one, full, personal mystery of the Word made flesh. Equally so, one must evaluate the extent to which he advances christomonism or a pneumatic christology.

NEWMAN'S PNEUMATIC CHRISTOLOGY

Newman's understanding of the office of the Holy Spirit in the life of Jesus Christ and, analogously, in the life of the Church has yet to be fully plumbed by scholars. To date, his pneumatic christology has been examined in isolation or relative to other concerns. Usually, the ecclesiological implications of these investigations have not been fully exploited. For example, Charles Stephen Dessain opened up many channels of inquiry by his work on Newman's appropriation of the Greek patristic doctrine of divinization (1962, 207-25; 269-88), Thomas Sheridan mapped the development in Newman's thought from his belief in justification by faith alone to justification as the office of the Spirit of Christ regenerating and sanctifying the believer through baptism (1967) and, Roderick Strange concentrated upon the Spirit insofar as this consideration clarified aspects of Newman's Alexandrian christology (1981). Similarly, Pierre Masson wrote about Newman's thought concerning the office of the Spirit in the life of Christ and the Church especially as regards the regenerate life of the baptized and the notes of the Church (1982); Michael Sharkey considered Newman's pneumatic christology as the source of the Church's sacramentality relative to the Easter mysteries (1976, 16-37); Gerald Dolan reflected upon Newman's understanding of the gift of the Spirit particularly

38 PS iii 10: 130-1.

39 PS ii 14: 155; PS iii 10: 131; PS iii 12: 170.

during his Tractarian years (1970, 77-130); Avery Dulles examined the ecumenical sources of Newman's pneumatology (1996, 1-9); and, Edward Jeremy Miller remarked upon Newman's pneumatology from the perspective of his ecclesiology (1996, 1-3). Notwithstanding the merit of these scholarly labours, Newman's view of the Holy Spirit in the life of Jesus Christ has neither been treated fully nor in its own right. This requires remedy because of the importance of pneumatic christology in the economy of salvation, its prominence in Newman's thought, and its extensive implications for his ecclesiology.

Scholars addressing Newman's view of the office of the Holy Spirit in the life of Christ have commonly acknowledged his equation of the economy of redemption with the one, full, personal mystery of the God-man in concert with his recovery of the Greek patristic doctrine of the indwelling of the Holy Spirit (Dessain 1977, 53-98; Strange 1981, 116-56; Masson 1982, 128; Blehl 1993, 81-100; Sharkey 1976, 16-37). The central theological position he advanced in "Righteousness the Fruit of our Lord's Resurrection," the ninth chapter of his *Lectures on the Doctrine of Justification*, and summarized in its opening section, has served as something of a *locus classicus* in this regard. In this memorable passage, Newman set forth the heart of his pneumatic christology.

> Christ's work of mercy has two chief parts; what He did for all men, what He does for each; what He did once for all, what He does for one by one continually; what He did externally to us, what He does within us; what He did on earth, what He does in heaven; what He did in His own Person, what He does by His Spirit; His death and the water and blood after it ... His Atonement, and the application of His Atonement ... He atones by the offering of Himself on the Cross; and as certainly (which is the point before us) He justifies us by the mission of His Spirit ..... The Holy Spirit realizes and completes the redemption which Christ has wrought in essence and virtue. The Atonement for sin took place during His own mission, and He was the chief Agent; the application of that Atonement takes place during the mission of His Spirit, who accordingly is the chief Agent in it .

This account of the redemptive actions of the divine agents is closely followed by Newman's specification of the office of the Holy Spirit in Christ's rising, ascending and imparting of the fire which sets the Church ablaze. The sacramental analogy is at the forefront of his thought as he moves from what the Spirit has done in Christ to what Christ's Spirit does in us.

> For He Himself was raised again and 'justified' by the Spirit; and what was wrought in Him is repeated in us who are His brethren, and the complement and ratification of His work. What took place in Him as an Origin, is continued on in the succession of those who inherit His fulness, and is the cause of its continuance. He is said to be 'justified by the Spirit,' because it was by the Spirit that He was raised again, proved innocent, made to triumph over His enemies, declared the Son of God, and exalted on the holy Hill of Sion ... This, I say, was His justification; and ours consists in our new birth also, and His was the beginning of ours. The Divine Life which raised Him, flowed over, and availed unto our rising again from sin and condemnation. It wrought a change in His Sacred Manhood, which became spiritual, without His ceasing to be man, and was in a wonderful way imparted to us as a new-creating, transforming Power in our hearts. This was the gift bestowed on the Church upon His ascension ....[40]

Several reasons explain why Newman's pneumatic christology and, consequently, his pneumatic ecclesiology have been examined predominantly from this perspective of his thought concerning the relationship between the atoning Christ and his justifying Spirit. Foremostly, the economy of redemption so closely concerns the mysteries of the cross and resurrection that without them there is no salvation (*1 Cor* 15). There is also the significant fact that Newman developed his understanding of Christ, the Holy Spirit, the Church and the sacraments in light of the issue of justification. Notwithstanding his criticism that Evangelical theology reduced the Gospel of Christ to certain justificatory passages in the letters of St. Paul, his own transposition of this matter, into the fuller context of his theology of the incarnate Word, continually referred to justification (Sheridan 1967; Komonckak 1976). Moreover, his personalist, neo-patristic presentation of these soteriological and ecclesiological matters in a simple yet elegant idiom made, and still makes, them accessible in a manner not readily found in either scholastic or contemporary theologies. In sum, the decision by scholars to emphasize the atoning Christ and his justifying Spirit in explanation of Newman's pneumatic christology corresponds to the data of revelation, his own narrative, a rich theme running throughout his writings, his persuasive prose as well as contemporary pastoral and theological needs.

Regardless of the real fruits and deep roots of this approach to Newman's pneumatic christology, it is not enough, because it has not been taken far enough. By focussing the spotlight too exclusively upon

40 Jfc. 203, 204, 206-7.

Christ who atones and his Spirit who justifies, other aspects of the Spirit's involvement in the life of the God-man have been placed in the shadows. Indeed, Pierre Masson, the sole scholar to attempt a major synthesis of Newman's pneumatology, christology and ecclesiology, treats scantily of his views concerning the office of the Holy Spirit in relation to the Mother of God, the Lord's temptation in the desert, baptism in the Jordan, ministry, transfiguration on Tabor, and his sacrificial offering on Calvary but, predictably, has much to say about Christ and the Spirit as agents of atonement and justification and the glorification of the Christian through the indwelling of the Holy Spirit (Masson 1982, 76-89, 127-90).

Masson is representative rather than exceptional in this regard. However, Newman quite properly equates the economy of redemption with the whole of the life of the God-man. This means that one needs to account for his views concerning the presence of the Spirit in representative moments of that life, not simply in the privileged, trans-historical moments of resurrection and glorification (Congar 1986, 85-100) or, indeed, subsequently, in moments of Christian rebirth through the indwelling of the Spirit of Christ. If this is left unattended, Newman's theology of the incarnation is subjected to the very reductionism he spent his life battling, for the extent to which the Holy Spirit of Christ truly renovates and restores fallen humanity is brought into question. On the other hand, the more thorough this accounting, the more Newman's pneumatic christology will be revealed as an integral theology of the perpetual presence of the Holy Spirit in the totality of the life of Christ. In turn, such an accounting promises to yield a broader field of 'data' from which new insights into his idea of the pneumatic Church can be derived. Additionally, in view of attention devoted by historical-critical scholarship to the Jesus of history, an examination of Newman's understanding of those pneumatic events in the life of Christ, which occupy a like place of importance in current exegesis, and systematics provides a means by which insights from his incarnate Word theology can be brought into conversation with contemporary thought. Inevitably, this accounting will bring forward further evidence for judgment concerning "the commonly-voiced criticism that Newman's high Alexandrian christology meant that he paid only notional attention to the humanity of Christ." (Ker 1993, 25-6; see Daly 1984, 289-90; Thomas 1991, 65; Strange 1990, 323-36). The prospective judgment involves an evaluation of the extent to which Newman's portrait of the Holy Spirit in the life of the God-man makes allowances for a genuinely free and human response to the Father in the Spirit.

Finally, a full accounting of Newman's pneumatic christology contributes to the history of theology. His achievement deserves to be better known. For example, the solitary 19th century figure cited by Anne Hunt in her fine study of the relationship between the Trinity and the paschal mystery (1997, 6) is Matthias Scheeben (1835-88). In spite of his original treatment of the subject-matter (Dessain 1966, 57), Newman is not mentioned by her, even parenthetically. Yet, on the basis of a renewed biblical theology (Coulson and Allchin 1967, 104-5; VCS 1990, 157-62), he underscores the one, saving, mystery of the suffering, death and resurrection of Jesus, and the office of the Holy Spirit in this work, more than a hundred years earlier than F.X. Durrwell whom Hunt credits with this ground-breaking achievement (Hunt 1997, 11-35; Durrwell, 1960; Dessain 1962, 277-8; 1977, 76; Strange 1981, 127-8; Ker, 1990 b, 48). Likewise, Ralph Del Colle, in his monograph, *Christ and the Spirit*, does not so much as allude to the pioneering work of Newman when he describes western theologians who have moved beyond neo-scholasticism by their identification of the indwelling of the Holy Spirit as a "pneumatic *proprium*" which is "not restricted to a trinitarian appropriation", a doctrine which he says that they recovered from Athanasius and the Cappadocians and, indirectly, from later Orthodox interpreters of this Alexandrian school (1994, 95-7). Maybe Del Colle omits Newman because he does not go this far. But, perhaps, this is Newman's very contribution. The Alexandrian Fathers were also influential in Newman's formation. Yet, he does not opt to speak of the indwelling of Holy Spirit as a "pneumatic *proprium*" in a manner that might blur the boundaries of appropriation. Rather Newman speaks about the special but non-exclusive role of the Holy Spirit in raising Christ from the dead and indwelling the justified in a manner which falls within the boundaries of appropriation, even though he avoids this scholastic terminology.[41] Nevertheless, his way of accenting the pneumatic dimension of this trinitarian appropriation revitalizes it from the 'homogenization' which can result from overemphasizing the common nature of appropriation at the expense of the divine person to whom the activity

41 Jfc. 144.

is appropriated (Fortman 1972, 309, 315). Divine activities are not arbitrarily appropriated to divine persons; rather the term appropriated has its foundation, albeit mysteriously, in the divine processions. Newman's language of congruity and fittingness certainly heads in this direction. His insistence that the Holy Spirit is particularly fitted for, and active in, the resurrection of the God-man, and the indwelling of believers, illustrates his conviction of the congruity between divine person and temporal office. Those mapping the history of trinitarian and pneumatic christology would do well to include Newman in this discussion.

CHAPTER THREE

SYNKATABASIS

John Henry Newman's understanding of the divine interaction between the Holy Spirit and eternal Son within the temporal missions prior to the birth of the Church requires us to 'unpack' his view of *synkatabasis*; that is, the Divine economy of salvation. Basically, Newman comprehends the Spirit to make present the Son in interpenetrating phases: preparatorily, in the formation of the cosmos; hypostatically, in the re-creation of all in and through the new Adam at the moment of incarnation by which the God-man becomes the personal, sacramental way of salvation; and, historically, in the unfurling of his life. Within this panorama, Mary, the Blessed Mother and perfect disciple, stands as the personal 'hinge' uniting preparatory and re-creative phases because the Lord and Giver of Life both prepares for, and brings about, the *enhominization* of God through his intimate relationship with *Theotokos*.[1] Here the concentration is upon the preparatory and re-creative phases of the economy of salvation. Later this effort is complemented by a consideration of the re-creative and historical phases of the tri-personal God's activity. Together these collective efforts show that Newman unites the distinct operations of the mediating Son and vivifying Spirit in a most complementary fashion to portray the Holy Spirit as the divine animator acting in concert with, and within, the God-man to exclude extrinsic, impersonal or diminutive interpretations of the Holy Spirit.

SYNKATABASIS

Newman believes it is the self-same triune God who acts both in the hidden glory of his inner life and in the economy of salvation. This

1 Newman's archaic spelling of *Theotocos* has been uniformly modified to meet current usage as *Theotokos*.

correspondence warrants speaking similarly of the eternal and temporal acts of the Son and Spirit as unified, complementary and distinct. This perspective also informs his vision of the Holy Spirit in the life of Christ in which temporal missions correspond intimately to divine offices: that is, existence in the Godhead *qua* eternal Son and *qua* Holy Spirit 'fits' each divine person to undertake his particular temporal mission in the one economy of salvation.[2] Newman tends to speak of this 'fittingness', 'suitability' or 'congruity' in terms of the analogy of faith in which aspects of belief are understood by their relation to other revealed truths.[3] Sometimes his understanding of this congruity between mission and office lies unarticulated in the background of his thought.

> The phrase 'Hand of God' is used as a title of the Son by Athanasius, Cyril and Augustine, and implies the Homoüsion, that is, that the Son and Spirit are included within, not external to the Divine Essence. Elsewhere, Irenaeus says in confirmation of this, 'All these things the Father made, not by Angels, nor by any powers divided from His own Intelligence, for God needs not any of these, but by His Word and Spirit.' (*contra. Haer.* i 22 I) .... Allowing then that the Second and Third Divine Persons have, in and since the creation, condescended to ministrative offices, no offence can be taken with statements, such as those of Irenaeus, which, assuming this, clearly maintain, on the other hand, Their co-existence in the Divine Unity.[4]

Sometimes his understanding of this congruity stands very much at the forefront of his thought. "Because our Lord is a Son, therefore it is that He could make Himself less than a Son; and, unless He had become less than a Son, we should not have learned that He was a Son, for his economical descent to the creature is the channel of our knowledge. This is what I have been insisting on; also, that since, His original Personality thus led on to His Temporal Procession, therefore it is not easy to determine when He acts the Son, and when merely as the Minister of the Father, and the Mediating Power of the Universe."[5]

2 Newman sometimes used the term "condescension" to speak of the temporal missions of the Spirit and the Son as an Anglican (PS ii 12: 132; 135; PS ii 19: 217-8) and as a Catholic (SN 306; Mix. 284-304).

3 See Mix. 360-1.

4 TT 217.

5 TT 199; see Ath. ii 269-70.

Now, in the case of the Holy Spirit, Newman's articulation of this congruity occupies a middle ground. While definitely acknowledging the particular fittingness of the Holy Spirit to undertake his temporal mission, Newman neither thoroughly nor exactly explains the meaningfulness of this congruity. This contrasts sharply with his sustained exploitation of congruity (or fittingness) as a means of penetrating the mission of the eternal Son. Moreover, even the specificity with which he acknowledges the congruity existing between temporal mission and the Holy Spirit fluctuates. In the passage below, Newman's reference to "Persons of the Ever-blessed and All-holy Trinity" ensures that all which precedes and follows is understood as applying equally to the Holy Spirit. However, relative to the Father and Son, his reference to the Holy Spirit is remote.

> As the Son was God, so on the other hand was the Son suitably made man; it belonged to Him to have the Father's perfections, it became Him to assume a servant's form. We must beware of supposing that the Persons of the Ever-blessed and All-holy Trinity differ from each other only in this, that the Father is not the Son, and the Son is not the Father. They differ in this besides, that the Father *is* the Father, and the Son *is* the Son. While They are one in substance, Each has distinct characteristics which the Other has not. Surely those sacred Names have a meaning in them, and must not be passed lightly over.[6]

Elsewhere Newman speaks proximately about this congruity by describing the eternal Spirit as the "very bond of love and peace dwelling and dwelt in by Father and Son," who enters history as the promise of peace vouchsafed by the Father and Son (*Lk* 24: 49). Still Newman suggests – rather than precisely affirms – that the presence of the Holy Spirit in history as the "peace" promised by the Father and Son is congruous to his eternal presence as the bond of peace between the Father and Son. "He did not bring into being peace and love as part of His creation, but He was Himself peace and love from eternity, and He blesses us by making us partakers of Himself, through the Son, by the Spirit, and so He works in temporal dispensations that He may bring us to that which is eternal."[7]

On one occasion, however, Newman refers immediately to the congruity between the person of the Holy Spirit and his temporal mission. In his 1853 sermon, "Order, the Witness and Instrument of

6 PS vi 5: 58.

7 PS vi 25: 368.

Unity," preached in St. Chad's Cathedral on the occasion of the first diocesan synod of Birmingham, his homily considers the unified but diverse nature of those gathered around the one altar of the bishop. He precedes these ecclesial comments by considering the tri-unity of the Divine Mystery wherein he asserts that the Godhead is "occupied and possessed wholly and unreservedly" by Father, Son and Holy Spirit who are "equal to Each Other in their Divinity" so "that not one of the Divine Persons is less infinite, less eternal, less all-sufficient than the Other Two". Then he specifies the distinctness of each divine person relative to the one economy of salvation at which juncture the congruity between the Spirit's person and office comes to the fore.

> [I]t is true also that, in the history of the Everlasting mystery, the Father comes first in order, as the Fountain-head of Divinity; the Son second, as being the Off-spring of the First; and the Holy Ghost third, as proceeding from the Father and the Son. And for this reason it would appear that the Second and the Third Persons hold certain offices, such as that of mission, which are fitting only in Them. Hence it was **fitting that the Son should be incarnate**, and not the Father; and **fitting that the Holy Ghost should be the energising life, both of the animate and rational creation**, rather than the Father or the Son.[8]

Employing the heuristic of congruity, Newman finds that the office of mediation suits the Son, and the office of life-giving suits the Spirit, in conformity with basic affirmations of the Nicene Creed (Tanner i: 24). This understanding invariably underpins his view of their temporal missions in the one economy of salvation. Newman consistently identified life-giving as the hypostatic hallmark of the temporal mission of the Holy Spirit. Consequently, his appropriation of animation to the Holy Spirit in his Catholic *Sermon Notes*[9] confirms previous Anglican practice.[10] Some later reflections intensify the identification. For example, in his *Meditations on Christian Doctrine*, Newman talks of the Paraclete expansively as "Life of all Things", specifically as "Life of the Church", intimately as "Life of My Soul" and eternally as "that Living Love, wherewith the Father and Son love each other."[11]

---

8 OS 183-94; both citations at 186, emphasis added.

9 SN 300 is part of Newman's (28 August 1849– 11 Jan. 1850) sermon notes on the articles of the Apostles Creed.

10 "On the Holy Spirit – His Nature and office," MS 339: 8 at Birmingham Oratory, A.17.1; see also PS ii 19: 218; VM ii 180; Jfc. 210.

11 PVD 414-20.

This designation of the eternal person of the Holy Spirit as "that Living Love" in the heart of the Trinity is atypical. As noted, although Newman speaks remotely, proximately, and immediately, about the fittingness of the Holy Spirit to fulfill His mission as the Lord and Giver of Life, he is usually silent about the deep meaning of His eternal proceeding and how this fits Him to be "the energising life, both of the animate and rational creation" – a silence which is typical of the Tradition (McDonnell 1985, 191-227).[12] In this regard, there exists real 'distance' between the foreground and middle ground of his thought about the Son and Spirit. Whereas he clarifies the Son's temporal mission directly in light of eternal sonship,[13] he clarifies the Spirit's temporal mission indirectly in light of the Son's temporal mission. Study of sacred scripture and, especially, doctrinal disputes of the early Church taught Newman that the revelation of the Spirit occurred in and through the historical revelation of Christ. This realization informs his pneumatology in which the Spirit makes present the Son [animation] who, paradoxically, is the *locus* in which the Spirit becomes manifest [mediation].[14] However, the equality of their persons and missions neither necessitates nor results in an equal sharing of the spotlight. In this manner, Newman reflects the record of sacred revelation in which the central content of the gospel is the person, work and mission of Jesus Christ crucified and risen. However, the Holy Spirit so animates, penetrates and is related to his person, work and mission as to be, at certain points, virtually indistinguishable from him.[15] In short, the perichoretic nature of their eternal relationship extends to the temporal missions.

Newman's view of the temporal relationship between the eternal Son and the Holy Spirit reflects his understanding of their joint task in creating the cosmos and re-creating fallen humanity.[16] He repeatedly calls this co-ministration the *synkatabasis* in his lengthy 1872 essay, "Causes of the Rise and Successes of Arianism."[17] After establishing an historical-doctrinal context in which to examine Arianism, his

12 OS 186.

13 See PS vi 5: 58; see TT 185-6.

14 PS iv 17: 254.

15 See Ath. ii 304; Jfc. 206, 207-8.

16 See SD v 61 (Christ); 53, 55 (Spirit).

17 TT 139-299.

essay focusses primarily upon the Father and Son and treats sparingly of the Spirit.[18] Mention of the Holy Spirit occurs mostly in relation to Newman's discussion of the historical development of the doctrine of the Trinity, the presence of the Son and Spirit in the *synkatabasis*, and the transferability of Old Testament titles such as Wisdom to their divine persons.[19] In spite of this comparative neglect, Newman writes that "this *synkatabasis*, or economy of condescension, on the part of the Son and Spirit, took place, not from the era of redemption merely, but, as I have remarked, from the beginning of all things . ."[20] This position articulates his belief that the Son and Spirit are equally involved in the cosmic drama which embraces creation, redemption, the Church and the wider world (McGrath 1997).

As mentioned, Newman perceives a special relationship between eternal office and temporal mission. In particular, he considers the *synkatabasis* as congruous with eternal sonship and the event of the incarnation as befitting eternal sonship. According to Newman, the congruity of temporal mission with divine sonship no more makes the *synkatabasis* a necessity than the incarnation (which supremely exemplifies that sonship) can be said to circumscribe it. Within this horizon, Newman indicates that the far-reaching mediatorial office of the Word arises from an affinity between eternal sonship and the possibility of creation as an idea in the mind of God.[21]

> [B]ut there is in Scripture a record of acts before the Incarnation, which the Church, following Scripture, has ever ascribed to Him, and which come short of His Supreme Majesty, – acts which belong to Him, not as man of course, nor yet simply as God, not to His Divine Nature, but, as I may say, to His Person, and to the special Office which it was congruous to His Person to undertake, and which He did voluntarily undertake, as being the Son and Word of the Father, – acts, which, if it was in the divine decrees that a universe of matter and spirit should be created, were *ipso facto* made obligatory on the Creator from the very idea of creation, and of necessity must proceed from Him, while they were in themselves of a ministrative character.

Again, he writes, "He was the Son of God, equal to the Father; He took works upon Him beneath that Divine Majesty; they were such

18 See TT 141-9 149-57, 158-66.

19 See TT 167-91 (Father); TT 192-299 (Son); TT 149-66; 199; 219-23 (Spirit).

20 TT 193; see 199-200.

21 TT 232, 232 ff.; Ath. ii 216-21.

as were not obligations of His Nature, nor of His Person, but they were congruous to His Person, and they might look very like what essentially belonged to Him; but after all, they were works such as God alone could undertake. He was Creator, Preserver, Archetype of all things, but not simply as God, but as God the Son, and further, as God the Son in an office of ministration ...."[22] Thus Newman insists that the eternal Son has a pivotal role in creation congruous to his sonship which is analogous but prior to, and differentiated from, his incarnation *per se*. Although he realizes that talk of the *synkatabasis* opens the door to Arianizing, Newman still stresses that the "first act of His *synkatabasis*" was creation. He describes how "in the hour of its coming into being [it] was raised into something higher than a divine work ... by the entrance, presence, manifestation in it of the Eternal Son"; and, he characterizes it as something "adopted into a divine family and sonship" conformed to the Son's divine fullness. Newman is careful to stipulate that this intimate relationship to creation does not involve any sort of pantheism or 'world-soul'. This originating, fashioning and elevating of creation by Christ anticipates and prepares for the incarnation and man's deification insofar as the Divine Word is the archetype and origin of the creation into which he first enters as divine Son and which, subsequently, he redeems as son of Mary. As Newman says, "the elevation of the universe in the Divine Son includes an impress of His own likeness upon it. He made Himself its Archetype, and stamped upon it the image of His own Wisdom ... He was the beginning of the creation of God, in respect of time, so was He its first principle or idea in respect to typical order."[23] Clearly he perceives God's relationship to the created order in terms of the congruity between the eternal *gennesis* and the origin of creation.

> Catholics, as we have seen in the extracts from Athanasius, were very explicit in teaching that the Divine Word was the Living Idea, the All-sufficient Archetype ... on which the universe was framed. The Son interprets and fulfils the designs of the Eternal Mind, not as copying them, when He forms the world, but as being Himself their very Original and Delineation within the Father. Such was the doctrine of the great Alexandrian School, before Athanasius as well as after ... Hence it was that He was fitted, and He alone, to become the First-born, of all things, and to exercise a *synkatabasis* which would be available for the conservation of the world.

22 TT 193-4, 197.

23 TT 202, 203, 204 n.1, 204-5.

By "First-born", Newman here refers directly to the eternal Son's involvement in the creation and preservation of the universe. Only analogously does the term refer to the incarnation itself. Moreover, he includes the very possibility of creation, incarnation, in fact, all of salvation history, in the divine act of the Father eternally begetting the Son, that is his *gennesis*.[24]

The significance of this theological move is hard to overestimate. Without making the world eternal or inserting necessity into the Godhead, Newman claims that creation at origin, and even from eternity, is related to the Son's generation. Inasmuch as creation receives existence in time from the Word who "interprets and fulfils the designs of the Eternal Mind" the relation is actual. Inasmuch as from eternity the Word is the "very Original and Delineation" of the plans upon which the universe is framed the relation is potential and congruous. Retrieval of the Alexandrian tradition enables Newman to describe the Son as originating, fashioning and elevating that which sacramentally mediates his own presence so that the transcendent, triune God is immanently present to the created order in a distinctly christocentric manner.[25]

Admittedly, Newman minimizes the role of the Spirit in his discussion of creation (and other matters) in his 1872 essay, "Causes of the Rise and Successes of Arianism". Apart from his standard treatment of the Holy Spirit in his explanation of the dogma of the Trinity, his pneumatological comments are reserved to insisting that the *synkatabasis* involves "the Son and Spirit" and occurs "from the beginning of all things" as well as observing that the multiple meanings and transferability of divine titles indicates the incomprehensibility of these temporal missions. In this investigation – described by Newman as an "inquiry into the historical origin of Arianism" – his relative neglect of the mission of the Holy Spirit signals his preoccupation with heresy rather than christocentricism.[26] In fact, the co-equality of the temporal missions holds a secure place in his trinitarian thought and, elsewhere, the invisible mission of the Holy Spirit shares the spotlight. Nearly forty years prior to writing "Causes of the Rise and Successes of Arianism" (1872), Newman described the missions of the Son and

24 TT 218-9, 199-207, 230-1.

25 TT 218; see PS ii 3: 30.

26 TT 149--66, 199, 220, 298.

Spirit as incomprehensible, trinitarian acts of loving condescension, distinguished by their outer and inner forms of communication, which equally evoke adoration, in the sermon, "The Indwelling Spirit" (1834).

"God the Son has graciously vouchsafed to reveal the Father to His creatures from without; God the Holy Ghost, by inward communications. Who can compare these separate works of condescension, either of them being beyond our understanding? We can but silently adore the Infinite Love which encompasses us on every side .... The condescension of the Blessed Spirit is as incomprehensible as that of the Son."[27] Newman's sensitivity to mystery is tempered by his openness to history. The temporal missions reveal the Father without compromising divine incomprehensibility. Trinitarian affirmation is coupled to apophaticism in order to emphasize that the incomprehensible God of love communicates His life and love by disclosing Himself as a holy Triad of distinct persons. As well, this presentation affords an insight into his view of the relationship between the invisible mission of the Holy Spirit and the visible mission of the eternal Son. The complexity of this view is revealed *via* a simple spacial metaphor which connotes that the Son-Spirit relationship involves unity insofar as 'outer' and 'inner' require each other for wholeness, complementarity insofar as 'outer' and 'inner' imply each other and distinction insofar as 'outer' and 'inner' are not each other.

Near the beginning of this 1834 sermon, Newman explores the *synkatabasis* in terms of the creative dimension of the mission of the Son using sacramental language very similar to that he employed years later in his 1872 "Causes of the Rise and Successes of Arianism".

> The Son of God is called the Word as declaring His glory throughout created nature, and impressing the evidence of it on every part of it. He has given us to read it in His works of goodness, holiness, and wisdom. He is the Living and Eternal Law of Truth and Perfection, that Image of God's unapproachable Attributes, which men have ever seen by glimpses on the face of the world, felt that it was sovereign, but knew not whether to say it was fundamental Rule and self-existing Destiny, or the Offspring and Mirror of the Divine Will. Such has He been from the beginning, graciously sent forth from the Father to reflect His glory upon all things, distinct from Him, while mysteriously one with Him; and in due time visiting us with an infinitely deeper mercy, when for our redemption He humbled

27 PS ii 19: 217-18.

> Himself to take upon Him that fallen nature which He had originally created after His own image.

Immediately after this christological passage, Newman presents the pneumatological component of the *synkatabasis* by speaking most vividly, although not exclusively, of the office of the Holy Spirit in the creative phase of the cosmos.

> The condescension of the Blessed Spirit is as incomprehensible as that of the Son. He has ever been the secret Presence of God within Creation: a source of life amid the chaos, bringing out into form and order what was at first shapeless and void, and the voice of Truth in the hearts of all rational beings, tuning them into harmony with the intimations of God's Law, which were externally made to them. Hence He is especially called the 'life-giving' Spirit; being (as it were) the Soul of universal nature, the Strength of man and beast, the Guide of the faith, the Witness against sin, the inward Light of patriarchs and prophets, the Grace abiding in the Christian soul, and the Lord and Ruler of the Church.

Prior to undertaking his preacher's task of describing "as scripturally as [he] can, the merciful office of God the Holy Ghost, toward us Christians," Newman notes how the Son impresses evidence of the Father's glory on every aspect of that creation which the Spirit vitalizes to emphasize again the oneness, complementarity and distinctiveness of the temporal missions in the creative dimension of the *synkatabasis*. Finally, he closes these prefatory remarks by re-inserting them into the same trinitarian context of adoration and love which framed his opening sentences: "Therefore let us ever praise the Father Almighty, who is the first Source of all perfection, in and together with His Co-equal Son and Spirit, through whose gracious ministrations we have been given to see 'what manner of love' it is wherewith the Father loved us."[28]

This glance at Newman's 1834 sermon, "The Indwelling Spirit" confirms that he accords the Holy Spirit a central role in the creative dimension of the *synkatabasis* early in his life. This suggests strongly that the comparative neglect which the Holy Spirit receives at his hands in the 1872 essay, "Causes of the Rise and Successes of Arianism," is unrepresentative of his pneumatology and signals not christocentrism but attention to Arianism. The consistency of Newman's pneumatological approach is further indicated by his 1849 Catholic sermon note on the Apostles Creed which stipulates that the life-giving mission

28 PS ii 19: 217, 218; see TT 201-7.

of the Holy Spirit sustains all mysteries associated with his original condescension – "On the condescension of the Holy Ghost. Creation implies ministration, and is the beginning of mysteries. It passes the line, and other mysteries are but its continuation."[29] Granted, over and against such clear assignation of the task of preserving creation to the office of the Holy Spirit, one must juxtapose other remarks like: "[c]reation and conservation must go together ... He [the Word] who was at the first instant external to it, must, without a moment's delay, enter into it and give it a supernatural strength by His, as it were, connatural Presence."[30] Yet, within the logic of Newman's trinitarian grammar, this attribution of life-giving to the Word is best explained in terms of *circumincessio* and the indivisibility of divine action; it does not diminish Newman's sense that it is fitting to assign the property of vitalization to the Spirit. In fact, the above reference to "continuation" clearly indicates Newman's belief that the invisible mission of the Lord and Giver of Life extends from the creative to the re-creative, that is, to the redemptive dimension of the economy of salvation.

THEOTOKOS

The task now is to illumine the indispensable place Newman assigns to the Holy Spirit in the life of Mary, Mother of God. Understanding the pneumatic dimension of Mary's person, privileges and office is vital for properly comprehending Newman's thought concerning her cooperative, co-redemptive role in the work of the Holy Spirit preparing for, and making present, the eternal Son in the event of incarnation itself, and beyond.

In the *Apologia pro Vita Sua*, Newman records his judgment concerning his religious convictions since becoming a Roman Catholic: "I was not conscious to myself, on my conversion, of any change, intellectual or moral, wrought in my mind. I was not conscious of firmer faith in the fundamental truths of Revelation, or of more self-command; I had not more fervour ... " Nonetheless, he is acutely conscious that ongoing inquiry into the depths of revelation amid shifting circumstances caused growth in thought.[31] Continuity and development are themes evident in his thought on the Blessed Virgin which bear upon

29 SN 306.

30 TT 202.

31 Apo. 214; see Dev. 1845: 27-8; Dev. 1878: 29-30.

his view of the Holy Spirit in the life of Jesus. One of his most original university sermons portrays Mary as "our pattern of Faith" in her reverent believing, loving, accepting, dwelling upon, receiving, studying, developing, assenting and submitting to God's revelation. Likewise, Newman understood his only book-length Marian work, *A Letter Addressed to the Rev. E. B. Pusey, D.D., on Occasion of his Eirenicon of 1864*, to be a popularized explication of terse arguments advanced decades earlier in his *Essay on the Development of Christian Doctrine.*[32] The Holy Spirit-Mary-revelation-development nexus is best explained, from Newman's vantage, by recalling his primary understanding of revelation as the Word made flesh and, only secondarily, as the intelligibility of this mystery expressed in propositional form. This differs from the propositional emphasis upon revelation at Vatican I and prefigures the incarnational emphasis at Vatican II (Tanner ii: 806; 971-81). For him, Mary embodies the Word incarnate, experiences him grow within her and grows by her openness to the Holy Spirit. In the most basic and profound terms, Mary is the living, personal temple within which the body of Christ is formed by the Holy Spirit.

As an Anglican, Newman's disdain for extravagant Marian devotion contributed to his judgment that Roman theology had displaced "Christ, the Son of God, the Author and Dispenser of all grace and pardon" by substituting "St. Mary and the saints" as "the prominent objects of regard and dispensers of mercy" (Dessain 1982, 235). However, this represents an exercise of Newman's anti-Roman reflex more than it states any lack of appreciation for Mary or her unique office in the economy of salvation. During his early days at Oxford, Richard Hurrell Froude and John Keble opened him up to the profound place of Mary in Christianity. Froude familiarized him with Mary as the Virgin of virgins and Keble, his spiritual mentor, published tender poems about Mary's person, dignity and office that he quite cherished. Of his time as vicar of St. Mary, the Virgin, before the Oxford Movement, Newman recalled, "I had a true devotion to the Blessed Virgin, in whose College I lived, whose Altar I served, and whose Immaculate Purity I had in one of my earliest printed Sermons made much of."[33] In the years immediately preceding his 1845 con-

32 US xv 313. *A Letter to Pusey* (1866) was later published as the first part of *Diff.* ii. On the connection of *Letter to Pusey* to Dev., see LD xxii 148-9.

33 Ess ii: 8; see Apo. 34, 35; LD xxi 96 n.2-3; Ess ii 421-53; Apo. 152 referring to PS ii 12: 127-138.

version, he corresponded with the Catholic theologian, Dr. Charles Russell of Maynooth, about his difficulties with Roman teaching about Mary. Russell advised him to distinguish between the permanence of dogma and the changeability of pious practice as influenced by epoch, culture and temperament.[34] Sensitivity to the relationship between dogma and pious practice was not limited to matters Marian, but recurred in Newman's thought on development of doctrine, *sensus fidelium* and the Church conformed to the triple office of Christ. Eventually, Newman concluded that his disaffection for continental devotions did not require him to reject the Marian teachings of the Catholic Church.[35]

By 1832, Newman ascribed a profound blessedness to the Virgin Mary based upon her office as *Theotokos*. Reflecting upon *Luke* in his sermon, "The Reverence Due to Her," he recounts how "the Angel Gabriel was sent to tell her that she was to be the Mother of our Lord" and "the Holy Ghost came upon her and overshadowed her with the power of the Most High". Exegeting this pericope (*Lk* 1: 42-3, 5), Newman posits a qualitative difference between the pneumatic experiences of Mary and Elizabeth.

"Though she was filled with the Holy Ghost at the time she spake, yet, far from thinking herself by such a gift equalled to Mary, she was thereby moved to use more reverent language. 'She spake out with a loud voice, and said, *Blessed art thou* among women, and blessed is the fruit of thy womb. And whence is this to me?' ... Then she repeated, 'Blessed is she that believed; for there shall be a performance of those things which were told her from the Lord.'" Evidence that Newman understands Mary's motherhood as the source of the singular reverence due to her also appears in his near acknowledgement of her Immaculate Conception as the necessary corollary of her office as *Theotokos*. Furthermore, he attributes this special gift that fits Mary to be Mother of God solely to the "miraculous presence" of the Creator Spirit.

> [W]hat must have been the transcendent purity of her, whom the Creator Spirit condescended to overshadow with His miraculous presence? What

---

34 Apo. 176-7; see Diff. ii 26-31.

35 See Dev. 1845: 407-10, 435-38; Dev. 1878: 143-8, 426-8; as well, Cons. 60, 70-3; *Preface to the Third Edition*, VM i: xl-xli; lxxxiv. This disaffection was life-long; see LD xx 470-1; LD xxi 165, 195.

> must have been her gifts, who was chosen to be the only near earthly relative of the Son of God, the only one appointed to train and educate Him ... This contemplation runs to a higher subject ... for what, think you, was the sanctified state of that human nature, of which God formed His sinless Son; knowing as we do, 'that which is born of the flesh is flesh' and that 'none can bring a clean thing out of an unclean?'[36]

Newman keenly perceives that the office of *Theotokos* is co-extensive with Mary's being; it is not limited to the biological arena. Under the shadow of the Holy Spirit, she conceives Christ in faith prior to conceiving him in the flesh – her *fiat* is a dynamic, epicletic response that engages and emerges from her entire person. "And, of these undefiled followers of the Lamb, the Blessed Mary is the chief. Strong in the Lord, and in the power of His might, she 'staggered not at the promise of God through unbelief;' she believed when Zacharias doubted, – with a faith like Abraham's she believed and was blessed for her belief, and had the performance of those things which were told her by the Lord."[37]

Newman also signals his awareness that the anointing of the Spirit totally penetrates Mary's life during his reflection upon the relative silence of sacred scripture concerning her life. He notes that sacred scripture records her presence at events involving the presence or imminent arrival of the Spirit: i.e., the nativity, the foot of the cross and the cenacle (*Lk* 1:35, *Mt* 1:20, *Jn* 19:26, *Acts* 1:14). By juxtaposing her pure, faith-filled, Spirit-assisted *fiat* with her active embrace of the cross, Newman intimates that Mary's indwelling by the Spirit is not simply a figure but a fulfilment of redemption : "And when sorrow came upon her afterwards, it was but the blessed participation of her Son's sacred sorrows, not the sorrow of those who suffer for their sins." Thus he implies that Mary is a personal embodiment of the Church. Granted, Newman's awareness of what was achieved in Mary personally needs to be balanced against his awareness of what needed to be achieved in the Church as a whole. Meditating upon Mary's Magnificat, he states, "What God began in her was a sort of type of His dealings with His Church"; His gracious favour to her is

---

36 PS ii 12: 127-38: citations at 127, 128, 135; corollary at 135 (see Ps v 7: 94-5; Lk 1:26-38, esp. v. 35).

37 PS ii 12: 137. Consider St. Augustine *Sermons* (PL 38: 1019, 1074; 46: 937-8) and chpt. 3, *De Sancta Virginitate* (PL 40: 398), over and against Mix. 351 and Diff. ii 36. On a fulsome Marian response, see US xv 312-14.

"a shadow or outline of that Kingdom of the Spirit, which was then coming on the earth."[38] Mindful of the sufficiency and uniqueness of the atonement, Newman touches upon the ecclesial participation in the paschal mystery, first mentioning the sword piercing Mary's heart (*Lk* 2:35) that he associates with his sermon text, the Pauline injunction to fill up what is lacking in Christ's sufferings for the sake of his body, the Church (*1 Cor* 1: 24). Though clear elsewhere that only God was equal to the "weight" of the passion of Christ, Newman still ventures to describe Mary as mysteriously participating in her Son's paschal mystery[39] as one who is already justified[40] by the indwelling of the Holy Spirit (Dessain 1982, 246). Sealed with the Spirit, Mary not only foreshadows but already perfectly embodies the relationship which will adhere between the justified, the Spirit and the risen Christ that Newman so movingly depicts in "Righteousness in us not of Us".

> Christ Himself vouchsafes to repeat in each of us in figure and mystery all that He did and suffered in the flesh. He is formed in us, born in us, suffers in us, rises again in us, lives in us; and this not by a succession of events, but all at once: for He comes to us as a Spirit, all dying, all rising again, all living. We are ever receiving our birth, our justification, our renewal ... ever rising to righteousness. His whole economy in all its parts is ever in us all at once; and this divine presence constitutes the title of each of us to heaven ... He impresses us with the seal of the Spirit, in order to avouch that we are His.[41]

In 1845, Newman again insists upon the direct relationship between the dignity of Mary and the mystery of the Word becoming flesh. Surveying this moment in the fullness of time (*Eph* 1:10), he characterizes her Spirit-filled 'yes' as a *sine qua non* of the incarnation: if Mary had "been disobedient or unbelieving on Gabriel's message, the Divine Economy would have been frustrated." Hence he accents the uniqueness of her personal co-operation with the Holy Spirit and attends to the indispensable place of human freedom in the encounter. In the wake of the dogmatic definition by Pius IX in 1854, he

38 PS ii 12: 132; PS vi 22: 314.

39 PS iii 11: 139-41; Mix. 338.

40 On his view that this 1832 sermon almost affirms the content of the dogma of the Immaculate Conception see LD xix: 346-7; see LD xix: 438, LD xxv 378-9. Note the fluidity of his Anglican views insofar as he says the Blessed Mother was "a sinner" in his 1834 sermon, "The Incarnation," PS ii 3: 32.

41 PS v 10:139.

replies to the perplexed by situating the privilege of the Immaculate Conception in the context of Mary's office as *Theotokos* thereby making it susceptible of a pneumatological and christological interpretation. The reason for the privilege of Mary's Immaculate Conception is christological, while its achievement is pneumatological.[42]

In the next decade, Newman's view of Mary's person, prerogatives and office finds its clearest expression ever in his 1866 *Letter to Pusey* where he speaks of the Holy Spirit preparing her, from the first moment of existence, to become Mother of the Redeemer.

> [W]e consider that in Adam she died, as others; that she was included, together with the whole race, in Adam's sentence; that she incurred his debt, as we do; but that, for the sake of Him who was to redeem her and us upon the Cross, to her the debt was remitted by anticipation, on her the sentence was not carried out ... Mary could not merit, any more than they [Adam and Eve], the restoration of that grace, but it was restored to her by God's free bounty, from the very first moment of her existence ... And she had this special privilege, in order to fit her to become the Mother of her and our Redeemer, to fit her **mentally, spiritually** for it; so that by that, by aid of the first grace, she might so grow in grace, that, when the Angel came and her Lord was at hand, she might be 'full of grace,' prepared as far as a creature could be prepared, to receive Him into her **bosom**.

Newman presents Mary's *fiat* as an integrally human response of mind, soul and body to the mission of the Holy Spirit.[43] Expanding his understanding of the all-encompassing nature of this work of the Spirit, he locates the 'privileged yes' of Mary amongst a series of lesser acts effected by the indwelling of the Holy Spirit. Consequently, he explicitly places individual, pneumatic episodes involving Mary – such as her preservation against original sin and *fiat* – in the context of her total anointing by the Lord and Giver of Life. He portrays her personal, plenary, pneumatically-charged gift of self as something salvific that transcends the partial and instrumental. Since Mary is "a cause of salvation to all", she merits high titles such as "the Second Eve" and "Mother of the living" which are to be taken "gravely and without any rhetoric". Indeed, as *Theotokos* she has "a real meritorious co-operation ... in the reversal of the fall."

> However, not to go beyond the doctrine of the Three Fathers, they unanimously declare that she was *not* a mere instrument in the Incarnation, such

42 Dev 1845: 384, Dev. 1878: 415, see Diff. ii 32; LD xix 362; 437-8.

43 Diff. ii 49; emphasis added; see PS ii 12: 137.

> as David, or Judah, may be considered; they declare she co-operated in our salvation not merely by the descent of the Holy Ghost upon her body, but by specific holy acts, the effect of the Holy Ghost within her soul; that, as Eve forfeited privileges by sin, so Mary earned privileges by the fruits of grace; that, as Eve was disobedient and unbelieving, so Mary was obedient and believing; that, as Eve was a cause of ruin to all, Mary was a cause of salvation to all; that as Eve made room for Adam's fall, so Mary made room for our Lord's reparation of it; and thus, whereas the free gift was not as the offence but much greater, it follows that, as Eve co-operated in effecting a great evil, Mary co-operated in effecting a much greater good.[44]

As an Anglican and Catholic, Newman portrays the Holy Spirit as preparing for, working through, and supporting Mary's free and integrally human *fiat* that culminates in her office as Mother of God. Since Mary's office as the New Eve rests upon the fact that her Son is the New Adam,[45] his pneumatological and mariological remarks constitute a christological commentary upon the restoration of all things in Him: "He left His Father's courts ... and, whereas an enemy is the god and tyrant of this world, as Adam made it, so, as far as He occupies it, does He restore it to His Father."[46] Hence Newman recognizes a special relationship between the Spirit and the bride insofar as the presence of the Holy Spirit in the life of Mary is anterior to, and necessary for, the incarnation. Newman's thorough-going sense of the intimate relationship between *Creator Spiritus* and *Theotokos* is epitomized by his observation that, "it should be borne in mind, then, when we are accused of giving our Lady the titles and offices of her Son, that St. Irenaeus bestows upon her the special Name and Office proper to the Holy Ghost": i.e., Advocate or Paraclete.[47]

Four significant matters concerning Newman's thought about the Holy Spirit making the eternal Son present in the preparatory and re-creative phases of the *synkatabasis* have been clarified. First, there is a congruity between the temporal mission of the eternal Son as mediator and the Holy Spirit as life-giver which corresponds to the

---

44 Diff. ii 36, 44, 43, 32, 34. The Fathers referenced are Justin Marytr (c. 100-65), Irenaeus (c.130-200) and Tertullian (c.160-c.225).

45 Newman favours the Pauline reference to Christ as the New Adam. See PS vi 5: 64; Jfc. 89, 93, 105, 157-62, 192-4, 202, 211; TT 214, 224, 378; Ath. ii 61, 120, 132, 187, 206, 274; Ess. i 250-2; Diff. i 277; LD xiii 342; LD xix 368; Mix. 64, 298-9, 305.

46 Jfc. 195.

47 Diff. ii 37.

hypostatic character of their divine persons. Second, the mission of the Holy Spirit is to be understood indirectly in light of the mission of the Son. Third, the unified, complementary, distinct and perichoretic nature of divine filial and pneumatic acts in the *synkatabasis* is, sometimes, conveyed by use of the spacial metaphor of inner-outer. Fourth, and finally, pneumatic preparation of Mary for the office of *Theotokos* is another way of speaking about her Immaculate Conception. Mary is full of the Holy Spirit and her pneumatic office as *Theotokos* is indispensable for the event of the incarnation. This office engages and respects her entire humanity and embodies a co-redemptive dimension, that is, a receptivity to the ongoing work of the Spirit in making present the redemptive work of Christ.

CHAPTER FOUR

THE HOLY SPIRIT IN THE LIFE OF JESUS

Perhaps one of the most underdeveloped areas of Newman studies is the question of how the Holy Spirit operates in the life of Jesus. Initially, the general difficulty of asserting that Newman possesses a potent theology of the Holy Spirit in the life of Jesus is examined, especially as it relates to his Athanasian-inspired christology. This prepares the way for a specific examination of possible shortcomings in the effectiveness of his pneumatic christology. In turn, this examination leads to a consideration of the charges that Newman does not adequately account for the human nature of the God-man in his christology. If true, these shortcomings and charges would undermine the integrity of his pneumatic christology.

Over and against these putative failings, the fundamental strength of Newman's pneumatic christology is then presented. First, a response is given to the aforementioned possible shortcomings and charges. Then, a positive argument is mounted which illumines the office of the Holy Spirit in the ontological constitution of the God-man, his transfiguration, baptism in the Jordan, flight to the desert, fasting and pasch. Concern that Newman advances an immanent christology dissipates in the face of this fulsome pneumatic christology. "Christ ... was born of the Spirit ... He was justified by the Spirit ... He was pronounced the well-beloved Son, when the Holy Ghost descended on Him ... He was led into the wilderness by the Spirit; He did great

---

The material in this chapter is a revised & extended version of Donald Graham, "The Pneumatic Christology of John Henry Newman," *Louvain Studies* 28 (2003): 275-94.

works by the Spirit; He offered Himself to death by the Eternal Spirit ...."[1]

SHORTCOMINGS

An opening of Newman's mind about the presence of the Holy Spirit in the life of Jesus appears in his brief gloss on the scriptural title, "Spirit of God," in his *Select Treatises on St. Athanasius* where he renders judgments rather than building arguments. At the outset, he strings together disparate historical observations and theological judgments concerning the Holy Spirit. The brevity and variety of these are worth noting, if only to demonstrate Newman's awareness of the pneumatological dimension of patristic thought. First, he lists "certain difficulties" encountered by patristic writers in applying this scriptural title to the persons, offices and acts of the triune God, particularly, as regards "the economy and mission of mercy" shared by the Son and Spirit. To surmount this difficulty, he recommends the heuristic of Athanasius: "the Holy Ghost is never in Scripture called simply 'Spirit' without the addition of 'God,' or 'of the Father,' or 'from Me,' or of the article, or of 'Holy,' or 'The Paraclete,' or 'of the truth,' or unless He has just been spoken of just before". Next, he observes that some Fathers used the term 'Spirit' to speak "more or less distinctly of our Lord's divine nature in itself or as incarnate". Then he proceeds to defend the hypostatic distinctness of the Holy Spirit against Macedonian and Arian assaults by reference to the trinitarian terms of origin: ingenerate, generate and proceeding. Finally, he contrasts patristic characterizations of the Holy Spirit as "God's gift" with heretical attempts to disassociate the Spirit of God in the Old Testament from the Paraclete in the New Testament (Prestige 1952, xxiii).[2]

In the midst of his *ad hoc* survey of pneumatological controversy, Newman pauses to consider the role of the Spirit in the sanctification of the Word made flesh. He enumerates several Fathers who regard "our Lord's Godhead" as "the immediate anointing or chrism of the manhood" over and against the "more common" judgment "that the anointing was the descent of the Spirit".[3] Knowledge of these varying views of the Lord's sanctification reveals Newman's sense of the

1 PS v 10: 139.

2 Ath. ii 304, 305-6, 307-9.

3 Ath ii 306-7; 307.

struggle in patristic thought to reconcile the genuinely human history of Jesus with the metaphysical fact of his perfect manhood and perfect divinity at moments like his conception and baptism. The Greek philosophy informing patristic theology tended to devalue the historical actualization of being seeing it simply as the *a priori* fulfilment of an ontological structure. This tendency was gradually tempered by eastern patristic theology (Meyendorff 1979, 24; Hill 1982, 50) which – nurtured by its biblical faith in the doctrine of *creatio ex nihilo* – transcended Greek ontological monism by identifying *hypostasis* with divine person (Zizioulas 1985, 27-65, Prestige 1952, 242-3). In turn, this trinitarian achievement opened the way to the discovery of the human being as a 'person', although appropriating the implications of the Cappadocian contribution remained the task of centuries (Zizioulas 1995, 44-60). In response to Arian claims that change meant Jesus could not be *homoousios* or adoptionist claims that he became God in virtue of his Spirit-baptism in the Jordan, orthodox theologians tended to transfer attention away from the historical unfolding of his life toward the ontological moment of his incarnation. As Raniero Cantalamessa argues pneumatic christology was attenuated by this undervaluation of the historical in the life of Jesus and the focus upon the self-sufficiency of the eternal Son.

> The problem of the *foundation* of salvation (that is, how the Saviour *is made*) becomes more important than the problem of the *unfolding* of salvation (that is, what the Saviour *does*). The baptism is now a Christological mystery only in the active sense (Christ operates in it) and not in the passive sense as well (it operates in Christ). Jesus' baptism in other words is important and efficacious for us, but not for him. 'The descent of the Holy Spirit on Jesus in the Jordan,' says St. Athanasius, 'was for our benefit because he bore our body; and it did not happen to make the Word perfect but to make us holy' .... The Holy Spirit intervenes at Jesus' baptism, we now see, more to attest to Christ's dignity than to anoint and consecrate his humanity ... The anointing loses it true Trinitarian character ... he who anoints is still and ever the Father, and he who is anointed is still and ever Christ's human nature, but the chrism with which he is still anointed is no longer, properly speaking, the Holy Spirit but the Word himself. In Christ, the human nature is anointed, that is to say sanctified by the divine nature, by the very fact of the hypostatic union ... The function of the Holy Spirit with regard to the person of Jesus is only that of causing his human nature, by miraculously effecting, in Mary, the incarnation of the Word .... The most obvious result of all this is a certain weakening of the pneumatic dimension of Christology, that is the attention accorded to the Holy Spirit's

activity in the life of Jesus (1994, 8-10; see Congar 1986, 83-100; 1997, i 21; Wilken 1972, 268-77).

This position advanced by Raniero Cantalamessa finds support in the work of David Coffey and Boris Bobrinskoy (1979, 91-141;1984, 49-65). Bobrinskoy cites Irenaeus as the exemplar of vigorous second-century pneumatic christology that, subsequently, is attenuated under Origen and, consequently, is inadequate to the theological challenges faced by Athanasius who did not have "the conceptual resources needed to define the relation of the Holy Spirit to the Son, other than by analogy with the relation of the Son to the Father (1984, 54; McDonnell 1998, 317-19; Smith 1998, 319-21)." Admittedly, Bobrinskoy parts ways with Cantalamessa's judgment when he lauds later Fathers, such as the Cappadocians, for developing a theology that is sound regarding the "specificity of the person and work of the Holy Spirit" especially as this concerns "the redemptive economy of the eternal Son"(1984, 52, 53). Nonetheless, Cantalamessa, Coffey, Bobrinskoy and others, such as R.P.C. Hanson, (1988, 748-53) find Athanasian pneumatology quite inadequate to the task of specifying the fulsome pneumatic dimension of christology.

Notwithstanding the earlier demonstration of Newman's lively sense that the eternal Son and Holy Spirit act in a unified, complementary and distinct manner in the *synkatabasis*, one is led to ask two questions: does this "certain weakening of the pneumatic dimension of Christology" spoken of by Cantalamessa inform Newman's Athanasian-inspired christology to preclude proper consideration of pneumatic activity? and, does his God-man possess a full humanity, especially as regards the human soul (Graef 1967, 51-3; Daly 1984, 289-90; Thomas 1991, 65)? The first question seeks to discover whether he perceives the Holy Spirit to operate in the life of the God-man in an effective or putative manner; the second question seeks to discover if he does justice to the dimensions of the arena – *enhypostasized* humanity – within which this pneumatic performance occurs.

Writing to Arthur Alleyne in the summer of 1860 on the matter of the Immaculate Conception, Newman states, "Our Lord, as Mediator in two natures, is called the only sinless, because he is sinless apart from grace; His divine nature sufficing to sanctify His human nature, independently of the operation of the Holy Ghost."[4] This

4 LD xix 367.

statement rightfully asserts that the *enhypostasizing* of human nature in the Person of the eternal Son effects an immediate and superabundant sanctification of that which is assumed. However, the qualifying phrase – "independently of the operation of the Holy Ghost" – dilutes Newman's insistence upon the co-inherent nature of the economic activity shared by the Spirit and Son. By speaking as if 'one' of the 'two hands of the Father' does not need the 'other', he suggests that the Spirit is secondary in the sanctification of the *enhypostasization* of the humanity of the eternal Son. Read in this light, his statement weakens the earlier claim of this study that he sees the economy of grace as an undivided mystery of crib, cross, empty tomb and descent of the dove. It is difficult not to read the phrase as downgrading the pneumatic contribution to the constitution of the God-man and distancing the invisible Spirit (uncreated grace) from the visible Son (incarnation).

Now Newman certainly believed in the non-exclusive, but proper, indwelling of the Holy Spirit in the souls of the justified. He states this forthrightly in his *Lectures on the Doctrine of Justification*: "our justification and sanctification ... is nothing short of the indwelling in us of God the Father and the Word Incarnate through the Holy Ghost. *This* is to be justified, to receive the Divine Presence within us, and be made a Temple of the Holy Ghost"(Guielmo 1959, 63).[5] Regardless of Newman's position on justification, his claim that he did not know Thomas well,[6] and the fact that he was not discernibly influenced by scholasticism, his phrase, "independently of the operation of the Holy Ghost" resembles, from a certain angle, the reified theology of grace advanced by some contemporary interpreters of St. Thomas. A few scholars argue that Newman knew the scholastic tradition better than sometimes supposed and advise one to treat cautiously the commonplace judgment that he possessed of Aquinas merely "an educated Catholic's second-hand knowledge"(Davis 1964,158; Evans 1979, 203). Others, even more speculatively, have moved in an opposite direction associating his theology of uncreated grace with aspects of Karl Rahner's transcendental Thomism (Testa 1993, 167-78). Thus clarifying Newman's position is necessary.

At one point in his work, Newman refers to Aquinas on the consequences of the hypostatic union from the same section of the *Summa*

5 Jfc. 144.

6 PN ii 177.

Theologica which speaks of the grace of union (ST IIIa, q. 16, a. 8).[7] Aquinas affirms that Christ "was filled with the grace of the Holy Ghost from the beginning of his conception"(ST IIIa q 39 a.2; see q 34 a.1.) but places this work of habitual grace after the grace of union (ST IIIa q 7 a.1, a.9.).

> For the grace of union is the personal being that is given *gratis* from above to the human nature in the Person of the Word, and is the term of the assumption. Whereas the habitual grace pertaining to the spiritual holiness of the man is an effect, following the union (ST IIIa q 6 a.6.).

The grace of union is first given to Christ personally (ST IIIa q7) and, subsequently, as Head of the Church (ST IIIa q8); and, the work of the Spirit is consequent upon the grace of union. This theological explanation safeguards the ontological perfection of the hypostatic union so that one does not slide into adoptionism (ST IIIa q 7 a.9).

Certainly one should neither distort Thomas' distinction by exaggeration nor force it into a false separation. It is a matter of priority and emphasis; the Angelic Doctor distinguishes but does not separate the operation of habitual grace and the person of the Spirit in the God-man. Yet measured against Newman's own understanding of the economic missions as united, complementary and distinct, his approach is not flawless. If the perfection of the hypostatic union does not immediately involve the Spirit then pneumatic activity in the *enhypostasis* is somehow subsequent and additive. If the pneumatic contribution to the ontological constitution of the God-man is foremostly the created effect of the Spirit (habitual grace) and, secondarily, the gift of the person of the Spirit (uncreated grace) then the impersonal takes priority over the personal (Coffey 1979, 124; Kasper, 1976, 249-52; von Balthasar 1992, 184-6). If the distinctive action of the eternal Son is not complemented by the distinctive action of the Spirit then the Lord and Giver of Life appears as a junior rather than as an equal. This approach is also inconsistent with Newman's theology of uncreated grace[8] (Dessain 1962) as worked out in his *Lectures on the Doctrine of Justification* which stands or falls with his understanding of the personal presence of the Holy Spirit preceding the bestowal of pneumatic gifts: if this is the case with the redeemed, how can it not be true of the Redeemer in his assumption of humanity through

7 LD xxix 10.

8 Jfc. 144.

which the gift of that Spirit is bestowed? Considered over and against Newman's awareness that Augustine "makes [gift] a personal characteristic of the Third Person", a characterization which becomes a mainstay of the western Tradition, and his references to the Holy Spirit as the Giver of gifts,[9] this point intensifies.

The letter of Newman to Alleyne speaks of the self-sanctification of the Word. As mentioned, it is unlikely that scholasticism moved him in this direction. More probably, the influence came from Athanasius. Entertaining this conjecture involves the scrutiny of selected passages of Athanasius that Newman had translated, commented upon and adopted in which the self-sufficiency of the eternal Son is stressed over and against the pneumatic anointing of his hypostasized humanity. That Newman was intimately aware of the Athanasian emphasis upon the self-sufficiency of the Word is apparent from his translation of the bishop of Alexandria's comments concerning the exaltation of Christ in *Philippians* 2: 8-9 (Dragas 1979, 51-72) and his own adoption of the Athanasian interpretation of the baptism of the Lord which highlights the divinity of the Son more than the action of the Spirit. Athanasius filters *Philippians* 2: 8-9 on the exaltation of the Lord through an immanent christology so that the power inherent in the resurrection is strictly attributed to the Word. Newman translated the passage as follows:

"[A]nd, as the Word, He gives what comes from the Father, for all things which the Father does and gives, He does and supplies through Him; and as being the Son of Man, He Himself is said, after the manner of men, to receive what proceeds from Himself, because His Body is none other than His, and is a natural recipient of grace, as has been said. For He received it as far as man's nature was exalted; which exaltation was its being deified. But such an exaltation the Word always had according to the Father's Godhead and perfection, which was His."[10] Although the sentence juxtaposing exaltation and deification connotes pneumatic activity, the prior and subsequent sentences specify the divinity of the Word as the immediate source of this elevation. Athanasius rightly resists reading pneumatic references into the pericope, but equally he refrains from placing it over and against scriptural texts (*Rms* 1:4, 8: 11; *1 Cor* 15: 45; *2 Cor* 3: 17-18) that assign the

9 SN 271-2; 285-7.

10 Ath. i 225 which is an exegesis of Philippians 2: 8-9.

Holy Spirit a significant role in the exaltation of Christ (Montague 1976, 204, 208-9, 141-2, 188-91).

Certainly this sort of immanent christology contrasts with Newman's celebration of the dynamic role of the Holy Spirit in raising Jesus from the dead in his *Lectures on Justification*. Regardless, the relevant resemblance remains: his letter to Alleyne and the Athanasian passage assert that the Word is the immediate source of the divinization of the Godmanhood at significant historical moments (ontological constitution/resurrection) to the comparative exclusion of the Holy Spirit. Athanasius understands the eternal Son's assumption of humanity as the permanent "means and guarantor" of the grace of deification. He understands the Holy Spirit to transmit and apply what the Son has secured to God's people through his incarnation (Petterson 1995, 105; Bobrinskoy 1999, 224). Similarly, Newman depicts Christ as the agent of atonement and the Holy Spirit as the agent of justification so that Christ is the one who brings the Spirit and the Spirit is the one who imparts the life of Christ to the Church.[11] Hence Athanasius and Newman both move gracefully from what Christ has done, to what His Spirit does *pro nobis*. Yet, in itself, this critical soteriological move assumes but does not adequately account for the effective presence of the Spirit in the life of the God-man.

There are further instances in which Newman, following Athanasius, directs attention toward the ontological perfection of the God-man overshadowing consideration of the consecration of his humanity by the Holy Spirit. For example, Newman's commentary upon the Athanasian exegesis of the baptism of the Lord in light of the messianic psalm verse, "'Therefore God, Thy God, hath anointed Thee,' & etc" fails to move beyond its focus upon the divinity of the One anointed. The possibility that this anointing equips the God-man for his historical mission is not contemplated. Newman adheres to the Athanasian line:

> "*Wherefore*," says Athan. [sic] "does not imply reward of virtue or conduct in the Word, but the reason why He came down to us, and of the Spirit's anointing which took place in Him for our sakes. For he says not, 'Wherefore He anointed Thee in order to Thy being God or King or Son or Word;' for so He was before and is for ever, as has been shown; but rather, 'Since Thou art God and King, therefore Thou wast anointed, since

11 Jfc. 202-22.

> none but Thou couldest unite man to the Holy Ghost, Thou Image of the Father, in which we were made in the beginning; for Thine also is the Spirit' .... That as through Him we have come to be, so also in Him all men might be redeemed from their sins and by Him all things might be ruled."

Athanasius stresses that the baptismal anointing in the Jordan does not make Christ into God, but occurs because He is God, after which he states that the unction "took place in Him for our sakes". Although the citation is extracted from a passage containing several references to the anointed humanity of Christ as the means by which "He might provide for us men, not only exaltation and resurrection, but the indwelling and intimacy of the Spirit,"[12] the meaning of this anointing in the historical life of the God-man himself never arises. Rather, the text considers the anointing exclusively *pro nobis* and relative to the fact that the One anointed is God. In the face of Gnosticism and Arianism (Petterson 1995, 110), Athanasius maximizes the truth of *homoousios* and minimizes that which potentially detracts from it – such as, a discussion of the Holy Spirit operative in the humanity of the God-man in a manner which hostile interpreters might construe as implying insufficiency. Leaving the Athanasian point of view unaltered in his commentary, Newman seems to make his own its concentration upon the self-sufficiency of the divinity of the Word.

Notwithstanding its real achievement, these examples of Athanasian-christology and Newman's appropriation of them are open to criticism. Sometimes, the Spirit is characterized statically and impersonally as the unction self-bestowed by the Son rather than dynamically as the third divine-person-acting. Fear of compromising the Word's perfection occasionally leads Athanasius to conceive his completeness in a manner which renders receiving, even from the Holy Spirit, superfluous. These incidents emphasize the self-sufficiency of the eternal Son relative to his assumed humanity *pro nobis* and diminish economic interplay between the divine actors. Consequently, the Holy Spirit is assigned an auxiliary place pre-empting queries about his role in helping to make effective the mission of the God-man (Dragas 1979, 70). However, according to Prestige, the same criticism does not apply to Athanasius' thought concerning coinherence *ad intra* (1952, 257-9). In this vein, R.P.C. Hanson charges Athanasius with treating the Holy Spirit as the "understudy" of Word, and contends

12 Ath. i 269-70, 269, 227, 228, 226.

that in his *Letters to Serapion*[13] one misses "any serious understanding of the distinct function of the Holy Spirit in salvation. This is partly because Athanasius, like all Christian writers from the third century onwards at least, has lost the eschatological note which the New Testament witness to the Spirit contains, so that it never occurs to him to relate the Holy Spirit to time, and partly because his christology has to some extent absorbed his soteriology" (1988, 751-2).[14]

Now Newman definitely acknowledges the presence of the Holy Spirit in the history of the incarnate Word. The pneumatological dimension of the mystery of the incarnate Word is dynamically present in his presentation of the God-man as the personal, sacramental *via* of salvation: Christian rebirth occurs precisely because the humanity sanctified and assumed by the Lord is communicated to humankind by that same Spirit. The Life-giver who hovers over the void of creation and over the womb of Mary, hovers over each of the sanctified because the Son of God "vouchsafed to give us His Holy Spirit through the breath of His human nature."

> He gives us abundantly of His Spirit; but still He gives It not at once from His Divine Nature, though from eternity the Holy Ghost proceeds from the Son as well as from the Father, but by means of that incorruptible flesh which He has taken on Him. For Christ is come a High Priest through the tabernacle which He assumed, a tabernacle not of this creation, or in the ordinary course of nature, but framed miraculously of the substance of the Virgin by the Holy Ghost; and therefore the streams of life flow to us from Him, as God indeed, but still as God incarnate. 'That which quickeneth us is the Spirit of the Second Adam, and His flesh is that wherewith He quickeneth.'[15]

Yet, beyond repeating the biblical testimony that the Spirit frames the flesh of Christ, Newman, in the examined passages, portrays pneumatic operations predominantly from a *pro nobis* perspective protecting the integrity of the hypostatic union at the expense of the person of the Holy Spirit. The letter to Alleyne speaks of the self-sanctification of the Word, a position which is conspicuous in passages of Athanasius that he had translated, commented upon and adopted.

13 *Four Letters of St. Athanasius to Bishop Serapion of Thmius.*

14 For more favourable assessments of Athanasian pneumatology, see Kannengiesser 1981,178-9; Campbell 1974, 408-40 and Kelly 1978, 255-8.

15 See PS v 7: 86, PS ii 19: 218, PS ii 12: 128, 132 and Heb 2:11 which is the sermon text of PS v 7 at 86. Citations at PS vi 5: 63, 64.

This position exposes his theology to the charge that the Holy Spirit operates in the life of the God-man less effectively than putatively, less co-inherently than additively, less as person than as power, less as peer than as subordinate. This runs against his view of the unified, complementary, distinct and perichoretic character of divine acts in the *synkatabasis*. It also is inconsistent with his theology of justification which insists upon the indwelling of the person of the Spirit in the redeemed and not simply the action of his grace in the soul. This theology is premised upon the belief that the person of the Spirit operates in every facet of the life of the God-man bestowing upon humanity that which was bestowed upon him from the first instant of his ontological constitution, that which was efficacious throughout his entire history, and revealed gloriously upon his exaltation – that is, the person-gift of his Holy Spirit.

Although a thorough assessment of Newman's christology reaches beyond the present discussion, one must also evaluate the completeness of the *enhypostasized* humanity within which he envisions the Holy Spirit operating for critics charge him with undermining Christ's humanity by overemphasizing his divinity. The tenor and substance of their charges are now examined. In several Anglican sermons, Newman speaks of the virgin birth in an austere tone suggesting that even redeemed human sexual activity remains tainted by original sin and that, for this reason, regular conception was removed from divine possibility in bringing about the incarnation (Strange 1980, 114-26).[16] For some, later disavowals do not staunch suspicions that his theology of the God-man is affected by that approach which initially permitted such a position to take hold.

In 1834, Newman wrote that the eternal Son took upon himself Adam's unfallen nature.[17] His 1881 notes on Athanasius record his Catholic change of position: "[Christ] assumed it as it is **after the fall**, -- though of course some explanations have to be made".[18] While writing to his former Anglican curate, W.J. Copeland, on the occasion of the latter's re-editing of his *Parochial and Plain Sermons* in 1877, he notes this same change of view and indicates that "the Anglican 9th Article" (Of Original or Birth Sin) was the likely source of his origi-

16 PS ii 3: 31; PS v 7: 90; Ps v 9: 120; JHNS i 33: 253.

17 JHNS i 33: 253.

18 Ath. ii 120; see 192, 294-5; emphasis added.

nal view.[19] Similar concern exists regarding Newman's shift from his Anglican belief that the Lord lacked perfect knowledge in virtue of his assumption of fallen human nature[20] to his Catholic belief that the Lord had perfect knowledge in virtue of the beatific vision enjoyed by the Godmanhood. Occurrences of the Lord's ignorance were apparent; they illustrated how he had assumed ignorance economically, not in fact. To argue otherwise is to associate the Lord with sin and oneself with heretics.[21] This led Newman in his re-publication of the *Parochial and Plain Sermons* (1868) to amend his words from Christ "was partially ignorant" to "apparently ignorant".[22] That he reaches this conclusion (Christ in his humanity is not at all ignorant) for the right reason (the desire not to predicate anything of the God-man which implicates him in sin), does not dispel questions about the adequacy of his understanding of the hypostatic union. Such difficulties multiply when one considers other situations in which Newman seems to denigrate human nature. For example, he describes the God-man within the immaculate womb of the Virgin, as "feeling the extreme irksomeness of the prison-house full of grace as it was".[23] Granted, benign interpretations are possible. Divine condescension necessarily involves acceptance of the limitations of space-time, and proximity to sin, neither of which denigrates human nature *in se*; moreover, the text in question conveys Newman's perception of the blessedness of living in eternity over and against the strictures accepted by the Son in becoming human. This is confirmed when he compares the Creator's immanent presence to the soul "polluted" by "sin" to a prison, as well as speaking of the fallen world "dimly show[ing] forth His glory". In these instances, proximity to sin rather than creation itself is pinpointed as the origin of the prison metaphor.[24] Nevertheless, on one occasion, he depicts the emotions of Christ in a mechanistic manner which makes one wonder how they are seated in his human existence.

> His mind was its own centre, and was never in the slightest degree thrown off its heavenly and most perfect balance. What he suffered, He suffered

19 LD xxviii 250-1.

20 PS v 21: 305.

21 Ath. ii 162, 165-7, 169, 170-1; see PVD 182.

22 PS iii 10: 129.

23 OS 82.

24 Mix. 291, 290.

> because He put Himself under suffering, and that calmly and deliberately ... His composure is but the proof how entirely He governed His own mind. He drew back, at the proper moment, the bolts and fastenings, and opened the gates, and the flood fell right upon His soul in all their fulness.[25]

Speaking metaphorically as to make suspect the capacity of human nature for redemption, attributing the beatific vision to Christ in a manner that renders cognitive development superfluous, and envisioning the field of human emotions as mechanically operated by a divine person are problematic if one insists that the God-man is 'like us in all things but sin'. Set in the context of Newman's sometime subjectivism,[26] and placed over and against his predilection to explain aspects of existence in idealistic (Weatherby 1973, 68-82) and Platonic terms (Bouyer 1963, 111-31),[27] these difficulties fire misgivings about whether he affirms, at the deepest level, the full assumption of humanity by God in Christ Jesus.

This range of difficulties has led critics like Stephen Thomas to relate without further qualification that "Apollinarianism, with its high Christology stressing the identity of Christ as Divine Logos has been suggested as an appropriate designation for Newman's *own* view of the person of Christ" (1991, 65). This accusation is a death-knell for any orthodox pneumatic christology. If Newman holds – theoretically or *de facto* – that the God-man possesses other than a real human soul, his soteriology impales upon his christology. What is not assumed is not saved. A soul-less, *enhypostasized* humanity is incapable of serving as a living icon into which enfleshed souls can be sacramentally immersed and deified. Admittedly, John Meyendorff affirms that Athanasius well understood there to be two natures in Christ (and thus a fully human soul) despite the ambiguities inherent in his theological vocabulary and Alvyn Petterson categorically rejects the "commonly received opinion of scholarship" that Athanasius admitted no human soul prior to 362 and gave the soul "no theological function" (1975, 154; 1995, 130). However, the judgment of R.P.C. Hanson and Aloys Grillmeier is that Athanasius significantly neglects or downplays the question of the soul of the God-man in his theological ruminations. Hanson claims that until 362, "it never crossed his mind that there

25 Mix. 333-4.

26 Apo. 74; US xv: 347-9, esp. 349 n.5.

27 Apo. 26, PS i 2: 18-20, PS ii 29: 362; PS iv 13: 200-13; Ess. ii 193.

was any point in maintaining that Jesus had a human soul or mind", describes his mention of a human soul as merely 'formal' and says that he "does not actually reach the point of envisaging two natures in Jesus Christ" as proclaimed a century later in the *Tome of Leo* (1988, 451, 452). Aloys Grillmeier, SJ, reaches a more restrained, proximate conclusion: "The soul of Christ was no 'theological factor' for Athanasius, but at the same time he may not have denied its 'physical' reality" (1975, 310 n.37). When the Hanson-Grillmeier judgment is placed alongside Newman's reverence for Athanasian christology and viewed in light of his own aforementioned 'difficulties', it is not possible to dismiss Apollinarian accusations out of hand. Given Newman's overt references to the soul of the God-man,[28] the criticism is levelled at his supposed failure to ensure that the *enhypostasized* human soul functions *qua* human soul, not his denial of its actual existence.

STRENGTH

Two pivotal questions have been asked of Newman's pneumatic christology: does the Holy Spirit operate in the life of the God-man in an effective or putative manner? is justice done to the *enhypostasized* humanity within which this pneumatic activity occurs? Now that supposed shortcomings and certain charges surrounding Newman's position have been presented, it is time to examine its fundamental strength.

Earlier the possible theological shortcomings of Newman's 1860 phrase "independently of the operation of the Holy Ghost" were enumerated. One possibility was left unexamined. Perhaps Newman envisions the phrase as a statement that brackets, but does not deny, the unity and complementarity of this distinct activity of the eternal Son with the Holy Spirit. Quite possibly he brackets as a means of distinguishing sharply between the *sui generis* sinlessness of the God-man who has no need of sanctification and the fallen state of human beings who are sorely in need of the Spirit. The reasonableness of this interpretation is upheld both by understanding the specific context of Newman's comment and examining more fully his understanding of the pneumatic dimension of the ontological constitution of Christ.

The historical context of this phrase renders Newman's use of it understandable, but does not remove the theological difficulties it

28 Mix. 324.

engenders. In his letter to Arthur Alleyne, Newman was eager to uphold the necessary distinction between Christ's assumption of a human nature with infirmities consequent upon the fall, and a fallen human nature with infirmities tantamount to sin. In so doing, he sought to avoid the mistake of Edward Irving, the founder of the Catholic Apostolic Church, who spoke of Christ assuming a fallen but sinful flesh subsequently sanctified by the Holy Spirit (Strange 1981, 81-4). As demonstrated immediately below, the special role which Newman assigns the Holy Spirit in the constitution of the hypostatic union confirms that his use of the phrase, "independently of the operation of Holy Ghost" is a context-specific adjustment not a methodological principle.

Though moderated by his respect for the prominent place of the eternal Son in the event of incarnation, Newman, nonetheless, affirms a distinct pneumatic role in the mystery. While he speaks of the "unsearchable Love" of God as the cause of the incarnation, the temporal fashioning of this most mysterious of mysteries is not a solitary activity but involves the eternal Son and Holy Spirit in virtually indistinguishable acts. In his Christmas sermon of 1834, "The Incarnation," he speaks of their roles in the ontological constitution of the God-man.

> He came by a new and living way; not, indeed, formed out of the ground, as Adam was at the first, lest He should miss the participation of our nature, but selecting and purifying unto Himself a tabernacle out of that which existed ... He was, as had been foretold, the immaculate 'seed of the woman' deriving His manhood from the substance of the Virgin Mary; as it is expressed in the articles of the Creed, 'conceived by the Holy Ghost, born of the Virgin Mary' .... Thus He came into this world , not in the clouds of heaven, but born into it, born of a woman; He, the Son of Mary, and she (if it may be said), the mother of God. Thus He came, selecting and setting apart for Himself the elements of body and soul; then, uniting them to Himself from their first origin of existence, pervading them, hallowing them by His own Divinity, spiritualizing them, and filling them with light and purity, the while they continued to be human, and for a time mortal and exposed to infirmity.[29]

The accent in this passage is upon the Word who comes, selects, purifies, sets apart, unites, pervades, hallows, spiritualizes and fills the human elements that constitute his complete humanity.[30] Yet, the

29 PS ii 3: 31, 32; see PS iii 12: 156-7.

30 On the complementarity of Spirit and Word in originating the hypostatic union, see PS vi 5: 61, 64 and PS v 7: 91-3; on the Word alone, see PS iv 17: 266 and LD

Word's assumption of a human nature also intimately involves the agency of the Holy Spirit "as it is expressed in the articles of the Creed, 'conceived by the Holy Ghost, born of the Virgin Mary.'" Although Newman elsewhere notes the practical impossibility of distinguishing between the actions of the Word and Spirit in the life of Jesus, here he discriminates by speaking of the Son assuming, entering and uniting to himself the earthly tabernacle vitalized by the Spirit.[31] Consequently, he associates the ontological constitution of the God-man with the eternal Son insofar as this activity is congruous with his mediatorial role as "the First-born of all things" fitting him to become the first–born of Mary.[32] Likewise, he associates the ontological constitution of the God-man with the Spirit insofar as this activity is congruous with his life-giving role, as the One who "has ever been the secret Presence of God within Creation: a source of life amid the chaos, bringing out into form and order what was at first shapeless and void." Newman conveys the perichoretic character of the constitution of the incarnation by qualifying the filial derivation of "manhood from the substance of the Virgin Mary" with the pneumatic phrase of the creed, "'conceived by the Holy Ghost, born of the Virgin Mary'". The invisible medium through which the Son mediates is the person of the Spirit. The life-giving Spirit overshadows the Virgin to form and enliven the human nature assumed by the Son. Newman associates the re-creation of the whole of humanity with the specific ontological constitution of the God-man which is depicted very much as a pneumatic event: "the Highest had taken a portion of that corrupt mass [of matter] upon Himself, in order to its sanctification ... as a firstfruits [sic] of His purpose, He had purified from all sin that very portion of it which He took into His Eternal Person, and thereunto had taken it from a Virgin Womb, which He had filled with the abundance of His Spirit."[33] While cognizant of patristic disagreement over "whether That which anointed the Manhood of the Saviour with the fulness of grace, was not rather the Divine Fulness of the Saviour Himself than the Holy Ghost," Newman believes that the "more common" patristic

---

xix 367.

31 On practical impossibility of distinguishing actions of the Word and Spirit see Ath. ii 304 and Jfc. 208-9; on distinguishing such actions see PS vi 5: 61, 64; PS v 7: 91-3; Dev. 1845: 378 and Dev. 1878: 401-2.

32 TT 218.

33 PS ii 19: 217, 218; Ps ii 12: 132; Dev. 1845: 378, Dev. 1878: 401-2.

testimony considers "the anointing" of the Godmanhood at conception as "the descent of the Spirit".[34] Hence he so situates the Spirit at the core of the constitution and assumption of humanity by the eternal Son that it is fitting to speak of this humanity as anointed from its first instant of existence. This claim is strengthened by recalling the Catholic sermon note in which he conceives the mission of the Holy Spirit to sustain all mysteries associated with his original condescension in the *synkatabasis*: "On the condescension of the Holy Ghost. Creation implies ministration, and is the beginning of mysteries. It passes the line, and other mysteries are but its continuation." There is no reason to exclude the mystery of the incarnation from this pneumatic sustenance. For the Holy Spirit, "ministers, like a servant, to the whole of creation."[35]

The deep impress of pneumatic christology upon Newman's thought is also displayed in that part of his sermon, "On the gift of the Spirit," in which he juxtaposes the encounter between Jesus and Nicodemus with comments upon the meaning of the incarnation, the transfiguration and the sacrament of baptism. The sermon illustrates powerfully his use of the sacramental analogy between pneumatic christology and pneumatic ecclesiology. More germane to the issue at hand, the sermon demonstrates his awareness of the Spirit as the agent who glorifies Jesus, who reveals him in history as the Christ, who has a role that neither replicates nor is reducible to that which belongs to the eternal Son made man.

While Newman's reason in the sermon for meditating upon Christ's words (concerning baptismal rebirth into the Kingdom by water and Spirit) is translucent, his reason for interspersing these matters with comments about the incarnation and the radiance of the transfiguration is more opaque. As the sermon unfolds, he specifies the common factor con-joining these events: the coming of the Kingdom of God through the Spirit, one's entrance into this Kingdom through baptism and the transfiguration are consequent upon the incarnation. He opens his clarification of this connection by discussing the glory forfeited by those who repudiate the gift of the Spirit.

> I would have you pay particular attention to this last passage, which, in speaking of those who thwart God's grace, runs through the various

34 Jfc. 209; Ath. ii 307.

35 SN 306; PVD 289.

> characteristics or titles of that glory which they forfeit: – illumination, the heavenly gift, the Holy Ghost, the Divine Word, the powers of the world to come; which all mean the same thing, viewed in different lights, viz., that unspeakable Gospel privilege, which is an earnest and portion of that glory, of the holiness and blessedness of the Angels – a present entrance into the next world, opened upon our souls through participation of the Word Incarnate, ministered to us by the Holy Ghost.

Here Newman makes explicit his view that the gift of the Spirit is the deification of the human person which he attributes to the distinct yet complementary missions of the Son and Spirit who together effect the Christian's participation in the glorified humanity of the risen Lord. After his discussion of the transfiguration, Newman unequivocally identifies this deification with the pneumatic rebirth spoken of by Christ in his discourse to Nicodemus and imparted in the Christian Church through baptism. Significantly, he proceeds to affirm that the glorification of the human person through the gift of the Spirit presupposes the substantial presence of that glory in the life of the God-man. That he understands the deifying gift of the Spirit as consequent upon the intimate presence of the Spirit in the life of Christ is very clear from his statement that this "greater Mystery of the Incarnate Word is made to envelope and pledge to us the mystery of the new birth." Elsewhere Newman is straightforward in identifying the Spirit as the source of Christ's glorification in the transfiguration rather than insisting that this glory be credited solely to the grace of union in the incarnation.[36]

Since Newman is resolute in his view that the indwelling of the Spirit in the human person is encompassed by the greater mystery of the presence of the Spirit in the life of the God-man, he describes the indwelling of the Spirit in the baptized in a manner which parallels the presence of the Spirit in Christ revealed during the transfiguration. He begins his discourse on baptism by characterizing it as imparting "the especial glory and 'dreadfulness' which attaches to the Christian Church." Then he states that baptism "… [is] the *only* means of entering into His Kingdom; so that, unless a man is thus, 'born of water and of the Spirit,' he is in no sense a member of His Kingdom at all. By this new birth the Divine Shechinah is set up within him, pervading soul and body … raising [the Christian] in the scale of being, drawing and fostering into life whatever remains in him of a higher nature, and

36 PS iii 18: 264-7, 263, 267, 265; see PS ii 19: 227.

imparting to him, in due season and measure, its own surpassing and heavenly virtue."[37] This description of the baptized as a member of God's kingdom in whom the Spirit of glory shines, a living tabernacle of the Divine Shechinah, is strikingly similar to that of his earlier radiant account of the transfiguration of the Lord as "a vision of the glorious Kingdom which He set up on the earth on His coming" stating that "[s]uch is the Kingdom of God; Christ the centre of it, His glory the light of it, the Just made perfect His companions, and the Apostles His witnesses to their brethren. It realizes what the ancient Saints saw by glimpses – Jacob at Bethel, Moses on Sinai."[38] The message is clear – the same Spirit who glorified Jesus on Tabor glorifies the baptized.

In the course of his sermon on the "Gift of the Spirit," Newman demonstrates that pneumatic christology is the lens through which much of his theological thought comes into focus. Through its aperture, Christ's discourse to Nicodemus about entering the Kingdom of God, the mystery of the transfiguration and the sacrament of baptism are bathed in the light of the "greater Mystery of the Word Incarnate". Within the ambit of this light, Jesus Christ is paradoxically revealed by the Spirit as the one who establishes the Kingdom in his own person because he is ultimate bearer of the glory which is the Spirit. For Newman, the mission of Jesus is revealed as the bestowal of the glorious gift of the Spirit who makes Christians to be living tabernacles radiating the same Light which glorified the Lord on Tabor, the same Spirit who was bestowed upon him from the first moment of his earthly existence.[39]

Now Newman in no way confines his understanding of the joint activity of the Son and the Spirit to trans-historical moments like Tabor or the specific act of the ontological constitution of the hypostatic union. Rather, he views the former as a revelatory moment within the totality of his life and the latter as a point of departure leading into an account of that life involving his ministry, passion, death, burial, resurrection, ascension and role as eschatological judge. The incarnation for which Son and Spirit are co-responsible, embraces not only the constitution and transfiguration of the God-man but his entire history. Careful reading of Newman conveys his sense of this intimate

37 PS iii 18: 265-6; italics belong to Newman.

38 PS iii 18: 265-6; see Jfc. 190.

39 PS ii 3: 38; PVD 392.

involvement of the Spirit in the life of the God-man.[40] For example, the One who is ontologically perfect the moment at which the hypostatic union comes into existence begins his public ministry at the hands of the Baptist in a pneumatological event *par excellence*. Newman's description of this event provides his christological thought with a pneumatological proportionality lacking in passages spotlighting the self-sufficiency of the Word.

> These blessings are commonly designated in Scripture as 'the Spirit,' or 'the gift of the Holy Ghost'. John the Baptist said of himself and Christ; 'I indeed baptize you with water unto repentance; but He shall baptize you with the Holy Ghost, and with fire' (*Mt* 3:11). In this respect, Christ's ministrations were above all that had ever been before Him, in bringing with them the gift of the Holy Ghost, that one gift, one, yet multiform, seven-fold in its operation, in which all spiritual blessedness is included. Accordingly, our Lord was solemnly anointed with the Holy Ghost Himself, as an initiation into His Ministerial office. He was manifested as receiving, that He might be believed on as giving. He was thus commissioned, according to the Prophet, 'to preach good tidings,' 'to heal the broken-hearted,' 'to give the oil of joy for mourning' [*Is* 61:1, 3]. Therefore, in like manner, the Apostles were also anointed with the same heavenly gift for the same Ministerial office. 'He breathed on them, and saith unto them, Receive ye the Holy Ghost' [*Jn* 20:22]. Such was the consecration of the Master, such was that of His Disciples; and such as His, were the offices to which they were admitted.[41]

Several points are embedded in this passage. The ministry of Christ is "above all" comprised by the bestowal of the "one gift" which contains all gifts, that is the "gift of the Holy Ghost". This is a clear statement that the gift of the Spirit is at the heart of why Christ came and comprises the core content of his ministrations. Of particular note, the anointing of the Spirit actually initiates Christ into "His Ministerial office". Without implying any ontological change, Newman speaks unabashedly of the historical moment in which the Spirit specially equips Christ for what lies ahead; the Spirit is no 'after word' from the cross.[42] The beginning of the public ministry on the banks of the river Jordan entails a bestowal of the Spirit. This bestowal corresponds to the new historical situation unfolding and opening up in the life of the God-man. This newness elicits a response, the Spirit. Yet, there

40 Ps ii 3: 31-2; Ess i. 247-8.

41 PS ii 25: 303.

42 See "On the Holy Spirit – His Nature and office," MS 339: 1 at Birmingham Oratory, A.17.1.

is no suggestion that the bestowal is 'new' in the sense of 'original' or 'initial' or 'first'. For the "ministrations" of Christ, consequent upon this baptism, are described by Newman as "above all that **had ever been** before Him, in bringing with them the gift of the Holy Ghost".[43] Use of the past perfect tense – **"had ever been"** – indicates that he perceives the Holy Spirit as ever-present in the life of Christ. Although the public nature of the baptism of the Lord serves to strengthen the faith of those who follow him – "He was manifested as receiving, that He might be believed on as giving" – this revelatory moment forms part of the sequence of private and public events that are the historical life of the one Word incarnate. Regarding the operation of the Spirit in that life, there is no schism in Newman's account between who Christ is *in se* and what he does *pro nobis*.

While illustrating that the mystery of the incarnation "lies as much in what we think we know, as in what we do not know",[44] Newman unveils his sense of the pneumatic presence in the life of Jesus by noting that the nexus between the baptism and temptation of Christ is, in fact, the person of the Spirit. He draws attention to the scripture portrait of the Spirit driving Jesus into the desert, inaugurating his confrontation with the tempter and signalling a new phase in the restoration of all things by the new Adam.

> Again, there is something of mystery in the connection of His temptation with the descent of the Holy Ghost upon Him on His baptism. After the voice from heaven had proclaimed, 'this is My beloved Son, in whom I am well pleased' [*Mt* 3:17], '*immediately*', as St. Mark says, 'the Spirit *driveth* Him into the wilderness' [*Mk* 1:12] as if there were some connection, beyond our understanding, between His baptism and temptation, the first act of the Holy Spirit is forthwith to 'drive' Him (whatever is meant by the word) into the wilderness. Observe, too, that it was almost from this solemn recognition, 'This is My beloved Son,' that the Devil took up the temptation, '*If* Thou be the Son of God, command that these stones be made 'bread' [*Mt* 4:3]; yet, what his thoughts and designs were we cannot even conjecture. All we see is a renewal, apparently, of Adam's temptation, in the person of the 'second Man.'

Newman refers to the Spirit driving the Son into the desert as "a renewal, apparently, of Adam's temptation, in the person of the 'second Man.'" Though he raises "questions" about the mystery of the

43 Emphasis added.

44 PS iii 12: 157.

hypostatic union which "admit of no satisfactory solution" his accent is upon the operation of the Spirit within the human mind and heart of the God-man. Discourse about the Spirit driving the Son into the desert in order to experience temptation is intelligible only if one understands him to possess a complete human nature. Though Newman recognizes the frailty of reason in the face of this mystery, he is unequivocal that the eternal Son takes "into Himself a creature's nature, which henceforth became as much one with Him, as much belonged to Him, as the divine attributes and powers which He had ever had."[45] That this assumed nature entails an individual human reason, affections and free will standing at a created distance from God is confirmed by his comments concerning both friendship and fasting. Thus, on one occasion Newman states, "we find our Saviour had a private friend; and this shows us, first, how entirely He was a man, as much as any of us, in His wants and feelings ..." And, considering the universal human experience of temptation, which touches body, mind and soul during fasting, he says,

> Yet, I have not mentioned the most distressing of the effects which may follow from even the moderate exercise of this great Christian duty. It is undeniably a means of temptation, and I say so lest persons should be surprised, and despond when they find it so. And the merciful Lord knows that so it is from experience; and that He has experienced and thus knows it, as Scripture records, is to us a thought full of comfort. I do not mean to say, God forbid, that aught of sinful infirmity sullied His immaculate soul; but it is plain from the sacred history, that in His case, as in ours, fasting opened the way to temptation.[46]

Newman's remarks in these sermons on fasting profile fundamental features of his pneumatic christology. He presents the Spirit as a sort of 'agent provocateur' compelling the new Adam to leave the banks of the Jordan, journey to the desert, fast, undergo temptation and face Satan, which leaves little doubt that he considers the Holy Spirit to operate effectively in the full humanity of the eternal Son. En route Newman juxtaposes three truths the logic of which ensures that the Spirit-filled life of the God-man is understood as the universal sacrament of salvation: he states that human acts are truly effective only in the power of the Spirit; he moves beyond a plain affirmation of Christ as fully human to invest each of his acts with the 'content' of grace;

45 PS iii 12: 158-9, 158, 157.

46 PS ii 5: 52; PS vi 1: 7.

and, he speaks of how events in his life are mystically reiterated in the believer. Thus the structure of his thought suggests that the Spirit present in the life of the God-man is responsible for making his saving history sacramentally accessible across history. Newman opens up a window into his understanding of how the Spirit-filled humanity of the eternal Son is capable of serving sacramentally as the vehicle of salvation when he mentions the manner in which his fasting differs from that other human beings. "His fasting was unlike ours, as in its intensity so in its object." While the Christian fasts to do penance, subdue the flesh, imitate the Saviour and receive grace, the Lord fasts to set an example, inaugurate his confrontation with Satan, prepare for his ministry and experience human temptation in a manner proportionate to his hypostatic being. The last point is of utmost importance. Newman observes that the difference issuing from the union of natures in the person of the Son enhances rather than vitiates his experience of the human condition.

> For if it be a trial to us creatures and sinners to have thoughts alien from our hearts presented to us, what must have been the suffering to the Eternal Word ... to have been so subjected to Satan, that he could inflict misery on Him short of sinning? Certainly it is a trial to us to have motives and feelings imputed to us before men, by the accuser of the brethren, which we never entertained; it is a trial to have ideas secretly suggested within, from which we shrink; it is a trial to us for Satan to be allowed so to mix his own thoughts with ours, that we feel guilty even when we are not; nay, to be able to set on fire our irrational nature, till in some sense we sin against our will; but has not One gone before us more awful in His trial, more glorious in His victory? He was tempted in all points 'like as we are, yet without sin.' Surely here, too, Christ's temptation speaks comfort and encouragement to us.[47]

Elsewhere Newman leaves no doubt that the ontological basis of this intensification of 'God's human experience' is due to the hypostatic union. "Christ felt bodily pain more keenly than any other man, because His soul was exalted by personal union with the Word of God. Christ felt bodily pain more keenly than any other man, as much as man feels pain more keenly than any other animal." Now there is no "comfort and encouragement to us" if Christ did not really imbibe from the chalice of human suffering. Newman is emphatic, "the God-man has gone before us more awful in His trial, more glorious in His

47 PS vi 1: 1, 8-9; see PS v 10: 139.

victory ... tempted in all points 'like as we are, yet without sin.'" He stresses the coming of the Lord occurs in the "course of ordinary human life ... in the fulness and exactness of human nature ... in that very flesh which had fallen in Adam, and with all our infirmities, all our feelings and sympathies, sin excepted."[48] Those who suggest that Newman's christology is compromised by Apollinarian tendencies, in the face of his confession of the complete humanity of Christ and condemnation of Apollinarianism,[49] never address his position on the unsurpassable intensification of human experience in the God-man. They do not account for Newman's position that the Spirit-filled *enhypostasized* humanity of the eternal Son amplifies his experience of the human condition in precise proportion to the immeasurable depth of his divine person to illumine the mysterious truth that God and man are reconciled in Christ. The clarity and insistence of Newman's insight into *enhypostazation* as the intensification not the vitiation of humanity reaches its apogee in his mediation on the "Familiarity of Jesus":

> O Jesu, it became Thee, the great God, thus abundantly and largely to do Thy work, for which the Father sent Thee. Thou didst not do it by halves – and, while that magnificence of Sacrifice is Thy glory as God, it is our consolation and aid as sinners. O dearest Lord, Thou art more fully man than the holy Baptist, than St. John, Apostle and Evangelist, than Thy own sweet Mother. As in Divine knowledge of me Thou art beyond them all, so also in experience and personal knowledge of my nature. Thou art my elder brother. How can I fear, how should I not repose my whole heart on one so gentle, so tender, so familiar, so unpretending, so modest, so natural, so humble? Thou art now, though in heaven, just the same as Thou wast on earth: the mighty God, yet the little child – the all-holy, yet the all-sensitive, all-human.[50]

PASCHAL PENTECOST

Four pneumatological moments in the New Testament particularly signal the transition from the earthly ministry of Christ to the beginning of the Church: the paschal pentecost of commendation (*Lk* 23:46), the Johannine pentecost of the upper room (*Jn* 19:30; 7:38-9), the ascension of the Lord (*Mt* 27:50), and the Lucan pentecost

48 PVD 355; 385-6; see PS iv 16: 242.

49 See TT 307-8, 317, 319; Ath. ii. 193.

50 PVD 386.

described in Acts (*Acts* 7:60; see *Ps* 31:5). These moments interpret the "same fundamental event of the history of salvation: the outpouring of the Spirit made possible by the paschal sacrifice of Christ." In them, "at different moments and in different ways ... Easter and Pentecost draw near to one another" (Cantalamessa 2001, 35). While each figures in Newman's theology of Christ and the Church, the moment most central to his christology is the paschal pentecost of commendation. Newman enters into this moment with actute psychological perception in his Catholic sermon, "The Mental Sufferings of our Lord in His Passion".

The cry of Christ, simultaneously drawing his last breath and breathing forth his Spirit, signals the close of Newman's pneumatic christology and the beginning of the sacred crossing into his pneumatic ecclesiology. By selecting the Lucan version of Christ's final words, "Father, into Thy hands I commend My Spirit,"(*Lk* 23: 46) [51] he associates the passion of the God-man with the sacred narrative known for its focus upon the Holy Spirit in the life of Jesus (TDN 1985, 887-8) and the Church (NJBC 1990, 675-7), as well as choosing the text most amenable to a trinitarian reading (see *Mt* 27: 50; *Mk* 15:37; *Jn* 7:39). In this sermon, Newman invests the climatic moment of the death of the God-man with pneumatological significance: "Nor did He die, except by an act of the will; for He bowed His head, in command as well as resignation, and said, 'Father, into Thy hands I commend My Spirit' [*Lk* 23: 46]; He gave the word, surrendered His soul, He did not lose it." The phrases, "commend My Spirit," and "surrendered His soul," are not an instance of reiteration. Rather Newman indicates that the first breathing forth of the Holy Spirit and the final human breath of God occur dynamically within the self-same act of the incarnate One. Other interpretations are ruled out by his use of the terms "Spirit" and "spirit" within this sermon. Newman twice refers to the human soul of the God-man as "spirit", but never as "Spirit." He refers to the person of the divine Son as the "Eternal and Divine Personality" of the Lord, but never as 'Spirit' or 'spirit'.[52]

Logic and context make it inconceivable that Newman's sense of the Lucan commendation of the "Spirit" refers generally to the divine substance rather than specifically to the relations of origin. This dramatic

51 Mix. 331 cites Lk 23: 46 though no reference is given; see 341.

52 Mix. 331, 329, 336.

event involves the person of the Son commending and the person of the Father receiving: "Spirit" here means 'the person of the Holy Spirit.' For Newman the redemptive death of God in the flesh[53] is concurrently the paschal pentecost of commendation. Recent commentators discerning the pneumatological content contained in this final, filial-paschal action have usually focussed upon *Jn* 19:30 (Brown 1970, 931; Coffey 1979, 154; Theological-Historical Commission 1998, 55). Working within the horizon of Tradition, Newman adopts an original interpretation of this paschal action that is trinitarian, perichoretic, incarnational, pneumatological and, more subtly, ecclesiological. The paschal action is trinitarian insofar as each of the divine persons is involved, perichoretic insofar as it is almost impossible to disentangle the roles of the Son and Spirit in the action and pneumatological and ecclesiological insofar as the perspective from which Newman views the pneumatological content of this paschal action is that of the author of *Luke-Acts* whose sacred writing emphasizes the work of the Holy Spirit in the *synkatabasis*, especially in mission of Jesus and the origin of his Church (Montague 1976, 253-301). As the incarnational dimension of the act is the 'personal context' in which the others are articulated it calls for closer analysis.

Newman takes care to characterize the pneumatological commendation as a total exercise of freedom in which the pressure of unimaginable mental-physical suffering does not determine the moment at which Christ surrenders his soul and commends His Spirit: that salvific moment is constituted by the free act of the God-man in which his human and divine wills move in perfect unison: "Nor did He die, except by an act of the will; for He bowed His head, in command as well as resignation, and said, 'Father, into Thy hands I commend My Spirit;' He gave the word, surrendered His soul, He did not lose it."[54]

Previously, three observations were made about Newman's preaching on the incarnation: it transcends Evangelical teaching without downgrading its emphasis upon atonement; the scope of this transcendence is shown by his Scotist belief that the incarnation would have occurred even if the Fall had not happened; and, finally, Divine Love chose to redeem by the cross when divine *dabar* would have sufficed. To these observations, one can now add Newman's intense

53 Mix. 336.

54 Mix. 331; see 341.

awareness of the dignity accorded every human being because Man for man salvation won. This reality is the foundation of the Catholic understanding that human beings have the awesome privilege of participating in their own redemption by uniting their acts of love to the passion of the God-man. The privilege is premised upon and made possible by the *enhypostasis*. The privilege is supremely illustrated in the paschal pentecost of commendation in which Newman accents the redemptive significance of the human dimension of the act whereby the God-man places his life in the hands of his Father, gives up his soul and breathes forth his Holy Spirit.

Sensitivity to the involvement of the Spirit in the pasch of the God-man as conveyed by Newman's particular rendering of *Lk* 23:46 in his sermon, "The Mental Sufferings of Christ," is representative of his view that the Lord and Giver of life penetrates every aspect of the God-man's work of mediation. This is attested by Newman's understanding of another text to which he sometimes refers – *Heb* 9:13-14:[55] "For if the blood of goats and bulls and the sprinkling of a heifer's ashes can sanctify those whose flesh is cleansed, how much more will the blood of Christ, who through the eternal **S**/**s**pirit offered himself up unblemished to God, cleanse our consciences from dead works to worship the living God." While translators of this text choose variously to use the upper or lower case, Newman always employs the upper-case [**S**] for his citations of *Heb* 9:14 to ensure he is unambiguously understood as including reference to the person of the Holy Spirit rather than focussing solely upon the divinity of the Son.

Although the source of Newman's interpretation of "eternal Spirit" is indeterminate, by the age of 16 he definitely understood *Heb* 9:14 to mean that the Holy Spirit "has the attributes of God". In fact, this is one of only three terse comments that he made upon his listing of 27 scriptural texts indicating the divinity of the Holy Spirit.[56] A year earlier, he had begun his life-long habit of reading the extensive scripture commentary of his evangelical mentor, Thomas Scott. In 1837, he wrote about his familiarity with Scott's *opus* and stressed his knowledge of the commentaries: "I am perfectly well acquainted with his Force of Truth, his Essays, his Son's life of him, and above all his Commentary. I will not say I have read it all through, but I cannot recollect the part

55 See PS v 10:139; PS iv 7: 108; PS v 12: 168, 171.

56 "1817 Texts for the Divinity of the Holy Ghost," Birmingham Oratory, A.9.1.

I have not read ... His commentaries on the Epistles and Revelations I have read again and again.[57] Unsurprisingly, Scott's massive commentary – *The Holy Bible containing The Old and New Testaments according to the Publick Version; with explanatory notes, practical observations and copious marginal references* (1814) – is to be found in Newman's library at the Birmingham Oratory. Since Newman constantly read Scott's commentary, as an Evangelical, Tractarian and Catholic, it is reasonable to surmise that he may have been influenced by the words of his old mentor on *Hebrews*:

> His entire divine nature, the entire purity of his human nature, the exalted dignity of his person, as Emmanuel; the honour put on the law of God by his most perfect obedience; and **the voluntary offering of himself, under the immediate influences of 'the eternal Spirit,'** as a spotless sacrifice to divine justice, in the stead of sinners, concurred to render it glorious in God, for his sake, fully to pardon, and freely to accept, all who were interested in him by faith ... Some expositors, by **'the eternal Spirit'** suppose the Deity of the Son to be meant: but this seems rather to be implied in the word CHRIST: and as the holiness and obedience of our Saviour, his miraculous powers, and the supports given to his human nature, are constantly ascribed to his immeasurable unction with the Holy Spirit, sealing his appointment to his mediatorial offices; and as he was carried through his last scene of sufferings, by his most perfect zeal and love, which gave value to his sacrifice ... so, **the Holy Spirit seems to be intended**, and his eternal Deity, (as well as the everlasting value and efficacy of Christ's atonement,) is attested by the epithet here employed (Notes for Hebrews, Chapter ix: verses 11-14; emphasis added).

The question of Scott's influence aside, Newman's practice of speaking about the breath of the Spirit, in conjunction with the mediatorial work of the God-man at the peak of his passion, indicates the degree to which he truly has a pneumatic christology that highlights the role of human freedom in the pasch.

Significantly, Newman's pneumatological reading of the pasch of Christ recurs in several sermons. Speaking of baptismal regeneration in his sermon, "The Indwelling Spirit," he aligns the passion of the eternal Mediator with the bestowal of his life-giving Spirit. He describes the Holy Spirit as "a spring of health and salvation" flowing from the redeemed heart of man because "streams of grace" and "'rivers of Living Water'" first flowed from the heart of the Redeemer. In this way, Newman echoes that portion of the patristic tradition which

57 LD vi 129.

speaks of the blood and water flowing from the pierced side of the crucified Christ as symbolizing the unified the work of the eternal Son and the Holy Spirit in the pasch of the Lamb (Durrwell 1960, 87-9).

> Instead of [the soul's] own bitter waters, a spring of health and salvation is brought within it; not the mere streams of that fountain, 'clear as crystal,' which is before the Throne of God, but as our Lord says, 'a well of water *in him*,' in a man's heart, 'springing up into everlasting life.' Hence He elsewhere describes the heart [of the God-man] as giving forth, not receiving, the streams of grace: 'Out of his belly shall flow rivers of Living Water.' St. John adds, 'This spake He of the Spirit.' ... Such is the inhabitation of the Holy Ghost within us applying to us individually the precious cleansing of Christ's blood ....[58]

The same line of thought appears in his sermon, "The Shepherd of our Souls," where Newman connects the daily sacrifice of Christ in his ministry with his expiatory sacrifice on the cross in order to characterize the passion of the God-man as the culmination of his ministry, both of which he places in pneumatological perspective. For example, he associates the sacrifice of the High Priest (*Heb* 9:14) with the Good Shepherd laying down his life for his sheep (*Jn* 10:11; 17-18) and alludes to the Holy Spirit flowing from his pierced side as the "living water" imparted to "lost sheep" (*Jn* 4:14; Durrwell 1960, 81-6). In turn, this set of associations is referred to the One, "who, in the evening and night of His passion, was forlorn in the bleak garden" and "stripped and bleeding in the cold judgment hall."[59]

The foregoing references to the distinct, complementary and common work of the eternal Son and the Holy Spirit indicate the manner in which Newman approaches the temporal missions in the paschal mystery. The same awareness suffuses his sermon, "The Mental Sufferings of our Lord in His Passion". Prior to the Son's act of commendation, he does not overtly mention the Spirit because the passion is specifically about the visible Mediator, the God-man, not the invisible Life-Giver. The inner mission of the Spirit is to vitalize the outer mission of the God-man, to help make it effective, not to displace it. In light of the aforementioned sermons referring to the presence of the Spirit in the pasch of the God-man, and clear demonstration of Newman's position on the intimate, incessant involvement of the

58 PS ii 19: 224.

59 PS viii 16: 235, 240. Newman cites Jn 7:38-9 in reference to the indwelling of the Spirit in Jcf. 142, 147.

Holy Spirit in the life of Christ, one can validly infer his belief that the Spirit operates in his climatic pasch: for the precise pneumatic act of commendation is, in fact, the realization of all that has preceded. Any construal of the presence of the Spirit in Christ's passion as episodic rather than perpetual is faulty. His pneumatic christology requires one to perceive that every moment in the passion of the God-man is penetrated by the presence of his Spirit. Every moment of suffering undergone by the God-man in the passion is, therefore, a moment in which the Lord and Giver of Life is co-present. This is not an heretical claim that the Holy Spirit suffers. God experiences suffering and death only in and through the humanity assumed by the eternal Son. Rather this is a valid application of *perichoresis* to the situation of the divine "I" of the eternal Son suffering in his humanity to whom the Spirit is always co-present.

Newman specifies that the "seat of suffering" in the God-man is his soul.[60] Refusal of "wine mixed with myrrh" occurs because the God-man is "bent on bearing the pain in all its bitterness". At the end, "it is His agonising soul which has broken up His framework of flesh and poured it forth." In fact, the duration of the passion is concurrent with the suffering of the soul; as his "passion had begun with His soul, with the soul did it end."[61] Nowhere else in his *opus* does Newman contend so forcefully that the human suffering of the God-man is proportionate to his immeasurable capacity to drink the paschal chalice. For where a soul exists, "pain is possible, and greater pain according to the quality of the gift"; again, "pain is to be measured by the power of realising it". Just as the pain realized by human beings is vastly superior to that realized by brute animals, so to is the pain realized by the God-man unimaginably superior to that of mere man. For the power of pain lies in the capacity of the subject to enter into the fullness of its reality. More concretely, to say that the power of realizing pain is proportionate to the capacity of the *enhypostasized* soul means that the God-man experiences in each successive moment the totality of suffering present in every preceding moment; it means that the torture which the innocent and holy feel relative to their perfection and proximity to sin is intensified in Him both in view of his unsurpassable purity and his most immediate exposure to the most forceful, various

60 PVD 356-7.

61 Mix. 325, 328, 340, 341.

and unrelenting of evils which assail him "through the medium of His humanity." In Newman's memorable words, "our Lord felt pain of the body, with an advertence and a consciousness, and therefore with a keenness and intensity, and with a unity of perception, which none of us can possibly fathom or compass because His soul was so absolutely in His power, so simply free from the influence of distractions, so fully directed *upon* pain, so utterly surrendered, so simply subjected to the suffering. And thus He may truly be said to have suffered the whole of His passion in every moment of it."[62]

This sermon is the highwater mark of Newman's pneumatic christology in which he shows the God-man in possession of a full humanity wherein His Spirit operates intimately. The paschal pentecost of commendation involves effective interplay between the Holy Spirit, the human soul of the God-man and the divinity of the eternal Son at that salvific moment which is at the centre of his historical life[63] and the life of the world: "He offered Himself wholly, a holocaust a whole-burnt offering ... as the whole body, stretched out upon the Cross, so the whole of his soul ... His passion was an action ... 'Father, into Thy hands I commend My Spirit.'"[64] The final expiration of the God-man coincides with his first exhalation of his Spirit. Out of the side of his pneumatic christology flows his pneumatic ecclesiology. This is no immanent christology, but a fulsome Spirit-filled christology: "Christ ... was born of the Spirit ... He was justified by the Spirit ... He was pronounced the well-beloved Son, when the Holy Ghost descended on Him ... He was led into the wilderness by the Spirit; He did great works by the Spirit; He offered Himself to death by the Eternal Spirit ...."[65]

62 Mix. 328, 331, 329, 327-8, 332-5, 336, 329.

63 SN 302; US ii 23.

64 Mix. 338-9, 331.

65 PS v 10: 139.

CHAPTER FIVE

FROM EASTERTIDE TO *ECCLESIA*

The movement from Eastertide to *ecclesia* courses through the veins of Newman's ecclesiology. All else leads to, or flows away from, his understanding that the Church is forged in the Easter Mystery wherein the crucified God-man rises, appears, ascends and sends his Holy Spirit. Here "Easter Mystery" refers to these four interpenetrating mysteries: the resurrection, the post-resurrection appearances, the ascension and the sending of the Holy Spirit. This crossover is the sacred passage from pneumatic christology to pneumatic ecclesiology.

So far, Newman's thought has been clarified relative to his view of the divine persons of the Trinity working in a distinct, complementary and unified manner, the hypostatic hallmarks of mediation and life-giving which comprise the distinctive contributions of the eternal Son and Holy Spirit in their respective temporal missions, and the real, wide-ranging operation of the Holy Spirit in the one, full, personal mystery of the God-man. Drawing upon these findings, one can now articulate his vision of the Church as the 'body of Christ' which is sacramentally configured to the form of the God-man and indwelt by his Holy Spirit. This vision of the Church comes into sharp focus by attending to Newman's view of the (1) Holy Spirit as the 'leading actor' in the Easter Mystery; (2) resurrection as the origin of *ecclesia*; (3) centrality of the ascension; and, (4) significance of the intermediate interval and pentecost. Initially, however, it is necessary to set forth the rationale for centering this investigation upon Newman's ninth lecture on justification.

LECTURES ON JUSTIFICATION

Perhaps the richest extended meditation in Newman's oeuvre upon the sacred passage from pneumatic christology to pneumatic ecclesiology is his ninth lecture, "Righteousness the Fruit of our Lord's Resurrection," in *Lectures on the Doctrine of Justification* (1838).[1] Situated near the centre of the 1826-53 period that is of special interest to this investigation, these twenty pages provide an unparalleled entrance into his mind on the nexus between the Easter Mystery and *ecclesia*. As noted earlier, several Newman scholars have made the ninth lecture central to their investigation of his pneumatic christology and ecclesiology. Consequently for reasons of content, chronology, and scholarly engagement, this passage serves as an 'theological hub' around which coalesce many of Newman's insights regarding the relationship between Christ, the Holy Spirit and the Church.

Full-scale inquiry into the *Lectures on the Doctrine of Justification* would require one to investigate the many exegetical, historical, doctrinal and hermeneutical questions surrounding the doctrine of justification, which is one of the most controverted issues in Christian history. These findings would need to be situated in the stream of Newman's life. This would entail examining the *Lectures* relative to his conversion from Evangelical to sacramental Christianity and his correspondence with Abbé Jager (Allen 1975) as well as assessing the adequacy of his knowledge of his Lutheran and Roman interlocutors (e.g. Neuhaus 1997, 277-88; Murray 1990, 155-78; McGrath 1984, 28-43, Toon 1980, 335-44; Newsome 1964, 32-45; O'Leary 1991, 153-93) and considering this work as part of his broader *via media* theological project in support of the collective effort of the Oxford Movement to emphasize the Anglo-Catholic character of the Church of England. A much more modest path is trod here. Recourse to the ninth lecture is sharply circumscribed by the question: what specific contribution does the text make to understanding Newman's fundamental pneumatic christology and ecclesiology? This methodological move is sound insofar as the lecture is consulted solely to clarify his view of the relationship between the Easter Mystery and *ecclesia* within the already established horizon of his pneumatological and christological thought and not to lay bare his view of justification *per se*.

1 Jfc. 202-22.

THE HOLY SPIRIT AS THE 'LEADING ACTOR'

Does Newman present the Holy Spirit as the 'leading actor' in effecting the resurrection of Jesus? This is an important and fascinating question. Subsequent to noting contemporary interest in this question, it is prudent to place it against the background and mid-ground of his thought. These preliminary steps make possible the investigation of the question against the foreground of his thought. After registering qualifications, the question is answered affirmatively by advancing an argument comprised of *a priori*, negative and positive strands.

Within the Easter Mystery, Newman characteristically acknowledges the interpenetrating missions of the eternal Son and the Holy Spirit, the consequent predicament of distinguishing between their particular contributions to the economy of salvation and the need to attribute every *ad extra* act to the indivisible Godhead.

> Here I would observe of this part of the wonderful Economy of Redemption, that God the Son and God the Holy Ghost have so acted together in their separate Persons, as to make it difficult for us creatures always to discriminate what belongs to each respectively. Christ rises by His own power, yet the Holy Ghost is said to raise Him; hence, the expression in St. Paul, 'according to the Spirit of Holiness,' as applied to His resurrection, may be taken to stand either for His Divine nature or for the Third Person in the Blessed Trinity .... I notice this merely by way of explaining myself, if in speaking upon this most sacred subject I have said, or may say, anything which would seem to 'confound the Persons' of the Son and Spirit, which are eternally distinct and complete in Themselves, though in nature and operation One.[2]

However, distinguishing between the contributions of divine persons, preserving the common nature of the work of the tripersonal God and recognizing that the Spirit is also the Spirit of the Father, as well as the Son, does not hinder Newman from assigning the Holy Spirit the 'leading role' in the drama of the Easter Mystery. Indeed, Newman's judgment that it belongs particularly to the economic mission of the Holy Spirit to take a 'leading role' in the resurrection of Jesus supplies a positive response to a question that only now seems to be attracting significant scholarly attention. As Tom Norris says, "[t]o use a metaphor from the theatre, it is the task of the Holy Spirit to interpret the action of the Son to us spectators who are then drawn into the action.

2 Jfc. 208, 209.

With the Holy Spirit revelation becomes a divine and human drama. Now drama is, in the memorable description of W.B. Yeats, 'character disclosed in an action which engrosses the present and dominates memory.' The Holy Spirit is the key to our perception of the drama of the incarnate Son revealing the heart of the Father and drawing us into communion with him and with one another" (1996, 22). In a recent essay reviewing the state of scholarship surrounding aspects of the mystery of the resurrection, Gerald O'Collins, SJ, states, "[a] traditional axiom holds that all three persons of the Trinity are inseparably involved in every external action (*opus ad extra*). Yet the 'term', or objective effect, within the finite, world nexus can be special to one or other divine persons ... should, we introduce a similar distinction in the case of the resurrection? While the causality exercised in the resurrection is common to all three persons, does the 'term' (the risen, 'spiritual' Christ) belong in a 'proper' way to the 'economic' mission of the Holy Spirit?" (Davis, Kendall, O'Collins, 1998, 23-4).

Discerning Newman's position that Holy Spirit has the 'leading role' in effecting the resurrection of Jesus requires one to situate the issue against its background and mid-ground in order properly to fix in one's sights what stands in the foreground. In the background lies his perichoretic theology and the belief that persons of the Trinity operate *ad extra* in a distinct, complementary and indivisible manner. Dominating the mid-ground is his conviction that the economic missions of the eternal Son and the Holy Spirit fit or suit their divine personhood: eternal sonship is congruous with the task of mediation; whereas, that which is most proper to the person of Holy Spirit is enlivening everything which the Son mediates. As Newman states elsewhere, "Hence it was fitting that the Son should be incarnate, and not the Father; and fitting that the Holy Ghost should be the energizing life, both of the animate and rational creation, rather than the Father or the Son."[3] To understand the 'leading role' of the Holy Spirit in the resurrection according to Newman, four further remarks need to be registered about other matters situated more prominently in the foreground of the ninth lecture: agency, co-operation, awe and love.

First, Newman does not engage in detailed speculation about which divine person has the 'leading role' in the drama of the resurrection. Rather, he approaches this mystery by distinguishing between the

3 OS 186.

Son as the agent who atones and the Spirit as the agent who justifies (sanctifies and divinizes) by applying the merits and fruits of that atonement.[4]

Second, Newman sometimes accents the co-operation of the Son and Spirit in the resurrection rather than distinguishing what is distinct in their efforts.[5] To neglect this fact misrepresents his effort and distorts his emphasis.

Third, Newman's reticence to distinguish is, at some level, related to his awe for the Divine Mystery, his apophatic sensibility and his wariness of the reductionism that can accompany reason in matters divine. Hence, he observes that doctrinal statements about the Mystery of the Trinity are mostly, "negative rather than positive; intended to forbid speculations, which are sure to spring up in the human mind, and to anticipate its attempts at systematic views by showing the ultimate abyss at which all rightly conducted inquiries arrive ...."[6]

Fourth, Newman holds that the Father, the unoriginate Origin, who sent His Son into the world, is central in the resurrection, even if this does not translate into what is termed here, 'the leading role.' This makes sense considering Newman's view that the love of the Father figures conspicuously in the drama of the crib, cross, empty tomb and descent of the dove. According to Newman, the Father would have asked the Son to become incarnate even if the Fall had not happened. Even though the Father could have redeemed humankind by a way other than the cross, He decided to redeem through the sacrifice of His only-begotten Son, "who dwelt in His bosom in bliss ineffable from all eternity, whose very smile has shed radiance and grace over the whole of creation, whose traces I see in the starry heavens and on the green earth, this glorious living God, it is He who looks at me so piteously, so tenderly from the Cross." Though the Father's purpose for redeeming in this manner is inscrutable, or as Newman puts it, for "wise reasons unrevealed," one can assert that he holds redemption to occur according to the Father's intentions, in a way immeasurably "more loving, generous" and "munificent" than required by divine justice.[7] As much as redemption is a matter of obediential, filial love, it

4 Jfc. 203-4.

5 Jfc. 208.

6 PS vi 24: 360-1; citation, Jfc. 316.

7 Mix. 321, 307; see Mix. 305, PS ii 3: 30; Ath ii 187-8.

is also, from eternity, a matter of paternal love. As an integral part of redemption, the resurrection is not only a matter filial exaltation, but also a revelation of divine paternal love.[8] Consequently, he sees the pneumatic justification of the Son as definitive recognition of his filial dignity from before the foundation of the world confirming his status "as the Dearly-Beloved of the Father …. " Now, there is no sign here that Newman, against the judgment of St. Thomas (ST IIIa q. 16, a.2, 9), alludes to the pre-existence of the man-God (that is, the heavenly man or divine man) posited in diverse ways by theologians like Karl Barth, Oscar Cullmann, Pierre Benoît and Louis Bouyer (Congar 1986, 94-7; Farrow 1996, 281-98). Rather Newman refers exclusively to the eternal, divine sonship of the second person of the Trinity. "He is said to be 'justified by the Spirit,' because it was by the Spirit that He was raised again, proved innocent, made to triumph over His enemies, declared the Son of God, and exalted on the holy Hill of Sion. It had been declared, 'Thou art My Son, this day I have begotten Thee,' and in these words He was justified or recognized, and owned before the world as the Dearly-beloved of the Father."[9]

By drawing attention to this divine filial recognition, Newman ensures that his frequent references to the Holy Spirit as the Spirit of the Son (that is, the Spirit of Christ)[10] are complemented by his clear acknowledgement that the Spirit is also the Spirit of the Father, who reveals his tender love towards his Only-Begotten by the glorious act of resurrection effected in the Spirit.

Now that the proper qualifications have been made, one can make the case that Newman assigns the Holy Spirit the 'leading role' in the resurrection. The strength of the case derives from its interwoven strands: the *a priori* expectation that the office of Life-giving encompasses the specific act of resurrection, the argument from silence, and Newman's straightforward identification of the Holy Spirit (as opposed to the Father or Son) as the 'leading actor' in the movement of the God-man from death to life. Considered collectively these arguments leave little doubt that Newman identifies the Holy Spirit as the most prominent trinitarian actor in the drama of raising of the God-man to life.

8 SD 141-2, 143.

9 Jfc. 207.

10 See Jfc. 203-8.

Consideration of Newman's understanding of the role of the Holy Spirit in the resurrection of Christ requires one to recollect the precise fit between this role and his basic position that the raison d'être of the pneumatic mission is to enliven the work of Christ. Examples of this understanding abound in the ninth lecture wherein Newman stresses that Christ is the agent of atonement and the Holy Spirit is the agent who applies the full reality of this atonement to the lives of Christians. Now this is critical for grasping the present discussion about the agency of the Holy Spirit in the resurrection. Newman says, "our justification ... is ... a work of the Spirit" and characterizes the very "mission of His Spirit" as justification. In this context, he defines justification as "the application of this precious Atonement to this person or that person ... accomplish[ed] by His Spirit." Over and against these statements stands his specification of the resurrection of Christ as the origin of the justification of believers: "This, I say, was His justification [that is, resurrection]; and ours consists in our new birth also, and His was the beginning of ours."[11] His is "the beginning of ours" precisely because applying the full reality of the atonement of Christ has as its first fruits, raising Christ himself from the dead. For Christ is the new Adam. Because He rises, all those inserted into his sacred humanity will also rise. Identifying the special economic mission of the Holy Spirit with justification, and specifying the origin of that justification as the resurrection of Christ, is another way of Newman saying that the Holy Spirit is the 'leading actor' in the resurrection.

This insight is confirmed from another angle in lecture. In his commentary on the Johannine discourse about the bread of life, in the context of connecting resurrection-ascension-eucharist, Newman highlights the verse: "'It is the Spirit that is the life-giver; the flesh profiteth nothing ... (*Jn* 6:63).'" Concentrating upon this verse, Newman emphasizes the life-giving nature of *ad extra* acts of the Holy Spirit remarking that "'It is the Spirit that quickeneth'" reiterating, "'It is the Spirit that is the Life-giver ....'"[12] At one point, Newman shifts from these general comments about the office of the Spirit to state specifically that the transformation of the crucified and humiliated humanity

11 Jfc. 203-4, 203, 204, 207.

12 Jfc. 209-10; citation 210. Use of double quotation marks reflect that Newman speaks imaginatively, as if he were the Lord, in this Gospel scene.

of Christ occurs "'by the power of the Spirit'".[13] Raising the God-man from the dead is presented as the supreme instance of the vitializing nature of the pneumatic mission. Presentation of the Holy Spirit as the 'leading actor' in the resurrection is consistent with the logic of Newman's theology.

Alongside the argument which proceeds from Newman's general understanding of the life-giving office of the Holy Spirit to the specific act of resurrection, there is the argument from silence. Alone this argument is weak but when woven into the preceding and subsequent evidence, it strengthens the whole. While Newman speaks eloquently about the work of Christ in securing atonement upon the cross, and comments clearly about his ongoing work through the person of His Spirit after the ascension, he never unambiguously says that Christ raises himself. The sole apparent exception does not involve Newman arguing that Christ is the 'leading actor' in his own exaltation. Rather, he observes how the Pauline testimony that "Christ rises by his own power" is qualified by the equally weighty assertion that "the Holy Ghost is said to raise Him". He notes the difficulty of distinguishing between divine actors in specific instances, recognizes their co-operation and stresses the unity of their operation in order to avoid either diminishing their divine persons or the tri-unity of the Godhead. Here Newman is preoccupied with following the grammar of trinitarian discourse rather than building a case for Christ as the 'leading' actor in his own resurrection.[14]

Finally, there is the specific, positive case. Over and against his relative silence about the Son effecting his own exaltation, there are numerous, frank statements by Newman attributing the act of resurrection directly to work of the Holy Spirit: "For He Himself was raised again and 'justified' by the Spirit"; "He is said to be 'justified by the Spirit,' because it was by the Spirit that He was raised again, proved innocent, made to triumph over His enemies, declared the Son of God, and exalted on the holy Hill of Sion"; and, "'But all this is at an end, now I have died and risen again in the power of the Spirit'".[15]

13 Jfc. 208.

14 Jfc. 203, 204; 205,206, 216, 218; 208.

15 206, 207, Jfc. 216. Again, the double quotations are attributable to Newman imaginatively taking the role of Christ; this time in conversation with Mary Magdalene.

Taken together, *a priori* expectation, the argument from silence and Newman's straightforward statements convincingly demonstrate that he holds the Holy Spirit to be the leading trinitarian actor in the resurrection. The focus now shifts from considering who is the 'leading actor,' to asking what is the ecclesial significance of this act?

RESURRECTION AS THE "ORIGIN" OF *ECCLESIA*

There are profound ecclesial implications arising out of this justification of the God-man. Newman's simple phrase – "to justify us as He had been justified" – conveys the radical, redemptive consequences of the total fact of the incarnation as realized in the cross and resurrection: that is, atonement and divinization.[16] The *enhominized* crucified and risen God swallows up sin and death and, through his Holy Spirit, incorporates other human beings into his glorified flesh permitting them, by participation in this reality, to share in his victory. The ninth lecture, "Righteousness the Fruit of our Lord's Resurrection," is replete with references to the Holy Spirit applying the merits of the atonement[17] to believers divinized by their pneumatic insertion into the glorified manhood of God.[18] In this manner, the pneumatic justification of the God-man concomitantly constitutes the pneumatic origin, means and continuing cause of the Church:

> And here I have touched upon another part of the harmony of the Divine Dispensation, which may be profitably dwelt upon. For He Himself was raised again and 'justified' by the Spirit; and what was wrought in Him is repeated in us who are His brethren, and the complement and ratification of His work. What took place in Him as an Origin, is continued on in the succession of those who inherit His fulness, and is the cause of its continuance .... This, I say, was His justification; and ours consists in our new birth also, and His was the beginning of ours. The Divine Life which raised Him, flowed over, and availed unto our rising again from sin and condemnation. It wrought a change in His Sacred Manhood, which became spiritual, without His ceasing to be man, and was in a wonderful way imparted to us as a new-creating, transforming Power in our hearts. This was the gift bestowed on the Church upon His ascension ....[19]

16 "Thus he died to purchase what he rose to apply." Jfc. 206.

17 Jfc. 203-6, 208, 216, 221, 222.

18 Jfc. 212, 217, 219, 222.

19 Jfc. 206-7.

According to this passage, the raising of the God-man inaugurates the crossover that ends in the birth of the Church. Admittedly, from another perspective, one can argue that the crucifixion starts the crossover. It is a matter of emphasis. The accent here is upon the movement ***to*** life from death, not ***from*** death to life. Newman contends that the justification of Christ by the Spirit is the personal "Origin" of *ecclesia*: that is, the Spirit who raises and the Son who is raised, together and in this way, constitute the origin of the pneumatic Church. It is significant that the life-giving action of raising, changing, and spiritualizing the sacred manhood of the God-man is not presented as an end in itself. Rather, "The Divine Life which raised Him, flowed over, and availed unto our rising again from sin and condemnation." Newman thereby signals that the pneumatic justification of the New Adam is inscribed with the means to communicate this transformation to the rest of humanity: "what was wrought in Him is repeated in us ... and [is] in a wonderful way imparted to us as a new-creating, transforming Power in our hearts." Consistent with his office as Life-Giver, the Spirit sustains what He has set in motion. The communication of the full fruits of the pneumatic justification of the New Adam is, in fact, an ongoing, historical process rather than a temporary boon: "What took place in Him as an Origin, is continued on in the succession of those who inherit His fulness, and is the cause of its continuance." As well, Newman's typical thought concerning the person of the Holy Spirit penetrates the passage: that which is transmitted as the means of spiritual transformation is foremostly a 'who' and secondarily a 'what'. The person-gift of the Holy Spirit complements and ratifies the atoning, divinizing work of Christ by inserting "His brethren" into the spiritualized sacred manhood of God and indwelling them.[20] Newman forecloses docetic readings of this spiritualizing by qualifying his comments with the phrase, "without His ceasing to be man." Hence glorification of the God-man in the resurrection transforms, spiritualizes and makes sacramentally communicable his sacred humanity without diminishing this humanity. The ecclesial significance of this qualification is sweeping for diminution of his *enhypostasized* humanity would necessarily and proportionately diminish the Church which is created by pneumatic insertion into that sacred humanity.

20 Jfc. 206-7.

In sum, Newman's discussion of the Holy Spirit in the event of the resurrection of Christ entails an intimate, significant, ecclesial dimension. He portrays the pneumatic christological event of resurrection as the justification of the God-man in which the New Adam destroys death bringing life to those in the grave. The pneumatic glorification of the *enhominized* eternal Son comprises the origin, means, continuing cause and, even, content of *ecclesia*: it is the event that enables believers to be immersed into the spiritualized sacred humanity of Christ by the Holy Spirit who indwells them like the light in a temple making them one body, one communion. In Newman's words, "To be joined as one spirit to Christ and to be a Temple of the Holy Ghost are spoken of as the same gift."[21]

ASCENSION

The ascension deserves close scrutiny in Newman's thought on the Easter Mystery and *ecclesia* for several reasons. His accent upon the ascension recalls an ancient tradition espoused by Church Fathers like Irenaeus, Origen, Augustine and Maximus (Farrow 1999, 1-164). Showing the importance of the ascension in Newman's oeuvre corroborates that his thought, even when not drawing directly from patristic sources, harmonizes with the teaching of the Fathers. Showing this harmony serves also to confirm the earlier claim that he views redemption as one mystery from crib, cross and empty tomb to the descent of the dove. Moreover, scholars commenting upon Newman's pneumatic christology and ecclesiology do not adequately account for the ascension, even though he refers to it no fewer than 26 times in the short space of the ninth lecture. After reviewing Newman scholarship on ascension, his understanding of the ascension is unveiled as the point of critical exchange in the Easter Mystery – that is, the original *epiclesis* in answer to which the Holy Spirit is simultaneously and sacramentally sent in order to constitute and configure the Church to Christ.

Michael Sharkey's dissertation – *The Sacramental Principle in the Thought of John Henry Cardinal Newman* – contains important sections focusing upon the sacred passage from pneumatic christology to pneumatic ecclesiology: namely, chapter four, "The Christological Foundation," and chapter five, "The Church". Sharkey cites at length from the ninth lecture, which he considers "Newman's finest piece of

---

21 Jfc. 212-13.

work." However, Sharkey does not really advance one's understanding on the significance of the ascension in the context of the Easter Mystery and *ecclesia*. For his citation of key texts is not sufficiently matched by sustained analysis to show the implications of Newman's thought (1976, 37). *Mutatis mutandis*, the same evaluation applies to the work of Pierre Masson, OP, Gerald Dolan, Vincent Ferrer Blehl, SJ and Edward Jeremy Miller. In his monograph, Masson also cites extensively from the ninth lecture (1982, 48-89) but he never delves into the theological significance of the ascension for Newman's pneumatic christology and ecclesiology. Likewise, Dolan's thoughtful article, "The Gift of the Holy Spirit According to John Henry Newman (1828—1839)," merely acknowledges in passing the place of the ascension in Newman's pneumatic ecclesiology (1970, 90). Blehl devotes a solitary paragraph to the topic consisting mostly of citation from the ninth lecture (1993, 94). Edward Jeremy Miller operates with an explicit understanding of Newman's pneumatic ecclesiology, although the nature of his work does not lead him to excavate the pneumatological and christological foundations of this position. In his very short unpublished paper, "Newman's Pneumatology from the Perspective of His Ecclesiology," he shows himself familiar with Newman's view of "the action of the Holy Spirit and the risen Christ active *in medio ecclesiae*" which observation he grounds in the ninth lecture (1996, 1-3, citation 1). Miller assumes that this lecture contains the substance of Newman's teaching wherein his pneumatology and ecclesiology intersect, but he does not advance the conversation.

In his authoritative article on the indwelling of the Holy Spirit, C.S. Dessain explains how Newman's recovery of this Johannine, Pauline and Greek patristic teaching precedes the 1950 work on the resurrection by F.X. Durrwell that so influenced continental theology. During his explanation, Dessain barely broaches the place of the ascension in Newman's thought relative to his theme (1962, 221), even though he cites liberally from *Lectures on the Doctrine of Justification* in which it figures prominently, and in spite of the fact that Durrwell refers to the ascension on more than 100 occasions (Durrwell 1960, 369). Though Dessain is more concerned here with uncreated grace than ecclesiology, he recognizes that these themes intersect in Newman's thought.

> ... Newman anticipated more recent developments ... namely, the fundamental importance he attaches to the Holy Spirit in the life of the Church. There can be no true theology of the Church unless the place of

> the Holy Spirit, the soul of the Church, is stressed; nor until we grant that what is given us by Christ comes to us through His Spirit can we understand how it is that the Church is taken up into the life of the most Holy Trinity .... Père Rondet remarks in his *De Gratia Christi* ... that, however fine our present-day devotion to the state of grace may be, it still remains imprisoned in the individualism of the modern age. It may bring out the indwelling of the Holy Spirit, but it does not sufficiently emphasize the union of all of us in Christ, *filii in Filo* (1962, 281-2).

Despite this critical acknowledgement, Dessain does not explore the pneumatic-ecclesial meaning of the ascension in his article. The same omission occurs in *Newman's Spiritual Themes*. At one point, Dessain draws near citing from the ninth lecture concerning the Spirit, Church and the ascension. Elsewhere he mentions the ascension and this mystery figures in the texts he cites. Dessain's numerous references to *Lectures on the Doctrine of Justification* signify his recognition of their importance for Newman's thought concerning the Holy Spirit and the Church. However, recognition in Dessain's work that the ascension has an important place in Newman's thought about the Holy Spirit and the Church falls short of explaining theologically what that place actually is (1977, 121 n.45, 85, 76-77 n.3, 77-8 n.5-6).

Healing the Wound of Humanity by Ian Ker shares common ground with *Newman's Spiritual Themes* by C. S. Dessain. Each publication grew out of material for retreatants; each preserves the unity between spirituality and theology that characterizes Newman's own work; each emphasizes the indwelling of the Holy Spirit relative to the individual in the Church; and, each fails to articulate the theological importance of the ascension relative to his ecclesiology. Ker addresses the Easter Mystery most fully in his chapter concerning the persons of the Trinity wherein he summarizes precisely and accurately Newman's view of the oneness of the mystery of redemption, the role of the Holy Spirit in the resurrection and ascension of Christ, as well as the sending of his Holy Spirit to indwell, divinize and cleanse human beings. However, this awareness of Newman's pneumatic christology, and its implications for the birth of the Church, does not go beyond observing that the ascension has a meaningful place in Newman's thought on Easter Mystery (1993, 51-9, 56 n.10, 57 n.11, 58 n.15). At no point does Ker plumb its ecclesial meaning for Newman. Ker assumes a similar stance in *Newman on Being a Christian*. His chapter on the Church is full of references to Newman attending to the Spirit-filled character of *ecclesia*. His most complete exposition of the risen Christ-Spirit-ascension-Church nexus occurs in his exploration of Newman's thought concerning the unity of redemption. There he stresses that "Newman, like modern theologians, emphasizes that the crucifixion, resurrection, ascension, and pentecost are to be seen not so much as separate events and actions but as constituting one single divine act unfolding in several closely connected stages." Ker situates these comments in the context of several of Newman's sermons stressing the role of the Spirit in the Easter Mystery. At the close, while discussing Newman's views concerning eternal life, he notes that the "traditional idea that heaven 'is a certain place, and not a mere state' is justified in Newman's eyes by the doctrine of the ascension of Christ 'to the right hand of God.'" Nonetheless, Ker's awareness that the ascension occupies a serious place in Newman's theology of the Holy Spirit and the Church never approaches a thorough articulation of its pneumatic, ecclesial significance (1990b, 50, 50-52 nn. 30-6; 156 n.7).

INTERMEDIATE INTERVAL

Prior to treating the ascension proper, the place of the intermediate interval in Newman's view of the Easter Mystery requires attention. In the ninth lecture, he thrice touches upon the meaning of the interval located between resurrection and ascension speaking plainly of the post-resurrection appearances as historical events. On the first occasion he says:

> This was the gift bestowed on the Church upon His ascension; for while He remained on earth, though risen, it was still withheld. During that interval, too, if we may speak without presumption, He seems to have been in an intermediate state, passing by an orderly course from what He had been during His humiliation to what He is in His glory. Then He was neither in His body of flesh simply, nor in His glorified body. He ate in the presence of His disciples; He suffered them to examine His hands and feet, and wounded side. Yet, on the other hand, He now appeared, and now vanished, came into the room, the doors being shut, and one occasion said, 'Touch Me not.' When, however, on His ascension, He became a life-giving Spirit, in the power of His Spirit He came to us, to justify us as He had been justified.[22]

By referring to the Church and ascension both at the beginning and the end of this passage, Newman binds the ecclesial significance of the

22 Jfc. 207-8.

interval to the anticipated event of ascension. During this interlude, he also says that the "gift" of justification to be "bestowed on the Church upon his Ascension" is currently "withheld" by the "risen" God-man. As the gift already belongs to the glorified God-man, his comment concerns its prospective distribution not its present possession for "while He was on the Cross, while in the tomb, while in hell, the treasure existed, the precious gift was perfected, but it lay hid; it was not yet available for its gracious ends; it was not diffused, communicated, shared in, enjoyed." When he speaks of the gradual change being wrought in the already perfectly glorified Christ, Newman is referring to a change *pro nobis* not *in se*. Communication of the spiritual fruits obtained in virtue of his death and resurrection await the completion of this "orderly" process by which the ascended God-man shall become a "life-giving Spirit". The change affecting Christ's *enhypostasized* manhood – which transforms it from being potentially to actually able to communicate the gift-person of His Spirit and insert others into His sacred manhood – commences with the raising up. The resurrection begins the change. According to Newman resurrection and ascension constitute the *terminus a quo*[23] and *terminus ad quem*[24] of the intermediate state which, itself, is oriented towards *ecclesia*.

Newman's refusal to de-historicize the intermediate state underscores his thorough-going commitment to the project of trinitarian love, the *enhominization* of God in Christ Jesus. He realizes that the reconciliation of immanence and transcendence in the Incarnate Son occurs in the fullness of time, but is not bound by time. "He ate in the presence of His disciples; He suffered them to examine His hands and feet, and wounded side. Yet, on the other hand, He now appeared, and now vanished, came into the room, the doors being shut, and on one occasion said, 'Touch Me not.'" Sensitivity to this reconciled tension in the life of the Word made flesh leads him to affirm the eternal dimension of events in the intermediate state without purging them of their mundaneness. The second time Newman addresses the post-resurrection appearances, he reiterates points made about the intermediate interval as that time inaugurated by the resurrection and looking

23 Jfc. 206, 207.

24 Imagining the dialogue between the risen Lord and Mary Magdalen, Newman places these words in the mouth of the Lord, "When I am ascended, then the change will be completed." Jfc. 216.

towards ascension (McKeating, 1992, 115, 123-9,150-4). On this occasion, Newman "venture[s] to paraphrase [Christ's] sacred words" to "St. Mary Magdalen – 'Touch Me not, for I am not yet ascended to My Father'".[25] The in-between-ness of this interlude is characterized by these eschatological 'now' and 'not yet' notes sounded in encounters with the risen Christ who "bid[s] you at one moment handle Me as possessed of flesh and bones" yet "repel[s] another with the words, 'Touch Me not.'" The 'not yet' but 'already' series of notes are also heard in the language tenses that Newman deploys. Thus, he has the risen Lord say that "a glorified state **is begun** in Me and **will soon be perfected**" as opposed to his earlier statement that "on the Cross, while in the tomb, while in hell, the treasure **existed**, the precious gift **was perfected**, but it **lay hid**; it was not yet available for its gracious ends; it was not diffused, communicated, shared in, enjoyed".[26] Newman never speaks of the justification of the God-man other than in terms of the event of the resurrection. He is committed to the view that the glorification of the God-man is fully accomplished upon his raising up. This represents his 'already', 'perfected,' or 'now' notes. Subsequent events in the Easter Mystery are concerned with communicating his glorified, assumed humanity across time and space. Newman describes the resultant process in decidedly sacramental language: "When I am thus changed, when I am thus present to you, more really present than now though invisibly, then you may touch Me, – may touch Me, more really though invisibly, by faith, in reverence, through such outward approaches as I shall assign."[27] This represents his 'not yet', 'being perfected' or 'almost' notes.

The third and final mention of the intermediate interval is notable as much for its context as its content: the New Testament book of eschatology, *Revelations*. Newman comments upon the intermediate period in the course of reflecting upon the vision of John of Patmos of the risen Lord saying that "Here we seem to see something of the meaning of the words, – "The Holy Ghost was not yet given, because Jesus was not yet glorified ...."" Once again, Newman injects into his lecture the 'now' and 'not yet' eschatological tension of the intermediate interval.[28]

25 Jfc. 216-17; quotation at 216 citing Jn 20:17.

26 Jfc. 216 and 206, emphasis added.

27 Jfc. 217.

28 Jfc. 220, 221.

In short, Newman views the intermediate interval as a dramatic pause between resurrection and ascension highlighting the change wrought to the glorified humanity of the God-man *pro nobis*, who spans time and eternity providing in himself a bridge over death. The interval is punctuated by embrace and rebuke[29] signalling the flux between the glorification of the risen Lord in himself and the sacramental communication of the fruit of this glorification to others. The fluctuating nature of the interval points toward the approaching ecclesial epoch when Christ will be communicated sacramentally by the Holy Spirit in a full, real, personal and intimate manner upon his ascension. The inherently transitory nature of this interval stresses that Eastertide is indeed a sacred crossing over from pneumatic christology to pneumatic ecclesiology: from the glorification of Christ in the Spirit to the sharing of this first fruits with his brothers and sisters.

EPICLESIS AND *ECCLESIA*: ASCENSION AND PENTECOST

The beginning of the Church is often associated with the outpouring of the Holy Spirit on the feast of Pentecost. Specifying this event as the 'birthday' of the Church is suggested by aspects of holy scripture (*Acts* 1-2), patristic tradition, divine liturgy, sacramental practice and sacred art. Pronounced emphasis upon the Holy Spirit emerges in the rite of baptism, and the singing of *Veni Creator Spiritus* on occasions of confirmation, ordination, and the opening of ecumenical councils, both of which speak to ever-new advents of the Spirit in the sacramental life of the Church. Nevertheless identifying the precise moment of ecclesial birth in the Easter Mystery was not a preoccupation of the early Church. Until the latter part of the fourth century, the Church emphasized the unity of the fifty day festival celebrating the Easter Mystery. At this point, however, the focus began to shift quite gradually towards the mysteries of resurrection, ascension and pentecost, considered more discretely, and less as a part of the entirety of the Easter Mystery (Burns and Fagin 1984, 32-4, 50, 95, 132, 157, 174, 196; Congar, 1997, 228-257; VCR 182-3). Newman, in fact, reverses the tide. He recovers the patristic sense of the wholeness of the Easter Mystery, particularly as it relates to the birth of the Church. Below the ecclesial relevance of the mysteries of ascension and pentecost in

29 Jfc. 216.

the ninth lecture are explored from the Newmanian perspective that ascension is the original *epiclesis* in answer to which the pentecostal Spirit is simultaneously sent in order to constitute and configure the Church to Christ by making it 'his body'.

ASCENSION AND PENTECOST: A CRITICAL POINT OF EXCHANGE

Newman discusses the ascension as a pneumatic ecclesial event *extraordinaire* early in the ninth lecture: "... I shall treat the matter thus: – whatever is now given to us by the Spirit is done within us; whatever is given us through the Church since Christ's ascension, is given by the Spirit ...."[30] The specificity, definitiveness and scope of his simple statement is breath-taking: the ecclesial mission of the Spirit begins "since" the ascension; the Spirit works internally through ecclesial mediation; reception of the gift of the Spirit is tied to Christ departing which, indirectly, identifies him as the ultimate bearer and immediate giver of the Spirit. The largess of this pneumatic endowment is signified by the seemingly limitless scope of the indefinite pronominal which Newman employs: "whatever" is gift in the Church since the ascension belongs to the realm of the Spirit. He presents the origin and purpose of the Church relative to the missions of Christ and the Spirit in the context of the mystery of the ascension. In this manner, he makes explicit the pneumatological and christological foundations of *ecclesia*. Finally, Newman's straightforward attribution of a mediatorial role to the Church specifies its sacramental nature: that is, the Church is constituted to carry and communicate the life of Christ in the Holy Spirit.

Newman develops his initial observations about the pneumatological and christological nature of the Church and the mystery of ascension relative to his discussion of the one, complementary and distinct nature of the economic missions.

> Whatever then is done in the Christian Church is done by the Spirit; Christ's mission ended when He left the world; He was to come again, but by His Spirit. The Holy Spirit realizes and completes the redemption which Christ has wrought in essence and virtue. If the justification, then, of a sinner be a continual work, a work under the New Covenant, it *must* be the Spirit's work and not simply Christ's. The Atonement for sin took place

30 Jfc. 202-3.

> during His own mission, and He was the chief Agent; the application of that Atonement takes place during the mission of His Spirit who accordingly is the chief agent in it.[31]

"Whatever then is done in the Christian Church is done by the Spirit ...." Again Newman stresses the pneumatic penetration of *ecclesia* and the relative priority of the pneumatological in the era of the New Covenant. The mission of the Church is so bound up with the mission of the Holy Spirit that no ecclesial work is effected apart from the work of the Spirit. However, pneumatic penetration of the Church, and the relative priority of the pneumatological, operate within the fuller context established by Newman which is neither pneumatological nor christological, but pneumatological and christological. This includes the joint effort of the Holy Spirit and Christ to create and communicate life in, and through, the Church. Hence Newman presents the Church as the sacramental means whereby the "Holy Spirit realizes and completes the redemption which Christ has wrought in essence and virtue." This description of the fundamental theological nature of the Church has several implications. One understands the constitution of the Church foremostly as the work of God because *ecclesia* is forged in the crucible of the Easter Mystery. Perceiving the pneumatological and christological nature of the Church helps to explain why the economic missions are capable of historical-ecclesial mediation. The Church is set forth as a communion of human and divine persons which neither compromises human freedom nor diminishes divine personhood (Zizioulas 1974, 145).

The logic of situating the origin of the Church within the ascension is embedded within Newman's thought about this mystery as the critical point of exchange within the Easter Mystery. This exchange entails two aspects of movement wherein movement denotes dynamic, gracious action more than temporal change. Distinguishing between these aspects of movement is analogous to differentiating between competing viewpoints offered to one in transit who, at any instant, glances behind or ahead. The first aspect of movement within the exchange involves the departure of the God-man and his virtually co-incident return in the person of His Holy Spirit. This aspect of movement demarcates the completion of what Christ has wrought by virtue of his life, death and resurrection and the inauguration of what

31 Jfc. 204.

his Holy Spirit is doing *pro nobis* by applying this redemption to the wound of humanity. The second aspect of this movement within the exchange is realized by entering into the newness it effects: that is, the advent of the Holy Spirit justifying, sanctifying, divinizing and uniting the faithful by making Christ to indwell them. These energetic verbs dominate Newman's description of the dynamic action of the Holy Spirit; they appear on almost every page of the ninth lecture; and, they help the reader to realize that the life-giving role of the Spirit encompasses diffusing, communicating, and empowering, the faithful to 'share in' and 'enjoy' the gift of redemption wrought by Christ. This is, in fact, another way of articulating that the ascension-pentecost event originates the pneumatic Church. "Further it would appear as if His going to the Father was, in fact, the same thing as His coming to us spiritually. I mean there is some mysterious unknown connection between His departing in His own Person, and His returning in the Person of His Spirit. He said that unless He went, His Spirit would not come to us; as though His ascending and the Spirit's descending, if not the same act, yet were very closely connected, and admitted of being spoken of as the same."[32]

ASCENSION AND 'BODY OF CHRIST'

Since Newman speaks of the mystery of the ascension as the point of exchange at which the departing Christ simultaneously sends his Holy Spirit in order to constitute the Church, one can say that he sees ascension as the 'supreme *epiclesis*': that is, the sacred moment in which Christ implores the Father to pour forth his Holy Spirit in order to create the body of Christ. Recently, the same insight was mentioned by The Theological-Historical Commission for the Great Jubilee of the Year 2000: "Thus, the ascension of Christ can be considered as the highest degree of *epiclesis* ('invocation,' or intercession to the Father so that he might send the Spirit)" (1998, 57). The ninth lecture also evinces evidence that Newman thinks of *ecclesia* especially in eucharistic terms. He moves nimbly within the spacious possibilities afforded by the sacramental-analogous reality, 'body of Christ', in order to refer to the: (i) crucified God-man; (ii) glorified humanity of the God-man; (iii) ecclesial body of believers indwelt, united and configured by the Holy Spirit to this glorified, divine-human form; and, (iv) sacrament

32 Jfc. 206.

of holy eucharist in which the baptized believer receives Christ, body and blood, soul and divinity.

Surprisingly no one has commented upon the eucharistic aspect of Newman's thought within the horizon of his ascension understanding. In his closing words of the eighth lecture on justification, "Righteousness viewed as a Gift and as a Quality,"[33] Newman establishes the body of Christ theme that threads through the ninth lecture. He concentrates the four-fold meaning of 'body of Christ' into one passage in which he refers to "Christ Crucified" (historical) indwelling believers as "the One principle in His Church" (ecclesial), in virtue of his "risen" humanity (glorified) encountered most intimately in the sacrament of "the grace of Holy Eucharist" (eucharistic), that is, "the Presence of Christ Crucified". Here, of course, 'historical body' is juxtaposed with, not opposed to, other historical meanings of 'body of Christ' in order to specify the Good Friday sacrifice of Jesus upon the cross of Calvary. During the ninth lecture, Newman trades upon the multiple and over-lapping meanings of body of Christ in the context of his ascension theology. He introduces the eucharistic significance of ascension at the outset of his exegesis of the Johannine Bread of Life discourse (*Jn* 6: 25-70) saying: "Let me then proceed to comment on several important texts of Scripture, what are adapted to throw light on the main doctrine which is now under review, that our ascended Lord, in ascending, has returned to us invisibly in the attributes of a Spirit." Here he stresses his understanding of ascension as virtually co-incident with pentecost and suggests that one read the rest of the lecture in "light" of this "main doctrine." His illumination of this "main doctrine" starts at the midpoint of the lecture and extends to the end comprising 65% of the whole.[34] The "several important texts of Scripture" he mentions are almost exclusively Johannine and Pauline.

In his exegesis of the Bread of Life discourse, Newman connects the body and blood of the God-man sacrificed on Calvary (historical) to the believer's reception of his body and blood (eucharistic) as capacitated by the office of the Lord and Giver of Life, who spiritualizes the sacred humanity of Christ (glorified) in resurrection-ascension and sacramentally communicates Him.[35] Newman then proceeds to join

---

33 Jfc. 201.

34 Jcf. 201, 209, 222. The 'body of Christ' section is Jfc. 209-222.

35 Jfc. 209-10, 210 paraphrasing Jn 6:54.

these Bread of Life remarks to his reflections on the New Adam by noting that St. Paul characterizes the New Adam as "a quickening or life-giving Spirit" (*1 Cor* 15: 46) which are "the very words our Saviour used in His [Bread of Life] discourse at Capernaum." He speaks of the one people bound together by the Holy Spirit in whom Christ dwells so intimately that the terms Body of Christ and Temple of the Holy Ghost are spoken of as "the same gift" (ecclesial). This is very much what theology has traditionally identified as the mystical 'body of Christ' (Robinson 1961, Mersch 1962, De Lubac 1988, 88-101). All the while Newman continues to insist that the critical point of exchange in the Easter Mystery, the ascension, is the fuller context in which one should interpret these related body of Christ passages: "And further, as our Lord referred to His ascension and exaltation, so here again the life-giving Spirit is said to be 'the Lord *from* heaven.' Thus, this passage, equally with the foregoing, speaks of our ascended Lord as a Spirit present in His people, and that, apparently, *because* He has ascended."[36]

THE MAGDALEN TEXT (*JN* 20:17)

Alongside the Bread of Life discourse and these Pauline passages one must add Newman's assessment of that "difficult passage" in *John* 20: 17 wherein "our Lord says to St. Mary Magdalen – 'Touch Me not, for I have not yet ascended to My Father'". Previously, this text has been evaluated from the eschatological perspective of Newman's theology of the intermediate interval. This reading is now enriched by considering Newman's eucharistic gloss.[37] Understanding the text requires that one realize three facts. This text forms part of his series of scriptures about the body of Christ. Second, the pre-eminent text in this series, the Johannine Bread of Life discourse, establishes Newman's commitment to the eucharistic dimension of the body of Christ. Finally, like the Bread of Life discourse passage, the Magdalen text is also a Johannine text. In light of these three facts, one can speculatively propose that the Magdalen text speaks about the body of Christ in its ecclesial sense and definitely assert that it speaks of the body of Christ in a eucharistic sense.

---

36 Jfc. 212, 213, 214; emphasis belongs to Newman.

37 Jfc. 216-17.

Newman presents his reading of the Magdalen text as an extended, imaginary dialogue between the Lord and the lady in answer to a specific question that occurs within his ascension theology. "'Touch Me not, for I am not yet ascended to My Father.' The question arises here, *Why* might not our Lord be touched *before* His ascension, and how *could* He be touched *after* it?"[38] The passage in which this text is situated (Jcf. 216- 17) is devoid of direct reference to the body of Christ as the mystical body, that is, the people of God. Possibly the passage indirectly presents the Magdalen as an eponymous figure representing, in a circumscribed fashion, the metaphorical, feminine person of the Church. As such, the Magdalen would be the universal penitent symbolizing the repentant body of believers standing under the cross in need of the salvation brought by Christ crucified – the Saviour who comes "to us in the power of the Spirit, as God, as Man, and as Atoning Sacrifice."[39] Naturally, this representation would need to be tempered by Newman's understanding of immaculate Mary symbolizing and embodying the purity of the pneumatic, bridal Church.[40]

While there is a slight possibility that the passage obliquely refers to the corporate reality of the penitent Church, as represented by Mary Magdalene, the primary, obvious and dominant 'body of Christ meaning' embedded in the text is eucharistic. Since Newman never separates the atoning sacrifice of Christ from the bright side of the Easter Mystery, his movement from Eastertide to *ecclesia* entails the insight that the eucharist (pasch) makes the Church (Zizioulas 1985, 110-20; Farrow 1999, 150-1).

> Touch Me not, for I am fast passing for your great benefit from earth to heaven, from flesh and into glory, from a natural body to a spiritual body. When I am ascended, then the change will be complete. To pass hence to the Father in My bodily presence, is to descend from the Father to you in spirit. When I am thus changed, when I am thus present to you, more really present than now though invisibly, then you may touch Me, – may touch Me, more really though invisibly, by faith, in reverence, through such outward approaches as I shall assign.

Here Newman speaks directly about the sacramental reception of Christ "by faith, in reverence, through such outward approaches as [the Lord]

38 Jfc. 216; emphasis belongs to Newman.

39 Jcf. 222.

40 See PS ii 8: 91, 93.

shall assign." While such a broad sacramental statement encompasses baptism, and other means by which the Lord and Giver of life makes Christ to indwell the faithful, his remaining words make palpable the special eucharistic meaning with which he invests the passage:

> Henceforth this shall be; when I am ascended thou shalt see nothing, thou shalt have everything. Thou shalt 'sit down under My shadow with great delight, and My fruit shall be sweet to thy taste.' Thou shalt have me whole and entire. I will be near thee, I will be in thee; I will come into thy heart a whole Saviour, a whole Christ, – in all My fulness as God and man, – in the awful virtue of that Body and Blood, which has been taken into the Divine Person of the Word, and is indivisible from it, and has atoned for the sins of the world, – not by external contact, not by partial possession, not by momentary approaches, not by a barren manifestation, but inward in presence, and intimate in fruition, a principle of life and a seed of immortality, that thou mayest 'bring forth fruit unto God.'[41]

This passage is part of Newman's greater commentary upon *John* 20:17; it also occurs in the context of his ascension theology stressing the relationship between his glorified body and his sacramentally, communicated body. Hence the passage resonates with the meaning of his commentary upon the Bread of Life discourse. He deepens its eucharistic dimension by poetic allusion to joyous feasting: "Thou shalt 'sit down under My shadow with great delight, and My fruit shall be sweet to thy taste.'". The eucharistic reception of Christ in this festal act is further denoted by remarks concerning intimacy, receiving the whole humanity of the spiritualized Christ, forgiveness of sins and divinization. This interpretation is strengthened by considering some of his closing remarks to the ninth lecture. Newman speaks of the resurrection as "the means by which the Atonement is applied to each of us, if it be our justification, if in it are conveyed all the gifts of grace and glory which Christ has purchased for us, if it be the commencement of His giving Himself to us for our spiritual sustenance, of His feeding us with that Bread which has already been perfected on the Cross, and is now a medicine of immortality, it is that very doctrine which is immediate to us, in which Christ most closely approaches us, from which we gain life, and out of which issue our hopes and duties."[42]

Together these factors lead one to conclude that the eucharistic body of Christ meaning is dominant in the Magdalen passage. Such a

41 Jfc. 216-17; 217.

42 Jfc. 209-10, 217, 222.

reading, naturally, is inclusive of other dimensions, for Newman understands the believer to be incorporated into the glorified body of Christ by the Holy Spirit through the sacrament of baptism. Only subsequently is the baptized member of the 'ecclesial body of Christ' entitled to receive the 'eucharistic body' of Christ.

CONCLUSION

The Easter Mystery is the mysterious event in which Newman situates his fundamental, theological understanding of the Church as the pneumatic body of Christ. Within his extensive oeuvre, his ninth lecture on justification, "Righteousness the Fruit of our Lord's Resurrection," affords unrivalled access to his view of the sacred transition *from* pneumatic christology *to* pneumatic ecclesiology. Four conclusions stand out. First, Newman holds the Holy Spirit to be the leading trinitarian actor in the pneumatic justification of the God-man, that is, the resurrection. Second, he emphasizes that this resurrection of the *enhominized* eternal Son comprises the origin, means, continuing cause and, even, content of *ecclesia*: it is the mystery that enables believers to be immersed into the spiritualized sacred humanity of Christ by the Holy Spirit. Third, Newman's theology of the intermediate interval resounds with a series of eschatological 'now' and 'not yet' notes as a way of relating and distinguishing the historical and transcendent dimensions both of the economic missions and the Church in the Easter Mystery. Fourth, and finally, Newman's understanding of the Church in light of the Easter Mystery is a theology of the ascension-pentecost *par excellence*. Ascension-pentecost is presented as the 'critical-point of exchange' between pneumatic christology and ecclesiology within Eastertide. Ascension is the original and supreme *epiclesis* in which the resurrected God-man calls upon the Father to send the Holy Spirit in order to constitute the body of Christ. Whereas pentecost is the virtually co-incidental theological moment in which the Holy Spirit, who has glorified Christ in the resurrection, responds to the *epiclesis* of the exalted God-man and inserts others into his spiritualized humanity, making them one body and preparing them for an intimate, eucharistic encounter. Newman judges the ecclesial implications of the ascension of the God-man to be as significant as other aspects of the economy of salvation. In short, he takes the departure of the God-man as seriously as his first coming.

CHAPTER SIX

PROLEGOMENA FOR DISCERNING THE VIVIFIED CHURCH IN THE *ESSAY ON DEVELOPMENT* (1845)

Having established Newman's fundamental view of the Church in terms of the Easter Mystery – that sacred crossing over from pneumatic-christology to pneumatic-ecclesiology – one can now ask about his vivified idea of the Church in *An Essay on the Development of Christian Doctrine*. This worthwhile task requires discernment and a gradual approach because Newman wrote the *Essay on Development* as an explanation of doctrinal development rather than as an exercise in ecclesiology. Indeed his celebrated insights on ecclesiological issues such as the *sensus fidelium* in *On Consulting the Faithful in Matters of Doctrine* (1859), on the participation of the Church in the priestly, prophetic and regal offices of Christ in *Preface to the Third Edition of the Via Media* (1877) and on papal infallibility in *Letter to the Duke of Norfolk* (1871) are not really explored in the 1845 or 1878 editions. Prior to examining Newman's vivified understanding of the Church in his *Essay on Development*, then, it is helpful to provide a rationale for focussing upon this particular text, to explain his purpose in writing it, and to note the limitations in his treatment of the Church and the Holy Spirit. This clearing away of the brush will permit one to see more easily the pneumatological and christological character of the Church in the *Essay on Development*.

COMPLEMENTARITY, CONTEMPORANEITY, CENTRALITY, CONTRIBUTION

Setting forth the fundamental pneumatological and christological character of the Church in the *Essay on Development* is important for reasons of complementarity, contemporaneity, centrality and contribution. First, examination of the *Essay on Development* permits the corporate dimension of Newman's pneumatic ecclesiology to come to the fore. This effort complements emphases elsewhere which have stressed the place of the individual believer baptized into Christ.

Second, the *Essay on Development* requires evaluation because it is one of Newman's most original, influential and enduring works. Ian Ker observes that this text "is the theological counterpart of the *Origin of Species* which it pre-dates by over a decade" (1988, 300). After more than a century and a half, Jaroslav Pelikan says that the *Essay on Development* retains a privileged place in the highwire task of reconciling the permanent truth of Christianity with modern historical consciousness and asserts that it remains "the almost inevitable starting point for an investigation of development of doctrine" (1969, 3). Although starting points are not finishing lines, scholars traversing this terrain still engage Newman as an interlocutor (Walgrave 1972; Chadwick 1987; Nichols 1990; Thiel 2000). By demonstrating how his thought on development of doctrine is inextricably linked to his vivified ecclesiology, one also indicates the contemporaneity of his view of the Church in the *Essay on Development*.

Third, the *Essay on Development on Development* holds within its pages more of Newman's self than any other work except, perhaps, his *Apologia* and *Grammar*. Forged in the crucible of his conversion, reflecting his tutelage at the feet of Bishop Butler and the Fathers, refuting his own argumentation from the *Via Media* and drawing upon epistemological insights from his *Oxford University Sermons*, the *Essay on Development* is a more than a landmark intellectual achievement: it is a kaleidoscope of Newman as a believer, historian, rhetorician, philosopher and theologian, as a "seeing, feeling, contemplating, acting" person.[1] Jan Walgrave confirms the central place of the *Essay on Development* in Newman's thought. "We began by reading through, and carefully analysing, all the works of Newman; but it soon became

1 DA 294.

evident that we should have to work out a complete synthesis of his thought with his *Essay on Development* of 1845 as the nucleus. For all the main arteries of his thought, during the Anglican period, converge on this book, at once so characteristic and so definite a turning-point in his life" (1960, 3). One reasonably expects the most consequential theological text written during the period in which Newman's sacramental idea of the Church solidifies to contain a potent pneumatic christology, if that christology actually is the primary theological analogue for his ecclesiology. Hence discerning this pneumatic dimension of Newman's ecclesiology in the *Essay on Development* is fundamental for validating the central argument of this book.

Finally, and most significantly, demonstration of the pneumatological and christological dimension of the *Essay on Development* contributes to Newman studies by resolving a hitherto largely unexamined problem. The theory of development of doctrine advanced in the *Essay on Development* assumes the operation of a penetrating pneumatic ecclesiology. For the historical communication of revelation requires the presence of the Holy Spirit in the Church to make possible and render effective the sacramental life and love of God poured forth in Christ Jesus (Rahner 1966, 12-15). While scholars regularly operate upon the assumption that Newman employs such a pneumatic ecclesiology in the *Essay on Development*, no one has adequately demonstrated it. This omission is present even in the work of those scholars who treat of his sacramental ecclesiology and confirm its pneumatic character but ignore, assume, state or only touch upon, rather than demonstrate how the idea of the vivified Church is actually present in the *Essay on Development*: e.g., Avery Dulles, Louis Bouyer, Pierre Masson, C.S. Dessain, Ian Ker, Edward Jeremy Miller, Rino La Delfa, Terrence Merrigan, H. Francis Davis, Jan Walgrave and Nicholas Lash. Moreover, these scholarly assumptions about Newman's potent pneumatology are not readily verifiable by direct reference to unambiguously pneumatological passages in the *Essay on Development*. The originality of this part of the investigation is, thus, threefold: it brings to the fore and documents the presence of this problematic scholarly assumption; it analyzes closely pneumatological references in the *Essay on Development* and, on the basis of this analysis, raises the question of a potential 'pneumatological deficit'.

The solution to the so-called 'potential pneumatological deficit' is presented at the close of the book by demonstrating that Newman invests his epistemological language with pneumatological and christological significance. While others have looked in this direction, none have moved beyond intuition to advance a careful, systematic, albeit speculative, solution. The survey, immediately below, considers whether scholars who have investigated this area are aware of a potential pneumatological deficit in the *Essay on Development* and if, like the solution proposed later, they suggest a theological reading of Newman's epistemological language as a solution to this quandary.

In his work, Avery Dulles favours a sacramental vision of the Church as the bearer of revelation based upon a balanced pneumatic christology (1978). He has written on Newman's understanding of revelation (1985; 1990a) aspects of his ecclesiology (Ker and Hill, 375-400; 1990b-c) , as well as his view of the Holy Spirit (1996). Dulles is conscious of the relationship between revelation, ecclesiology, and epistemology in Newman's thought generally, and the *Essay on Development* particularly. Yet he never amplifies the pneumatological and christological significance of Newman's epistemological language in the *Essay on Development,* although he recognizes its theological import (Ker and Hill, 378; 1990a, 252-5).

Louis Bouyer has written a biography on Newman, produced a work that indicates his appreciation of Newman's view of the sacramental nature of the Church as rooted in a vibrant pneumatic christology and, like Newman, his own ecclesiology is informed by the Fathers and can justly be described as a pneumatic ecclesiology. However, Bouyer's closest look at the *Essay on Development* in an ecclesiological context does not touch upon the theological significance of Newman's epistemological language (1960; 1986; 1982, 191-214).

Pierre Masson has written the sole study devoted to Newman's pneumatology, *Newman and the Holy Spirit*. The work's subtitle – *Christian Life and the Church in our Times* – confirms his interest in Newman's pneumatic ecclesiology. Nonetheless Masson neither addresses Newman's ecclesiology in the *Essay on Development,* nor shows that he uses philosophical terms to communicate his theological meaning in the area of pneumatic christology and ecclesiology, even in his culminating chapter, "The Vital Environment: The Church Animated by the Spirit" (1982, 191-214).

C.S. Dessain substantiated and made widely known the prominent place of Greek patristic pneumatology in Newman's thought, especially, on the issues of divinization and justification, particularly, in his influential article, "Cardinal Newman and the Doctrine of Uncreated Grace." Though Dessain's reflections on Newman's theology of the Holy Spirit include a meaningful ecclesiological component, his efforts in this article do not engage the *Essay on Development* which is cited only once in this lengthy article (1962, 284 n.1). The same comments apply, *mutatis mutandis*, to his biography of Newman in which Dessain comments upon the *Essay on Development*, the Holy Spirit, the indwelling presence of God, the Church, revelation and shows an intimate knowledge of Newman's pneumatic ecclesiology. Yet his only consideration of the theological dimension of Newman's epistemological language in the *Essay on Development* is a brief comment upon the identification of Christ with the "idea of Christianity" (1966, 82-3). The Holy Spirit is not mentioned at this juncture. Dessain also investigates Newman's thought on several matters – including those christological, pneumatological and ecclesiological – in his posthumously published *Spiritual Themes*. However, this work does not examine Newman's use of philosophical language in the *Essay on Development* to convey his pneumatological, christological and ecclesiological meanings (1977).

Ian Ker has written the most comprehensive, substantive biography on Newman. In spite of masterfully considering the relevant issues separately, his references to Newman's ecclesiological thought, the Holy Spirit, the *Essay on Development*, revelation and development of doctrine contain only indirect, brief or elliptical mention of the manner in which his epistemological language in the *Essay on Development* communicates his theology of the vivified Church (1988, 268-9; 302-4, 314-15, 707). Elsewhere in his oeuvre, Ker considers Newman's epistemology, idea of revelation, theory of development of doctrine, sense of sacramentality, debt to the Greek Fathers, ecclesiology, and the pneumatic christological dimension of his personalism. Nonetheless, the doyen of Newman studies has little to say specifically about the nexus of matters epistemological-christological-pneumatological-ecclesiological in the *Essay on Development* (1990c; 1985; 1990b; 1989; 1978; 1993).

Edward Jeremy Miller's monograph, *John Henry Newman. On the Idea of Church,* has been described by Terrence Merrigan as "a clear and comprehensive presentation of Newman's thought on the Church" which "has few, if any, rivals in English"(1990, 79). Jan Walgrave states that "picturing in actual detail this essential image of the church" constitutes "the unique merit of Miller's book" (1987, xii). In his section on the "The Church as Sacrament," Miller speaks knowledgeably of the several sources of Newman's sacramental vision and describes his understanding of the Church as "the visible expression of the invisible Spirit of Jesus". He discusses Newman's grasp of the *sensus fidei* stating that his understanding of the "dialectical movement between the magisterium and the baptized faithful ... at the level of grace" can "be described in terms of the original unity that is the Holy Spirit." Miller also depicts Newman's understanding of the *consensus fidelium* in pneumatological terms saying that this "is Newman's *theological* vision of the church in terms of the Holy Spirit" (1987, 131-2, 120, 121). At times, Miller strongly affirms the pneumatological and christological character of the sacramental Church in the thought of Newman (1996). Nevertheless his closest examination of "The Church as the Oracle of Revelation" in *The Essay on Development on Development* does not address the manner in which Newman's philosophical language contributes to communicating his theology of the vivified Church (1987, 36-42).

Rino La Delfa's *A Personal Church? The Foundation of Newman's Ecclesiological Thought* addresses the sacramental nature of Newman's idea of the Church as grounded in the mystery of the God-man and his Holy Spirit. La Delfa specifies that "for Newman, what the illative sense achieves on the natural plane in the individual, the supernatural illative sense, or as he names it the *phronesis* of the Holy Spirit, does in the supernatural higher context of the Spirit-filled Christian community." La Delfa is aware that this view has antecedents in the *Essay on Development* (1845). He locates Newman's objectification of this insight in the *Newman-Perrone Paper* (1847) and *On Consulting the Faithful in Matters of Doctrine* (1859). At no point, however, does La Delfa demonstrate how Newman affirms the pneumatological and christological character of the ecclesial bearer of the idea of Christianity in the *Essay on Development* or even raise this as a question for inquiry (1997, 26-57, 103-4, 137-8, 123).

In *Clear Heads and Holy Hearts,* Terrence Merrigan analyses Newman's epistemology by way of the model of polarity to clarify how much of what seems opposite, discordant or contradictory in human thought is, in fact, reconciled in the unified, dynamic tension existing in the mind of the living subject. His project stands in the tradition of, and develops, the Leuven school of thought identified with the work of Jan Hendrick Walgrave (1911-1986) and Paul Sobry (1895-1954). In his concluding chapter – subtitled, "The Illative Sense in the Church" – Merrigan applies his model of polarity to the ecclesial mind in order to illumine Newman's sense of how the Church, as a communal subject, grows in faith and knowledge of religious truth (1991, 229-54).

In this final chapter, the *Essay on Development* is briefly mentioned. Here Merrigan does not discuss the pneumatological and christological character of the ecclesial subject who bears the Christian idea through history or the identity of the Christian idea in terms of the temporal missions of the Word and Spirit. By and large, Merrigan illustrates the pneumatological dimension of Newman's ecclesiology vis-a-vis *On Consulting the Faithful,* without treating the *Essay on Development* (1991, 232-36). At one point, however, he makes clear reference to the *Essay on Development.* "The most significant anticipation of the thought of the 1859 treatise remains, however, *The Essay on Development on Development.* Indeed, *Consulting the Faithful* restates one of the major insights of the *Essay on Development,* one considered earlier in this study, namely, that the contours of the Christian idea are to be discerned not merely in dogmatic definitions, but in all the variegated forms of the whole complex reality of the believing community's life" (1991, 235-6). This mention of an "earlier" discussion almost certainly refers to chapter three, "The Christian Idea," where Merrigan situates Newman's understanding of the Church and the Christian idea in an explicit pneumatological and christological context. He notes others who follow the same path, specifically, H. Francis Davis, Jan Walgrave and Nicholas Lash (1991, 82-100, esp. 98 n.42, 44). Merrigan, and those whom he cites, correctly judge the pneumatological and christological meaning of the Christian idea. However, these scholars do not sufficiently ground their correct judgements in an analysis of the *Essay on Development* that demonstrates (and, therefore, opens to evaluation) the manner in which Newman's philosophical language carries his theological meaning.

H. Francis Davis explains cogently that Newman's epistemological language of idea (and related terms), speaks about the believer's sacramental-ecclesial encounter with the living person of Christ and the subsequent objectification of this experience in creed, doctrine and the like. Notwithstanding his perceptive reading of Newman's theology, Davis' concentration upon the christological practically eclipses his consideration of the pneumatological. He mentions the Holy Spirit in relation to Newman's theology of revelation once, briefly, and outside of his analysis of the idea of Christianity in the *Essay on Development* (1964, 168).

In his article, "L'orignalité de l'idée Newmanienne du dévelopment, Jan Walgrave locates, though never excavates, the pneumatological dimension of Newman's ecclesiology relative to his discussion of the Christian idea in the *Essay on Development* (1960a, 83-96). Moreover, his major work addressing Newman's theory of development, *Newman the Theologian,* closely confines his comments on the Holy Spirit to the question of infallibility and exercise of the magisterium in regards to doctrinal definition (1960 74-5; 108-9).

Nicholas Lash in *Newman on Development* is the most insistent of commentators that the epistemological language of 'principle-idea' in the *Essay on Development* should be read on several levels including the theological. In this regard, he contends that 'principle-idea' should be placed in a pneumatological and christological context in order for Newman's meaning to be plumbed. Lash accurately judges this point and identifies numerous references outside the *Essay* which support his reading. Nevertheless his terse treatment occurs tangentially within the sweep of his methodological exploration of the *Essay on Development* rather than in relation to Newman's sacramental ecclesiology and pneumatic christology proper. Without framing the question in this way, he points towards the solution for any who might suggest the presence of a potential 'pneumatological deficit' in the *Essay on Development*. However, Lash does not himself provide the solution by sustained analysis of the text (1976, 48, 74-5, 108-9, 180 n.6).

WHY THE *ESSAY ON DEVELOPMENT* WAS COMPOSED

This examination of Newman's understanding of the Holy Spirit within the Church in the *Essay on Development* needs to be placed within the horizon of historical factors which led him to write it. No one event led the Anglican Newman to doubt the claim of the Church of England to apostolicity and originate his theory of development in support of the claim of the Catholic Church to be the Church of Fathers. However, his 1839 reading of the *Dublin Review* article, "Anglican Claim of Apostolic Succession," by Nicholas Wiseman, the future Cardinal Archbishop of Westminster, played a pivotal role. In the article, Newman discovered that the criterion of orthodoxy wielded by Augustine against the Donatists told against others (like the Monophysites and Anglicans) who also appealed to antiquity against the witness of those Churches in communion with Rome: namely, *securus judicat orbis terrarum* or as Newman later translated, "the judgment of the entire church has no chance of being wrong." In the *Apologia* he says that this discovery "pulverized" his *Via Media*.[2] Thereafter he gave greater credence to the Roman claim based upon catholicity, grew suspicious of the Anglican claim based upon apostolicity and thought Roman developments of the *depositum* plausible and, even necessary, in light of the role of Leo and his Tome in shaping the christological solution of the Council of Chalcedon (451).[3]

The *Tract 90* and Jerusalem bishopric incidents of 1841 further corroded Newman's confidence in the Church of England's apostolicity.[4] *Tract 90* was Newman's attempt to see if a catholic reading of the Thirty-Nine Articles would be acceptable within the Anglican communion. He distinguished three possible senses of "Catholic": (i) the common patristic teaching of the early centuries; (ii) the formal dogmas of later councils, especially Trent, as summarized in the creed of Pope Pius IV; and, (iii) the popular beliefs and usages sanctioned by Rome. Newman said that a catholic reading of the Articles obliged Anglicans to accept fully the dogmas in (i); some of the dogmas in (ii); and, hardly any teaching contained in (iii). He realized that the Articles were framed with an eye for compromise and intended to supply subscribers with interpretative latitude. Moreover, he believed that his positions were supported by the Caroline and primitive divines. Thus, the seminal question was set: would the Church of England permit a reading of the Articles which was commensurate with the

2 LD xxv 220; Apo. 111

3 Dev 1845: 295-308; Dev. 1878: 299-313.

4 Apo. 78-9, 131-6, 139, 141-2.

teaching of the primitive Church? If not, how could one maintain that Anglicanism was a continuation of the latter? Newman realized that the Church of England's reaction to *Tract 90* was "a matter of life and death", that he "was engaged in an *experimentum crucis*." The hostile, overwhelming rejection of *Tract 90* by the bishops and the establishment gave Newman his answer.[5]

In the same year, the idea of a bishopric in Jerusalem was advanced by the Prussian ambassador in London, Chevalier Bunsen. He saw the bishopric as an opportunity for the Church of England to recognize the state Lutheran Church of Prussia. The proposal involved alternate appointments by England and Prussia of a prelate to exercise jurisdiction over English Anglicans and Prussian Protestants in Palestine. Ordinands had to accept either the Thirty-nine Articles or the Confession of Augsburg. The bill was passed in parliament on 5 October 1841. Michael Alexander was consecrated bishop of the Church of St. James at Jerusalem on 5 November 1841. This arrangement remained in effect until 1881 when no attempt was made to find a successor upon the death of the see's third bishop. Newman was appalled that the Church of England would so willingly enter into communion with the Lutheran Church which he regarded as heretical. The arrangement typified for him the Erastian, non-apostolic character of Anglicanism that substantially weakened its claims to be a branch of the Catholic Church.[6]

Subsequently, Newman adopted an interim theory viewing Anglicanism as a contemporary Samaria, a schismatic ecclesial body justified by the witness of its holy ones.[7] This situation proved untenable when friends objected to the tone of the series he was editing on *English Lives of the Saints*. Gradually these circumstances brought him to a new place. Disillusioned with the apostolic claims of Canterbury, his mind turned toward the question of the apostolic claims of Rome. This led him to re-examine his understanding of development with an eye to understanding doctrinal changes within Catholicism as positive growths rather than as corruptions of the *depositum*.

Before 1843, Newman had understood the notion of development primarily as the deepening of one's knowledge of sacred scripture or

5 Apo. 79, 122.

6 SD xxii 324-42; especially, 335 n.1.

7 Apo. 139 ff.; SD xxi 308-80.

the growth of creedal formulae guarding the original meaning of foundational gospel truths under siege from hostile forces (Byrne 1937, 230-86).[8] By 1843, his thought on development of doctrine had acquired new dynamism. Now Newman approached development of doctrine as the growth of the Christian idea. This third strand emerged in his fifteenth University Sermon, "The Theory of Developments in Religious Doctrine," (1843) and found full expression in *An Essay on Development on the Development of Christian Doctrine* (1845) though Lash (1976, 129) warns against making this sermon 'the leap' in his thought from a static to dynamic notion of development claiming that this process actually had its seeds in his *Via Media* (1837).

After resigning his living and retiring to Littlemore, Newman laboured over the *Essay on Development on Development* from March of 1844 until September of 1845. He spoke of the fruit of his labours to Mrs. William Froude as "a sort of obscure philosophical work ... with little to interest, and much to disappoint." Intended as "a book of some sort to advertise to people how things stood with me" prior to going over to Rome, Newman described the incomplete state in which he left the text, "Before I got to the end, I resolved to be received, and the book remains in the state in which it was then, unfinished."[9] He characterized the *Essay on Development on Development* as "an hypothesis to account for a difficulty" – an hypothesis to convince himself that the Church of Rome was the authentic heir to the Church of the Fathers, that so-called Roman corruptions were actually realizations of the deposit of the faith. On 8 October 1845, having ascertained this reality to his own satisfaction, Newman was received into the Catholic Communion by the Passionist, Blessed Dominic Barberi.[10]

8 On deepening knowledge of sacred scripture see PS vii 18: 247, 252; PS i 4: 53; PS ii 17: 183-205; PS i 16: 208-9; PS i 2: 21-2; 2 US i 1; VM i 158-9, 309 ff. & Ari. 58-9; on growth of creedal formulae see US iv 64-5; PS iii 12: 161-2; PS ii 22: 256-7; *Essay* ii 14-15; Ari. 36-7, 146; VM i 225-6.

9 US xv 312-51; Moz. ii 365; KC 379, 378; Apo. 211.

10 Dev. 1845: 27, Dev. 1878: 30; Dev. 1878: 169. On "realization of the faith," see US 330-33 as the basis for Dev. 1845: 54-7.

ECCLESIOLOGICAL LIMITATIONS OF THE *ESSAY ON DEVELOPMENT*

Before examining Newman's pneumatological and christological understanding of the Church in the *Essay on Development* as the historical bearer of the idea of Christianity, it is necessary to examine how his construction of an hypothesis concerning development of doctrine imposes four specific limitations upon his ecclesiology. More generally, one needs to keep in mind Nicholas Lash's assertion that the "argument of the Essay on Development remains 'an hypothesis to account for a difficulty' ... [it] *starts* with assuming the historical identity of the present and past Church, and does not set out to establish that identity. Not only does it not seek to 'demonstrate' where demonstration is impossible ... it does not claim to provide a systematically elaborated explanation of variations in church teaching and practice" (1976, 19).

First, the overwhelming task of formulating a theory of doctrinal development that applies to nineteen centuries of human history is more than even the erudite Newman can manage. His relative ignorance of byzantine, medieval and reformed Christianity narrows in practice his theoretic appeal to a broad field of data (Chadwick 1987, 143; Lash 1976, 44; Ker and Hill, 1990, 294-8, 322). While he purports to address many manifestations of Christianity, he really concentrates attention upon two terms in the process of development – patristic and nineteenth century Roman Catholicism.[11] The personal exigency to reach moral certainty about where he can find the 'one, true Church of Christ' guides his method of proceeding so that his theological exposition of the Church is subordinated to his methodological justification of Roman Catholicism as the legitimate heir of patristic Christianity (Lash 1976, 42-5).

Second, the *Essay on Development* is largely written as a rebuttal (Lash 1971, 228). As his latest answer to the question of where one finds apostolic Christianity in the nineteenth-century, the *Essay on Development* is Newman's rejoinder to his earlier 'Anglican answer' in the *Via Media*. In part, this accounts for his frequent citation of the *Via Media*, the Fathers, and Butler. These authorities were held in high esteem by the many Tractarians for whom he felt a pastoral

11 Dev. 1845: 43-57; 203-317; Dev. 1878: 41-54, 207-322.

obligation. Thus Newman's theological exposition of the Church is circumscribed by the degree to which his apologetic aim superintends his efforts.

Third, in an effort to establish a correspondence between primitive Christianity and nineteenth-century Roman Catholicism, Newman naturally stresses continuity of doctrine. Thus he neither explores the degree to which discontinuity is possible without betraying the gospel nor forges a 'theology of abuses' in which the mistakes of the Church and sins of her members are explained. Some three decades later, these concerns will find a voice in his *Preface to the Third Edition of the Via Media* (1877).

Fourth, since Newman considers the Church of the Fathers to be authentic Christianity, his equation of the patristic Church with nineteenth-century Roman Catholicism results in the total identification of genuine Christianity with this Catholicism (Lash 1976, 44). The *Essay on Development* tends to stylize those features of patristic Christianity which approximate features of nineteenth-century Roman Catholicism and ignore those which are dissimilar.[12] *De facto,* Newman incorporates into the *Essay on Development* what had been the Roman definition of the Church since Cardinal Bellarmine and the Counter-Reformation: namely, "The one and true Church is the community of men brought together by the profession of the same Christian faith and conjoined in the communion of the same sacraments, under the government of the legitimate pastors and especially the one vicar of Christ on earth, the Roman pontiff." While laudable in some respects, this definition of the Church totally excludes unbelievers and heretics by reference to creed, schismatics by reference to code and excommunicated persons by reference to cult. Any Christian body that does not manifest these visible marks is completely outside of the one, true Church. Although Newman's acceptance of the ecclesiology of the Council of Trent reasonably reflects what one might expect from a nineteenth-century English convert to Catholicism as a man of his age, it remains that his theory of development reinforces rather than modifies this Tridentine understanding of the Church. This is somewhat surprising considering the resources present in Newman's pneumatic ecclesiology for an understanding of the Church as communion, as the vivified Body of Christ. Therefore, the ecclesiology

12 E.g.: Dev. 1845: 138-9, Dev. 1878: 97-8; see also, LD xiii 295-7.

of the *Essay on Development* precludes positive consideration of the activity of grace in Churches and ecclesial bodies outside of Roman Catholicism. According to its view, one is in or out of the ark of salvation (Miller 1987, 143-4).

In sum, during his discussion of the Church in the *Essay on Development*, Newman *de facto* narrows his field of data, constructs his argument to address his apologetic aim, omits discussion of a theology of abuses and renders a negative judgment concerning the operation of God's grace in those Christian bodies not in communion with Rome. Although these limitations show the insufficiency of certain aspects of Newman's developing vision of the Church, they do not compromise the value of his fundamental view of the Church as the Spirit-filled bearer of the deposit of faith across history.

PNEUMATOLOGICAL DEFICIT?

The central problem encountered in the suggestion that the *Essay on Development* contains a potent pneumatic ecclesiology is that Newman rarely refers directly to the Holy Spirit, even though his theory of development requires belief in the animation of the Church by the Lord and Giver of Life. Without this pneumatic element his thought on development lacks theological coherence. For discussion about the capacity of the Church to mediate the truth and grace of revelation is premised upon the fundamental belief that the Holy Spirit makes Christ present in his body across time and space; that is, the Spirt of Christ enables his body to carry, understand, appropriate, live in and through, as well as communicate, the reality of revelation in specific times and places. A comprehensive word search of the titles 'Holy Spirit,' 'Holy Ghost', 'Paraclete,' 'Comforter,' 'Advocate,' 'Divinity,' 'Lord,' 'Lord and Giver of Life,' 'Trinity,' 'God,' 'Providence,' 'grace' and 'Third Person' in the 1845 and 1878 editions reveals that Newman hardly ever explicitly focusses upon pneumatic agency in his explanation of the dynamic of development or his view of the Church. His thought touching upon the Holy Spirit in the *Essay on Development* involves interwoven strands: (i) several remarks distinctly mention the Holy Spirit without reference to the third person as the agent of development or animator of the mind of the Church; (ii) some remarks attribute the process of development or the animation of the mind of the Church to divine agency without distinctly referring to the Holy

Spirit; (iii) and, a smattering of remarks distinctly mention the Spirit as the agent of development or animator of the mind of the Church.

Most of Newman's pneumatological references illustrate his hypothesis accounting for the historical phenomenon of doctrinal change. For example, he uses the historical unfolding of the particular doctrine of the person of the Holy Spirit in order to illustrate the general dynamic of development.[13] Corresponding to his observation that the divinity of the Holy Spirit makes him an object of faith,[14] Newman proceeds to illustrate "ethical"[15] developments by explaining how worship of the Holy Spirit testifies to this divinity.[16] From a methodological point of view, he observes that proof for the divinity of the second person of the Trinity lightens the burden for showing the divinity of the third person in the Godhead.[17] Commenting upon fourth-century controversies involving schism/heresy, Newman mentions the Holy Spirit in a standard reference to the baptismal formula.[18] In order to illustrate his criticism of the Antiochene over-emphasis of the literal sense, Newman cites from the works of Theodore of Mopsuestia (*c.*350–428). In the process, he parts ways with Theodore's gloss that the apostles' reception of the Holy Spirit in the upper room[19] was merely "as an anticipation of the day of Pentecost".[20] While advocating the pre-eminence of the mystical interpretation of scripture in the Church, Newman, *inter alia,* affirms his belief in the *Filioque,* as well as his understanding that the Holy Spirit is the primary author of sacred scripture.[21] Elsewhere he grounds the sacrament of extreme unction in the scriptural account of Christ's own anointing of the sick (*Jas*

13 Dev. 1845: 16 ff., see 298 n.2; Dev. 1878: 18 ff., see 302-3 n.8.

14 Dev. 1845: 54-5; Dev. 1878: 52. Here Newman cites US xv 329-32; reference to the Holy Spirit at 329.

15 In Newman's terminology "ethical" developments are "natural and personal, substituting what is congruous, desirable, pious, appropriate, generous, for strictly logical inference." Dev. 1845: 50; Dev. 1878: 47.

16 Dev. 1845: 50-1; Dev. 1878: 47-8. Newman refers generally to the second part of *Analogy*, for example, II ii 135 ff.

17 Dev. 1845: 155; Dev. 1878: 107.

18 Dev. 1845: 267; Dev. 1878: 270. The reference occurs in Newman's brief citation of the north African bishop, St. Fulgentius of Ruspe (c. 462-527).

19 See Jn 20: 19-23; esp., v. 22.

20 Dev. 1845: 285; Dev. 1878: 289.

21 Dev. 1845: 322; Dev. 341.

5:14).[22] This emerges out of his argument that the terseness of, and design "gaps" in, scripture provide the antecedent probability that the Church will grow both in understanding and applying the meanings of the sacred page to Christian living.[23] Given his pneumatic understanding of the anointing of the Lord at his baptism, one wonders: does his mention of this account of unction allude to, or ascribe, a pneumatological and christological dimension to the sacramental office of the Church? However, there is no support for this supposition in the text.

Newman also cites Athanasius on deification which, indirectly, affirms his understanding of the Church as the Body of Christ and Temple of the Holy Spirit.[24] Even here, however, Newman draws upon Athanasian pneumatology in order to illustrate the gradual realization by the Church of the implications of the doctrine of the incarnation. The pneumatological reference in question neither illustrates the office of the Holy Spirit in assisting the mind of the Church in this realization nor unfolds the implications attendant upon this indirect confirmation of the divinized nature of the Church. Other similar remarks about the Spirit take place within the horizon of Newman's comments upon the incarnation[25] and mariology.[26] In this array of texts there are no explicit references to pneumatic agency relative to the process of doctrinal development or vivification of the Church.

Other passages in the *Essay on Development* correlate divine agency, doctrinal development and Church without any particular pneumatological accent. At one juncture, Newman speaks of the self-same identity of "the Author of Nature" and "the Author of Grace".[27] He reasons (according to divine consistency) that the living God, who operates according to one set of discernible principles in the order of nature, will likely operate according to a similar set of principles in the order of grace. For example, as creation in nature implies an accompanying means of preservation, so too, there exists the antecedent

22 Dev. 1845: 112; Dev. 1878: 73.

23 Dev. 1845: 102, 103; Dev. 1878: 63, 65.

24 Dev. 1845: 404; Dev. 1878: 142.

25 Dev. 1845: 400; Dev. 1878: 137.

26 Newman cites "one of the Fathers of Ephesus" (431) who speaks of *Theotokos* as filled with "the Fount of Life" and St. Peter Chrysologus, bishop of Ravenna, (c. 400-50) who speaks likewise. Dev. 1845: 409; Dev. 1878: 147.

27 Dev. 1845:123; Dev. 1878: 85.

probability that an objective, infallible authority has accompanied the gift of revelation to preserve its life and integrity in history.[28] In light of his propensity to identify life-giving as a hypostatic hallmark of the Holy Spirit, one is attracted to the notion that this parallelism (the Author of Nature is the Author of Grace) contains specific pneumatic content. Yet absent evidence to the contrary, the parallelism is more properly construed as referring to an essential act of divinity common to all three triune persons not as a pneumatic *proprium*. Similarly, Newman's discussion of "merciful Providence" supplying diverse means (e.g., prayer, obedience, antecedent probability) by which one decides what constitutes the evidence upon which to cogitate in order to come to belief in matters of revelation, development of doctrine and the Church does not allude to the Holy Spirit.[29] On another occasion, citing Butler, he generically entitles God, as "'the Giver of prophecy'" without alluding to the fact that prophecy is often associated with the Holy Spirit in sacred scripture and tradition.[30] Possibly Newman refers to the Holy Spirit as that "perspicacious intellect" who "ruled the theological discussion from first to last" in connection with his comments upon the development of the doctrine of the incarnation.[31] However, there is no marker in the text signalling distinctive pneumatic activity. Hence, on numerous occasions referring to themes usually associated with the work of the Holy Spirit – such as the relationship between the orders of grace and nature, revelation, the Church as the bearer of revelation, prophecy, faith and belief and divine guidance in doctrinal development – Newman makes no distinctive mention of the third divine person.

Finally, there are a few places in the *Essay on Development* where Newman probably assigns the Holy Spirit a prominent place. Conceivably he implies pneumatic activity in the mind of the Church *via* his comparison of development of doctrine to the parables of the sower of the mustard seed and the leaven (*Mt* 13: 31-2; *Mk* 4:26-8).[32] He interprets these parables of physical growth as illustrative of the expansion of the Kingdom of Heaven. In turn, he says that this divine

28 Dev. 1845: 123-4 and Dev. 1878: 85-7.

29 Dev. 1845: 179-81; citation, 180; Dev. 1878: 110-12; citation, 111.

30 Dev. 1845: 151; Dev. 1878: 104. *Analogy* II vii 220.

31 Dev. 1845: 448; Dev. 1878: 440.

32 Dev. 1845: 112-13; Dev. 1878: 73-4.

process "distinctly anticipates the development of Christianity both as a polity and as a doctrine", a development which he subsequently characterizes as "expand[ing] within the mind in its season" due to "its own innate power". In short, the organic biblical metaphor is understood in terms of his ecclesial analogy of mind.[33] Although this work of Providence is not specifically appropriated to the Paraclete, the assumption is valid given that Newman later cites Tertullian who refers to "'this dispensation of the Paraclete'" animating the Church *via* precisely such an organic analogy.[34] Moreover, recent scholarship seems to support Newman's sense that Tertullian understood 'Holy Spirit' to refer to the divine person rather than simply pointing to divine power or presence (Hinze and Dabney, 2001, 109, 117 n. 16; 296). Surmising that Newman follows his own principle of interpreting earlier texts in light of later developments, one might argue that his use of Tertullian illuminates earlier passages that omit specific reference to the Holy Spirit. If this argument is accepted, the scope of potential pneumatological passages could include Newman's talk of "Christianity ... [as] informed and quickened by what is more than intellect, by a Divine Spirit'"; his description of the Church as "'the pillar and ground of Truth'" to whom is promised perpetually by covenant, "'the Spirit of the Lord'" (*1 Tim* 3: 15 & *Is* 59: 21);[35] his identification of "the definition passed at Chalcedon" as "the Apostolic Truth once delivered to the Saints" due to "that overruling Providence which is by special promise extended over acts of the Church;"[36]and, his numerous references to grace and truth as gifts of God residing in, enlivening, and flowing out of, the missionary Church into the wider world.[37] Nevertheless, examination of this third group of texts confirms that the *Essay on Development* has fewer direct references to the Holy Spirit as the divine agent of development, as the animator of the ecclesial mind, than one might expect for a theological work which specifically addresses the historical communication of revelation by the Church.

---

33 Dev. 1845: 112; 113; Dev. 1878: 73.

34 Dev. 1845: 350; Dev. 1878: 363.

35 Dev. 1845: 96; Dev. 1878: 57; Dev. 1845: 127; see Dev. 1878: 89.

36 Dev. 1845: 307; Dev. 1878: 312.

37 E.g. Dev. 1845: 401, 62, 208-9, 337-44; 347-8, 352, 354-6, 360, 363, 365, 366; Dev. 1878: 139, 177, 212, 347-51; 359-60, 365, 368-9, 374, 377, 379, 380.

The relative paucity of direct pneumatological references in the *Essay on Development* places in question the extent to which Newman assigns the Holy Spirit a key role in communicating revelation across time and space. Minimal explicit discussion concerning the agency of the Holy Spirit is also puzzling given Newman's sense of the vivified Church at the time he composed this work. In this limited context, Newman's presentation of the Church in the *Essay on Development* seems to fall short of his own fulsome pneumatic ecclesiology. While the lament of modern theology concerning the forgetfulness of the Holy Spirit does not precisely apply here, Newman appears vulnerable to what Bernd Hilberath calls "pneumatological 'deficit'" – the term designates situations in which "the Holy Spirit is subordinate, not properly valued ... repressed or controlled ...." (2001, 265). In his revisionist biography of Newman, Frank Turner contends that a pneumatological deficit characterizes the *Essay on Development*.

> The profoundly naturalistic vision of both human and ecclesiastical history that characterizes Newman's *Essay on Development* was recognized immediately upon its publication. Brownson claimed that Newman had removed the Roman Catholic Church from the order of grace and left it merely part of the order of nature .... Just as Darwin, privately in the late 1830's and early 1840's and then publicly in *On The Origin of Species* in 1859, appropriated much of the vision and rhetoric of natural theology but excluded from it the presence of the Creator, Newman effectively naturalized the history of the Christian church, interpreting it with all of its usual features except the presence of divine Providence or the guidance of the Holy Spirit (2001, 583, 584).

Notwithstanding the fact that Orestes Brownson came to regret his intemperate remarks concerning the *Essay on Development* (Newman eventually offered him a position at the Catholic University of Ireland!)[38] or that Turner's accusation is situated in a psychologizing polemic, it needs to be met. For, if true, the accusation weakens the claim advanced by this author concerning the pivotal connection between Newman's pneumatic christology and his pneumatic ecclesiology. Furthermore the presence of such a "pneumatological deficit" in the *Essay on Development* would strengthen the charge that Newman's theology of revelation is extrinicist (Misner 1970, 44-7). The answer

38 On the original attacks see LD xii, 77-78; on Newman and Brownson's rapprochement, see Campaign xxxi-v.

to this accusation emerges by close examination of Newman's sacramental analogy of mind in the *Essay on Development*.

CHAPTER SEVEN

THE VIVIFIED CHURCH IN THE *ESSAY ON DEVELOPMENT* (1845)

Newman's *Essay on Development* definitely contains a potent pneumatic christology. Fears of a 'pneumatological deficit' dissipate to the degree that one realizes how thoroughly he invests his epistemological language of the Christian idea with pneumatological and christological significance. The truth of this assertion is achieved by one's insight that Newman's sacramental vision, which permeates practically every ecclesiological aspect of his work post-1826, is dynamically operative in the *Essay*. This realization requires one to make three moves on the 'theological chessboard'.

The first move is to describe Newman's analogy of mind, illustrate its operation and clarify his phenomenology of ecclesial cognition which presents the Church as a metaphorical person sacramentally bearing the idea of Christianity across history. The second move is to examine the isomorphism that Newman employs between epistemological [object-principle-idea-subject] and theological [God-Holy Spirit-Christ-Church] terms, relations and networks. Then, after explaining the meaning and limits of this isomorphism, his characterization of the 'Christian idea' as real, medial, vital, historically-conditioned, permanent and whole needs to be considered. The third move is to specify the pneumatological and christological likeness of 'principle-idea' relative to eight specific theses which, themselves, are anchored in already established positions concerning his pneumatic christology and ecclesiology. At the conclusion of these three moves, one sees clearly that Newman accords the Holy Spirit a perpetual, life-giving role in the historical, ecclesial task of bearing Christ and the Gospel across the corridors of history in his *Essay on Development*.

THE MIND OF THE CHURCH

In the *Essay on Development*, Newman conjoins the fecundity of human knowing to the working of Providence in order to explain that so-called "additions" to the gospel are not corruptions of its apostolic integrity, but the outcome of the mind of the Church gradually unfolding the implicit meaning of the word of God – an ecclesial explication of aspects of the Divine Mystery held pre-reflexively by the community of faith. For example, he describes the development of the doctrine of the incarnation "under the fiercest controversies" by reference to the providential permeation of the entire ecclesial reasoning process: "but it was as if some one individual and perspicacious intellect, to speak humanly, ruled the theological discussion from first to last." He refers to the mind of the Church or, more frequently, to the performance of that mind, in order to present it as a personal unity-whole patiently and labouriously striving to "know revelation" like a human person strives to "know a great idea."

"[F]rom the nature of the human mind, time is necessary for the full comprehension and perfection of great ideas; and that the highest and most wonderful truths, though communicated to the world once for all by inspired teachers could not be comprehended all at once by the recipients, but, as received and transmitted by minds not inspired and through media which were human, have required only the longer time and deeper thought for their full elucidation. This may be called the *Theory of Developments* ...."[1] Now Newman's analogy of mind rests upon his understanding of person and Church as structured unities of body-soul-spirit comprised of an equilibrium of functions. His sense of the Church as a structured unity is reflected in the type of developmental analogies which he employs. His analogy of mind stresses the role of reason in the Church's explication of the gospel. This analogy is complemented by an analogy of growth that describes the same process via an organic metaphor, the physicality of which metaphor

1 Dev 1845: 428-9, 135, 448, 320, 352-4, 27; Dev. 1878: 420, 93, 440, 339, 365-8, 29-30.

alludes to the corporeal dimension of the Church.[2] The cognitional and organic analogies both assume the role of the Spirit. Together they present the Church as a unity-whole comprised of body, soul and Spirit; that is, a corporate person. Newman's analogy of mind is grounded in the sacramental analogy that applies between the incarnate Word and the Church constituted by a proportionality consisting of four terms: the human nature of Christ is to the eternal Son what the natural dimension of the Church is to the Holy Spirit. This analogy is limited inasmuch as the human dimension of the incarnation is not a pre-existing person, but an assumed nature, and the personality is that of the eternal Son (Dulles 1987, 44; Tanner ii 854). Hence, there is not a multiplicity of persons in Christ. In the Church, diverse persons are drawn into a communion of faith and love that respects their uniqueness as subjects. Within this framework, Newman exploits the possibilities inherent in this proportionality to speak of the individual and ecclesial mind analogously. Consequently, he is comfortable speaking of "[t]he process of thought of which [the doctrine of Purgatory] is the result" as "an instance of the mind of the Church working out dogmatic truths from implicit feelings under secret supernatural guidance."[3]

Newman's idea that the Church explicates its pre-reflexive knowledge of revelation, as prompted by the circumstances and exigencies of successive epochs, requires some elaboration. He situates specific acts of ecclesial reasoning within the context of the Church's entire historical life.[4] Such operations are never explicable solely in virtue of isolated, external evidence for this activity occurs under the tacit tutelage of penetrating and, sometimes, indeterminable factors such as ethnicity, cultural milieu and the intellectual-moral calibre of those believers comprising the Church. This is true quite apart from the often undetectable and always unquantifiable agency of the Holy Spirit in ecclesial cognition. As a Catholic, Newman spoke about the positive effect of ethnicity upon the mind of the Church designating national diversity as a safeguard of catholicity.[5] In the *Essay on Development* he also states that the character of the age in which the Church dwells

2 Dev. 1845: 44, 112-13; Dev. 1878: 41, 73-4, 171-4.

3 Dev. 1845: 417.

4 *Preface to the Third Edition* (1871), US xi-xvii.

5 Apo. 240-1.

can distort its grasp of the idea of revelation. For example, he asserts that the Church's "accurate apprehension of the consequences of the fall" was blurred by "the fatalism so prevalent, in various shapes pagan and heretical, in the first centuries."[6] Thus, he specifies cultural milieu as another factor which may inhibit a lucid understanding of implicit aspects of revelation. Finally, he asserts that the Church's penetration of the Divine Mystery is influenced by the intellectual and moral disposition of its members. In so doing, Newman emphasizes that moments in ecclesial thought, however important in themselves, must eventually be evaluated in the context of the life of the Church considered as a whole. For "[d]octrines expand variously according to the mind, individual or social, into which they are received; and the peculiarities of the recipient are the regulating power, the law, the organization, or, as it may be called, the form of the development."[7]

Newman also observes that one's fundamental judgments about reality condition one's future judgments (Walgrave 1960, 115). Such judgments are often reducible to more primary ones, but in the concrete they usually remain unconscious and unquestioned. He calls these influential convictions 'first principles' and assigns responsibility for their acquisition to the knowing subject who determines, by acquiescence or deliberative choice, which principles will exercise hegemony and be given dominion. In turn, the vibrancy of mind induced by first principles creates a *habitus* which qualifies how one acts. Similarly, first principles operate in that dynamic grid of minds which comprise the human intelligence of the Church. These principles establish an ethos that qualifies the character of the ecclesial mind and influences its reasoning. Notably, the Divine Mystery is not exhausted by its embodiment in any one culture. By its very nature revelation requires unfolding within many host cultures. Newman's account of the unfolding of a great idea supports this position (Walgrave 1960, 79-80).[8]

In spite of its elasticity, Newman invariably uses the term, first principle, to refer to "a multitude of analogues, whose common characteristic is that they are, *in fact*, the *first* grounds of our thinking and judging". Some ecclesial first principles arise from the Church's experience of the Divine Mystery; others are imbibed from the public arena and

6 Dev. 1878: 126.

7 Dev. 1845: 67, 81; Dev. 1878: 178, 190.

8 Dev. 1845: 29, 37-9; Dev. 1878: 31, 38-40.

worn more as an outer garment than an inner reflection of real, ecclesial apprehension and realization. In each instance, first principles function as prime movers and as sources for judgments (Walgrave 1960, 116; 1975-76-77, 35-81). In this vein, Newman speaks of "Catholic principles" as the often subterranean first grounds of ecclesial thought on matters revelatory:

> And, lastly, it might be expected that the Catholic principles would be later in development than the Catholic doctrines, as lying deeper in the mind, and as being its assumptions rather than its objective professions. This has been the case. The Protestant controversy has mainly turned, or is turning, on one or other of the principles of Catholicity; and to this day the rule of Scripture Interpretation, the doctrine of Inspiration, the relation of Faith to Reason, moral responsibility, private judgment, inherent grace, the seat of infallibility, remain, I suppose, more or less undeveloped, or, at least undefined, by the Church.[9]

Accordingly, Newman suggests that a set of fundamental principles stimulate and energize the ecclesial mind when, according to circumstance and exigency, some implicit aspect of revelation requires concrete doctrinal expression.[10] Although not exhaustive about the content of ecclesial principles, which qualify and direct the operations of the ecclesial mind, Newman indicates in the 1878 version of the *Essay on Development* that they emerge from the incarnate Word, and he lists ten of them: dogma, faith, theology, sacramentality, the mystical interpretation of scripture, grace, asceticism, the recognition of the malignity of sin, the capacity of mind and matter to be sanctified and development.[11]

Newman's belief that the operations of the ecclesial mind emerge from a *habitus* influenced by natural and supernatural first principles makes him wary of appraisals of its actions in strictly logical terms based on deductive reason.[12] He refuses to confine its life of the mind, particularly in the matter of doctrinal development, to the realm of syllogism or scientific method.[13] For these processes, which abstract from the exigencies of daily living, neither inspire belief in God, trust in the Church, nor fully account for the concreteness of reality.

9 Dev. 1845: 368; Dev. 1878: 179-80.

10 Dev. 1845: 74, 71, 67; Dev. 1878: 186, 180, 178.

11 Dev. 1878: 324-6.

12 US v 88 n.7.

13 Dev. 1845: 397, Dev. 1878: 383; US xii 223; LD xxix 116.

Conversely, Newman situates the empirical paradigm of reason in a broader context to conclude that the operations of the mind of the Church are both explicit and implicit, that they are founded on secular and sacred assumptions and that they are concerned with method as well as the genius of its members. He presents ecclesial reasoning as a force which betrays a breadth and depth beyond, but not independent of, the strictly logical (Jost 1989, 56).

THREE STAGES: HISTORICAL VIGNETTES

References by Newman to the performance of the mind of the Church suggest that ecclesial cognition unfolds in three stages. To begin, a real but diffuse knowledge of revelation is present within the mind of the Church, especially with the Apostles.[14] The apprehension of this revelation by the faithful causes them to adopt certain positions and postures on matters revelatory. Second, on occasion, some event, often a crisis,[15] prompts certain persons within the Church to explicate this pre-reflexive knowledge. "Thus, the pressure of the [Arian] controversy elicited and developed a truth, which till then was held indeed by Christians, but less perfectly realized and not publicly recognized."[16] This explication focusses the diffuse knowledge of revelation present within the mind of the Church. Third, a judgment crystallizes as to the correctness of this clarified understanding like the decision of the Church about the canon. "On what ground, then, do we receive the Canon as it comes to us, but on the authority of the Church of the fourth and fifth centuries? The Church at that era **decided**, -- not merely bore testimony, but **passed a judgment** on former testimony, -- **decided**, that certain books were of authority ...."[17] Although Newman does not overtly schematize this tripartite method, it penetrates his historical vignettes as an examination of his discussion of Mary, "Mother of God" and infant baptism testifies (Norris 1977, 29-35; Walgrave 1960, 106-14).

In the context of discussing the development of the doctrine of the incarnation, Newman reflects upon the dignity of Mary. "[I]n order to do honour to Christ, in order to defend the true doctrine of the

14 Dev. 1845: 83, Dev. 1878: 191-2; TP ii 158-9.

15 "No doctrine is defined till it is violated." Dev. 1845: 167; Dev. 1878: 151.

16 Dev. 1845: 402; Dev. 1878: 140.

17 Dev. 1845: 160; Dev. 1878: 125. Emphasis added.

Incarnation, in order to secure a right faith in the manhood of the Eternal Son, the Council of Ephesus determined the Blessed Virgin to be the Mother of God .... But the spontaneous or traditional feeling of Christians ... had in great measure anticipated the formal ecclesiastical decision. Thus, the title *Theotocos*, or Mother of God, was familiar to Christians from primitive times ...."[18] Within the framework of his reflections on how the conciliar Fathers fashioned incarnational dogma at Ephesus, Newman reveals something fundamental about his understanding of how the ecclesial mind operates. He suggests that the lively, pious knowledge of Christians about Mary's place in the plan of salvation, what he likes to call real knowledge, prepares the way for, and provides the substance from which, the Fathers of Ephesus were able to derive the notional and dogmatic title, *Theotokos*. In this manner, Newman indicates that real and notional apprehensions of revelation by the Church share a common starting point, that is, impressions made by the content of concrete experience. His remarks permit one to distinguish between these complementary forms of knowing in terms of the knowledge to which they attain, the quality of their content, as well as the way in which they focus the concern of the Church, and the degree to which each type of knowledge resonates within, and commands the attention of, different members of the Church. Real apprehension concerns the relation between the mind of the Church and a concrete object, such as the Mother of God. Such apprehension "transcends immediate impressions by an act *sui generis*" in which the ecclesial mind "attains to a communion with substantial and concrete realities which are not explicable in terms of these impressions."[19] In terms of content, the object in its entirety engages the Church's imagination and engraves an impression upon its memory; in terms of attention, the Church focusses exclusively on the object itself as a whole; and, in terms of reality or value, the encounter of the Church perceiving and the concrete object perceived remains the source of ecclesial motivation. In contrast, notional apprehension involves the mind of the Church relating realities to each other. In terms of content, the Church focusses on aspects of objects as they are abstractly and theoretically related to each other; in terms of attention, the preoccupation of the Church is with certain aspects of reality and not the whole; in

18 Dev. 1845: 407; Dev. 1878: 145.

19 See GA 22-7; 73.

terms of reality or value, these abstractions do not move the Church with the same vitality as objects really apprehended (Walgrave 1960, 112, 106-14; Norris 1977, 29-35).

Newman's understanding of the performance of the ecclesial mind also comes to the fore in his discussion of the transition in Christianity from the custom of adult baptism to that of infant baptism which, he asserts, has its origins in the spontaneous desire of "any Christian father, in the absence of express direction, to bring his children for baptism" as "the practical development of his faith in Christ and love for his offspring ...."[20] The discussion highlights his understanding of the personal quality of the deliberative process within the mind of the Church that precedes, prepares for and, at length, issues forth in an act of judgment. "[N]either in Dalmatia nor in Cappadocia, neither in Rome, nor in Africa, was it then imperative on Christian parents, as it is now, to give baptism to their young children. It was on retrospect and after the truths of the Creed had sunk into the Christian mind, that the authority of such men as St. Cyprian, St. Chrysostom, and St. Augustine brought the *orbis terrarum* to the conclusion, which the infallible Church confirmed, that observance of the rite was the rule, and the non-observance the exception."[21] Significantly, Newman introduces the baptismal question by an affirmation that its core meaning is found in those truths which reside in the Christian mind and are summarized by the creed. Hence, he places the emergent historical question – about the age at which one ought to be baptized – in the more basic primal understanding of the mind of the Church concerning the relation of baptism to the mystery of the incarnation. In the process, he indicates that ongoing ecclesial reflection upon the meaning of divine revelation is the very method by which the mind of the Church moves from implicit to explicit knowledge. Hence, Newman invites one to view the development of the baptismal practice from within the dynamic stream of that "retrospect[ive] process" by which "the truths of the Creed" sink into the Christian mind. Moreover, this passage emphasizes that ecclesial reasoning on the matter of baptism did not achieve clarity in an impersonal fashion. Rather it was a personal process that integrated the efforts, talents and idiosyncrasies of specific individuals in various cultures – Cyprian (d. 258),

20 Dev. 1845: 99, Dev. 1878: 61.

21 Dev. 1878: 129.

Chrysostom (347-407) and Augustine (354-430) – to achieve a fuller, more vivid grasp of the meaning of baptism. In turn, insights articulated by prominent thinkers gradually garnered the approval of the faithful and, subsequently, were "confirmed" by the authority of the Church.

Newman's discussions of *Theotokos* and infant baptism suggest that the mind of the Church incessantly reflects upon its grasp of revelation of which the entire body of Christ is the repository; that members of the Church are prodded by exigency and circumstance to clarify this understanding; and, that a judgment eventually crystallizes as to the correctness of this clarified understanding.

> Doctrine too is percolated, as it were, through different minds, beginning with writers of inferior authority in the Church, and issuing at length in the enunciation of her Doctors .... The deep meditation which seems to have been exercised by the Fathers on points of doctrine, the debate and turbulence yet lucid determination of Councils, the indecision of Popes, are all in different ways, at least when viewed together, portions and indications of the same process. The theology of the Church is no random combination of various opinions, but a diligent, patient working out of one doctrine out of many materials. The conduct of Popes, Councils, Fathers, betokens the slow, painful, anxious taking up of new elements into an existing body of belief.[22]

The form and subject of this judgment, as the case warrants, is either doctrinal definition by the teaching office of the Church or the acceptance of a new practice by the Church universal. Thus, the Church, in the unity of its communal relations, functions much like the human person who moves from apprehension of the content of concrete experience to a more explicit understanding of that experience to a judgment about the correctness of that understanding. In this fashion, the Church operates as a conscious, living vessel who bears and imparts a real and notional knowledge of revelation.

CLEARING AWAY OBSTRUCTIONS

Further entrance into Newman's analogy of mind is opened up by clearing away two possible obstructions. To begin with, he does not view the person of the Church as an hypostasized entity. Second, the cognitive emphasis present in his analogy of mind does not signal an

22 Dev. 1845: 352; 353; Dev. 1878: 365; 366.

intellectualist understanding of the ecclesial subject who carries the idea of revelation.

METAPHORICAL PERSON

First, Newman does not conceive of the Church as some supra-human person existing and operating over and against that aggregate of minds comprising the human intelligence of the Church. He sidesteps pitfalls inherent in the idea of the Church as an hypostasized person by speaking of it as a "metaphorical" person as early as 1830.[23] Any concept of pneumatic personation that hypostasizes the Church transforms it into a supernatural entity somehow situated 'above' human persons, but 'below' the persons of the Trinity. At best, this concept blurs the nature of the communion that adheres between 'human persons' and the 'persons' of the Trinity. At worst, this concept places the Church on par with the divine persons of the Trinity. Such personation tends to threaten the freedom and identity of the human person by subsuming the individual within the hypostasized person of the Church. Conversely, a proper understanding of divine indwelling involves a communion in which human freedom and identity is enhanced not subsumed.

Enhancement rather than subsumption runs through Newman's understanding of the united aggregate of human minds to whom the deposit of faith has been committed over the ages. Although the ecclesial mind is a much more complex reality than an individual mind, this increased complexity does not result in grace over-riding the operations of human intelligence. Rather, Newman predicates analogously of the person of the Church the cognitive performance of the human person. Accordingly, he claims that the ecclesial mind operates on the same basic principles of cognition as the individual mind even when the object of cognition is revelation. Barring "some special ground of exception" Christianity "will develope [sic] in the minds of recipients, as that it conforms in other respects, in its external propagation or its political framework, to the general methods by which the course of things is carried forward."[24] His insight that the Church contains the "treasure" of revelation within its mind shows a thorough regard for, and understanding of, the integrated character of its divine-hu-

23 US ii 28-30.

24 Dev. 1845: 96; Dev. 1878: 57.

man form. Thus, his candid observation of Christianity's supernatural "powers" and "miraculous nativity" is offset by an equally frank recognition that, like the "Lord Himself", the message and its bearer are incarnate:

> Certainly it is a sort of degradation of a divine work to consider it under an earthly form; but it is no irreverence, since the Lord Himself, its Author and Owner, bore one also. Christianity differs from other religions and philosophies, in what it has in addition to them; not in kind, but in origin; not in its nature, but in its personal characteristics; being informed and quickened by what is more than intellect, by a Divine Spirit. It is externally what the Apostle calls an 'earthly vessel,'[25] being the religion of men. And, considered as such, it grows 'in wisdom and stature;'[26] but the powers which it wields, and the words which proceed out of its mouth, attest its miraculous nativity.[27]

Here Newman underscores the incarnate form of Christianity by reference to the apostle Paul's metaphor that he is an "earthly vessel" bearing a precious "treasure" (the gospel of Christ) whose "transcendent power" reveals its divine origins (2 *Cor* 4:7). This reference is intriguingly juxtaposed with the Lucan phrase about growing "in wisdom and stature" by which Newman compares the Church's ongoing and gradual growth in its understanding of the gospel to the eternal Son's natural maturation as a human being. In the process, he is careful neither to compromise the divinity of the eternal Son nor the permanence of divine revelation. The comparison is evocative. Newman manages the tension between the historicity and permanence of the gospel borne by the pilgrim Church by placing both within the mystery of the historicity of the Word made flesh in whom immanence and transcendence are reconciled without being dissolved. Newman does not seek to relieve this tension by analysis, rather he situates it in a sacramental context. He seeks to preserve the tension inherent in the sacramental truth that the Church is both an "earthly vessel" subject to the laws, limits and foibles of human nature as well as a graced reality "quickened by what is more than intellect, by a Divine Spirit."

---

25 2 Cor 4:5-7.

26 Lk 2:52.

27 Dev. 1845: 96; Dev. 1878: 57.

ECCLESIAL IDENTITY: PERSONAL, HISTORICAL, CORPOREAL AND COGNITIVE

Second, Newman's analogy of mind requires that the idea of Christianity be understood in the context of his concrete portrait of the sacramental Church. This idea is entrusted to the ecclesial subject who labours in the vineyard of time not in Platonic realms of contemplation. In the course of his discussion about the phenomenon of development, he speaks about how the office of Mary, the confession of martyrs, the toil of the Fathers and doctors of the Church, the penitential life of monks, the cult of the saints and angels, the example of virgins, the exercise of the episcopal office, the activity of Councils and the movements of the Christian body *in toto* make contributions to the unity-whole.[28] Moreover, he refers to the Church as a feminine reality, to Christianity as a fact of history and development of doctrine as that organic growth illustrated in the parable of the mustard seed about the Kingdom of Heaven in order to emphasize that the ecclesial bearer of revelation is in the form of the Word made flesh.[29] The Church, then, is a graced unity-whole possessing a personal, historical, corporeal, as well as a cognitive identity (Merrigan 1991, 89-90).[30] While Newman believes that the non-discursive operations of the human person have a vital role in the Church's task of bearing revelation, he stresses that "intellectual action" is "the organ of development". His recurrent description of the concreteness of the Church provides a hedge against reductionistic interpretations of the Christian idea viewed solely through the lens of the philosophies that influenced him: English empiricism, Romanticism, Platonic idealism and Aristotelianism. Far from denying that Newman is influenced

28 Dev. 1845: 384-7; Dev. 1878: 415-18 (Mary); Dev. 1845:348; 1878: 361 (martyrs); Dev. 1845: 349 ff., 448-9; Dev. 1878: 361 ff., 440 (Fathers); Dev. 1845: 423-8; Dev. 1878: 395-9 (monks); Dev. 1845: 376-81; Dev. 1878: 410-15 (saints and angels); Dev. 1845: 381-3; Dev. 1878: 407-10 (virgins); Dev. 1845: 258-69; Dev.1878: 265-72 (bishops); Dev. 1845: 281, 288, 293-317; Dev. 1878: 284, 292, 297-322 (Councils) ; Dev. 1845: 348; Dev. 1878: 360 (whole Church).

29 Dev. 1845: 126, 160, 164, 167, 219, 256, 264, 314, 320, 323, 348, 352, 362, 428, 449, 452; Dev. 1878: 88, 125, 133, 151, 223, 263, 266, 320, 339, 342, 362, 365, 376, 419, 440, 444 (Church as feminine); Dev. 1845: 94, 115, 123, 227; Dev. 1878: 55, 76, 85, 231 (Christianity as Fact); Dev. 1845: 112, Dev. 1878: 73 (mustard seed).

30 Dev. 1878: 92; Dev. 1845: 81, 349, 440 & Dev. 1878: 190, 362, 449.

by the traditions of Locke (Cameron 1960, 99-117; 1967, 76-96), Hume, Coleridge (Coulson 1970, 57-82; Prickett 1976, 152-210; Knox 1934, 35-52), Plato (Newsome 1974, 57-72; Weatherby 1973, 69-82)[31] and Aristotle[32] one needs to attend to the commonplace that the history of philosophy is a history of terms acquiring new meanings in changing contexts. As Owen Chadwick opines, "To adopt a word is not to adopt a philosophy which that word has often represented, though it may be to communicate ideas the more easily to persons who habitually think in those terms" (1987, 98). This is precisely what the Fathers did as they borrowed, adapted and changed terms and ideas from Aristotelian, Platonic, Middle Platonic and Stoic philosophy (Pelikan 1971, 1:27-41). In this case, the primary context in which one should interpret 'the Christian idea' is Newman's theology of the Church wherein the corporate subject is understood as a sacramental, personal, historical, corporeal, cognitive entity. In this regard, his understanding of divine revelation as an 'idea' in the mind of the Church involves much more transformation than repetition of his philosophical mentors. Terrence Merrigan makes this very point: "Newman, convinced of the living presence of the risen Christ, has woven Romantic and empiricist notions of ideas into a perspective peculiarly his own. It is only by bearing the essential features of all these elements in mind that one can do justice to the Newmanian synthesis (1991, 73)." Even J.M. Cameron, who sees Newman very much as an empiricist, readily admits that the use of the term 'idea' in the *Essay on Development*, "transcends the limiting model within which Newman, following Locke and Hume, is always thinking" (1974, 40-1). By taking into account the full identity of the ecclesial bearer of revelation one avoids intellectualist, ahistorical or impersonal interpretations of Newman's living idea of Christianity in his *Essay on Development* (Misner 1970, 32-47). Now this matter of "bearing the essential features of all these elements in mind" is more (though certainly not less) than arriving at the proper assessment of the epistemological underpinnings of the Christian idea. Essentially, it is a matter of arriving at the proper assessment of the sacramental underpinnings of the idea of Christianity – a matter of realizing the pneumatological and christological character of the idea of Christianity.

31 Apo. 23; PS i 2: 18-20; PS ii 29: 362; PS iv 13: 200-13; Ess. ii 193.

32 *Idea* 102.

COMMUNION WITH GOD THROUGH THE IDEA OF CHRISTIANITY

In light of the remarks, one can begin to examine how pneumatological and christological features are inscribed into Newman's cognitional language in the *Essay on Development*. Determining and detailing the entire landscape of Newman's epistemology, as it relates to his theology of revelation and ecclesiology, is an immense task. Here it is enough to give a modest account of the issues at hand with an eye to clarifying Newman's view of the Holy Spirit and the God-man in the *Essay on Development* relative to the idea of Christianity by setting forth his understanding of the idea as isomorphic, real, medial, vital, historically-conditioned, permanent and whole. By this sixfold characterization one can survey the contours of Newman's idea and enter into its reality without claiming, in the process, to have completely unravelled the "notoriously complex description of the history of a 'real' and 'living idea'" (Lash, 1971, 232). Mapping the contours of the idea of Christianity, then, is preparatory to illumining its pneumatological and christological likeness.

ISOMORPHIC

Newman speaks about the idea of Christianity in a theological manner which represents both the totality of that which the Church apprehends about revelation and the living presence of that revelation within the mind of the Church.[33] In point of fact, Newman sometimes makes the network of epistemological relations within which his analogy of mind operates isomorphic to the network of theological relations by which the Church herself is constituted and sustained. Bernard Lonergan supplies a useful definition of isomorphism. "Isomorphism, then, supposes different sets of terms, it neither affirms nor denies similarity between the terms of one set and those of other sets; but it does assert that the network of relations in one set of terms is similar to the networks of relations in other sets" (1988, 133). In the *Essay on Development*, Newman posits a similarity between the form of, and dynamics within, an epistemological network of relations [object-idea-principle-subject] and the form of, and dynamics within, a theological network of relations [God-incarnate Word-Holy

33 Dev. 1845: 34-5; Dev. 1878: 35-6; US xv 329-32.

Spirit-Church]. In virtue of his analogy of mind, this similarity extends beyond a mere similarity of the networks considered as self-contained units [isomorphism proper] to a more intricate similarity in which there is also a similarity between the sets of terms and relations within the two networks: that is, God is also analogous to object, idea to incarnate Word, principle to Holy Spirit and subject to Church.

Here one must register a caveat. The isomorphism between Newman's epistemological and theological terms and relations is not perfectly geometrical for at least three reasons. First, his own use of epistemological terms is fluid and, on occasion, inconsistent. One only has to consider the categorization of Newman's first principles by Walter Jost in order to appreciate their elastic, multivalent nature as: (1) true or false; (2) strict or loose as the principle is/is not grounded in a more fundamental principle; (3) determinate or indeterminate as the principle corresponds to a permanent or changing reality; (4) and, consequently, as universally or relatively applicable (1989, 46-54). Furthermore, there is no evidence that Newman thought through and systematically applied this isomorphism, although various of his writings suggest he was conscious of the correspondence and often found it congenial to convey his theological insights using cognitional language. Finally, Newman's theory of development was devised by him to apply to all manner and forms of ideas. Hence he is concerned at the outset of the first chapter of the *Essay on Development* to describe the generic nature of ideas and categorize certain kinds of ideas based upon this description.[34] The importance of establishing this common platform may even account for his 1878 decision to limit chapter one to these initial two sections of his 1845 work.[35] Only after establishing this common platform does Newman intensively begin to address the question of the "idea of Christianity". Yet one cannot forget – nor does Newman set aside – the fact that the idea of Christianity is *sui generis* not generic: "The doctrine of the Incarnation is a fact, and cannot be paralleled by anything in nature ...."[36] The Word of God who forms and enters into his own creation by becoming Man, who redeems and saves man, and who remains sacramentally-historically present to man in his Church through the person-gift of his Holy Spirit, is a great

---

34 Dev. 1845: 30-57.

35 Dev. 1878: 33-54.

36 Dev. 1845: 123; Dev. 1878: 85.

mystery. One should not expect such a great mystery to be reducible in every respect to the contours of isomorphism.

The inherent challenge of speaking about the great mystery of the incarnation *via* this epistemological-theological isomorphism manifests itself in Terrence Merrigan's statement that "the object of Christian faith is prior to the Christian idea and distinct from it, just as the ideas of sense perception are distinct from sensible impressions and their corresponding objects" (1991, 73). The epistemological set of relations [object-idea-principle-subject] demands the anteriority of object, as well as its distinction from idea, in order to safeguard the ontological ground upon which the network operates and to preserve the possibility of a philosophical realism. The corresponding position arising from the theological set of relations [God-incarnate Word-Holy Spirit-Church] is the understanding of God *in se*, along with related notions such as *creatio ex nihilo*. These theological truths safeguard the integrity of the Godhead by insisting upon his absolute existence prior to, and independent from all that is not Him.

So far the symmetry of the isomorphism is intact. Yet the great mystery of the incarnation, which Newman practically identifies as the idea of Christianity, requires more than a declaration about the anteriority of the Godhead and its distinction from creation. Insofar as Newman ascribes to the idea of Christianity the mediatorial role of making possible participation in the reality of the object of Christian faith, the idea of Christianity shares in what it communicates. From a theological perspective this is only possible if, in some fashion, the idea of Christianity **is** what it communicates, if it communicates the life of the Divine Object because it shares in its divine communion of life and love. As the Fathers of Vatican II declared, "The most intimate truth which this revelation gives us about God and the salvation of man shines forth in Christ, who is himself both the mediator and the sum total of Revelation" (Tanner ii 972).

Now insistence upon the priority of object, and its distinction from idea, must be matched by an equal insistence upon the mediation of object to subject *via* idea; that is, subject participates in object through idea. On the theological side of the isomorphism, this involves God becoming man without ceasing to be God in order to permit human beings to participate in the life of the Trinity, the divine Object of faith. Without the 'mediation' effected and the 'participation' made possible by 'idea', there is no bridge from (Divine) object to (ecclesial) subject. According to the logic of the isomorphism the Christian idea is, with the qualifications noted immediately below, the God-man.

One can find problems in the other direction. Under the broad canopy of the 'idea of Christianity', one could confuse bride and groom and efface the necessary distinction between the sacramental union of the spousal Church and the God-man. Newman is in no danger of making this error. Perhaps his sensitivity to this error stands behind his understanding of the Church as a 'metaphorical' rather than 'hypostasized' person, an understanding that enables him to distinguish the Lord from his Church, yet still speak intimately about her participation in His divine life through His Holy Spirit.

> When our Lord went up on high, he left His representative behind Him. This was Holy Church, His mystical Body and Bride, a Divine Institution, and the shrine and organ of the Paraclete, who speaks through her till the end comes. She, to use an Anglican poet's words, is 'His very self below,' as far as men on earth are equal to the discharge and fulfilment of high offices, which primarily and supremely are His. These offices, which specially belong to Him as Mediator, are commonly considered to be three; He is Prophet, Priest, and King; and after His pattern, and in human measure, Holy Church has a triple office too ....[37]

The challenge put by the great mystery of the incarnation to the isomorphism comprised of epistemological-theological networks of relations reminds one that every analogy involves dissimilarity as well as similarity and this is never more so than when that analogy concerns Creator and creature (Tanner i 232).

REAL AND MEDIAL

The belief pervades the *Essay on Development* that one can truly know being as such. From the epistemological perspective, then, Newman's idea corresponds to the object which it represents in one's mind. Recognition that an idea is real occurs in one's correct judgment that the idea serves to signify accurately and make present, in some manner, the object under consideration. "It is characteristic of our minds to be ever engaged in passing judgment on the things which come before us. No sooner do we apprehend than we judge: we allow nothing to stand by itself .... Of the judgments thus made, which become aspects

37 *Preface to the Third Edition* of the VM i: xxxix-xl.

in our minds of the things which meet us ... some, as being actually incompatible with each other, are, one or other, falsely associated in our minds with their object, and in any case may be nothing more than ideas which we mistake for things."[38] Here idea mediates the reality of the object that the subject seeks to know and stands as a middle term between object and subject. While some ideas do not correspond to reality and, therefore, are derisively called "nothing more than" ideas,[39] failure on the part of the knowing subject to grasp reality in certain situations does not impugn the potential for the authentic mediation of reality *via* ideas. Newman is clear that an idea can "claim to be the representative of an objective truth."[40] His sense of the idea within the mind of the subject is neither that of an object impressing itself upon the passive tablet of the mind (empiricism) nor the remaking of reality according to the categories of the mind (Kantianism). For the idea is "not only passively admitted in this or that form into the minds of men but it becomes a living principle within them, leading them to an ever-new contemplation of itself, an acting upon it and a propagation of it."[41] After discarding Platonic and Coleridgian thought as the source of the idea's vitality and subsistence, Cameron comments, "[o]ne thing is clear: in his preference for the term *idea* Newman is not offering a reductive analysis of religion in which we remain, as it were, in unredeemed subjectivity, playing with ideas but cut off from the reality which alone gives sense to religious utterances. On the contrary, [Newman's] idea is an instrument of discovery, a means of getting a more secure purchase on reality, a prism through which we see more of the rich detail of the in the end ineffable object" (1974, 40-1). In other words, idea is a medial term in the dynamic process of knowing/ revealing in which both the integrity of subject and object are preserved in a communion of being. This approach attests to Newman's insight into the unified but pluralistic reality of being: the knowing subject (individual or communal) is understood as a structured unity-whole comprised of an equilibrium of functions; the process of knowing itself involves several interwoven strands such as first principles, antecedent probabilities, ethos and the moral-intellectual character of

38 Dev. 1878: 33-4; Dev. 1845: 30.

39 Dev. 1845: 30-1; Dev. 1878: 34.

40 Dev. 1845: 32.

41 Dev. 1845: 35; Dev. 1878: 36.

the subject who knows really and notionally; and, finally, the known results from the communion of object-subject mediated by the idea which enters into the imagination to become a living principle within the mind. Thus, Newman's 'idea' is one of four terms comprising a unity of epistemological relations: object- idea-principle-subject. The nature of this communion is further clarified by grasping Newman's view of the vitality, wholeness, historicity and permanence of the idea of Christianity.

VITAL

Newman also emphasizes the ability of the idea "to arrest and possess the mind."[42] In this manner, he accents the vitality and objectivity of God's revealing and redeeming. As subject, the Church is presented with a revelation which both moulds and moves it. Even further, this revelation becomes an active principle within the Church and leads it to an ever new contemplation of that which has been given. Revelation is seen to possess a power, life and objectivity which animates the Church. Insofar as Newman presents the idea of Christianity as affecting the Church on every level of its being, and exercising its own personal presence, the idea ceases to be explainable solely as an ecclesial mental phenomenon (Merrigan 1991, 71). Obversely, the subjective dimension of this communion is highlighted by the dynamism of human consciousness which apprehends and appropriates the revelatory idea that has been gifted to the Church. The foregoing indicates that the density of the Christian idea is related to, and revealed by, the complementary meaning of mind implicit to Newman's prose in the *Essay on Development*. Broadly-speaking two meanings of this term are discernible. First, 'mind' is the ecclesial 'space' in which God makes known the objective reality of revelation. Second, 'mind' refers to the 'drive' of the ecclesial subject to know fully revelation. Ignoring either of these facets of 'mind' distorts that which is known and the process of knowing. Overemphasizing the impressing capability of revelation leads to an extrinsicist notion of the Divine Mystery as something known apart from, or even in spite of, the dynamic activity of the human mind, which is the source of culture, ever-changing social situations and human meaning. When this happens revelation assumes a Platonic bearing, ceases to be the outcome of a communion

42 Dev. 1878: 36; Dev. 1845: 35.

between God and the human spirit and functions as an imperial power. Alternatively, a lopsided emphasis on the Church's dynamism, at length, isolates it from the ontological ground of all meaning, the Divine Mystery. This isolation occurs precisely in attempts to treat ecclesial knowing as an invention of reason rather than a discovery that issues forth from a recognition of the correspondence that obtains between ecclesial knowing and the Divine Mystery which is known. Consequently, the structure of Newman's phenomenology of ecclesial cognition intimates that it is only by holding the objectivity of God and the subjectivity of the Church in creative tension that one appreciates the ultimate reality of the Divine Mystery, acknowledges the historical, mediatorial role of Christ Jesus and respects the dynamism of the human spirit operative within the Church.

HISTORICALLY-CONDITIONED AND WHOLE

Other important characteristics denoted by Newman's view of idea are that of historicity and wholeness. His references to the wholeness of the idea of Christianity opens up both his view of the historically-conditioned and permanent nature of God's revelation in Christ Jesus. The issue of historicity underlies Newman's observation that the fullness of the Christian idea is only asymptotically realized by the Church which, over time, and with much effort, gradually assembles the countless aspects constituting the completeness of the idea:

> Let one such idea get possession of the popular mind, or the mind of any set of persons, and it is not difficult to understand the effects which will ensue. There will be a general agitation of thought, and an action of mind both upon itself and other minds. New lights will be brought to bear upon the original idea, aspects will multiply, and judgments accumulate. There will be a time of confusion .... After a while some definite form of doctrine emerges; and, as time proceeds, one view of it will be modified or expanded by another, and then, combined with a third, till the idea in which they centre will be to each mind separately what at first it was only to all altogether .... It will be questioned by and criticized by enemies, and explained by well-wishers. The multitude of opinions formed concerning it, in these respects and many others, will be collected, compared, sorted, shifted, selected, or rejected, and gradually attached to it, or separated from it , in the minds of individuals and of the community. It will, in proportion to its native vigour and subtlety, introduce itself into the framework and details of social life, changing public opinion and supporting or undermining the foundations of established order. Thus in time it has grown into an ethical

> code, or into a system of government, or into a theology, or into a ritual according to its capabilities ....[43]

Further evidence of Newman's sensitivity to the historicity of these efforts appears in his statement that a living idea "not only modifies, but, ... is modified, or at least influenced, by the state of things in which it is carried out, and depends in various ways on the circumstances around it."[44] In essence, he declares that the Church's grasp of God's revelation in Christ Jesus is not entombed within the ahistorical world of disembodied Cartesianism or decadent scholasticism but affected by the world in which the Church resides. Intercourse with the world can corrupt the Church's understanding of the Divine Mystery. However, this is the only way in which the ecclesial subject can appropriate its true meaning.[45] For the Christ-event has life in the consciousness of the Church, a consciousness which is personal, historical, embodied and, as such, not immune to the vagaries of time.

Nonetheless, historicity does not mean discontinuity or relativism. Newman draws attention to the idea's quality of wholeness to speak about the permanency of revelation. He indicates that the final body of thought with which the idea of Christianity can be equated "will after all be only the adequate representation of the original idea, being nothing else than what that very idea *meant* from the first, its exact image as seen in a combination of the most diversified aspects, with the suggestions and corrections of many minds, and the illustrations of many trials." Hence, wholeness expresses not only the fullness of knowledge to which the Church will attain over time [historicity], but also, the fullness which properly belongs to the objective nature of revelation that the Church has pre-reflexively grasped from the start [permanence]. The reconciliation of permanency and historicity, achieved within the comprehensive nature of an idea, is itself related to Newman's anthropological principle that "the nature of the human mind" requires time "for the full comprehension and perfection of great ideas.".[46] Finally, the wholeness of the idea of Christianity testifies to the fundamental unity inherent in revelation, a unity that precedes and grounds every aspect of revelation upon which the ecclesial

43 Dev. 1845: 36; Dev. 1878: 37-8.

44 Dev. 1845: 37-8; Dev. 1878: 39.

45 Dev. 1845: 38; Dev. 1878: 39-40.

46 Dev. 1845: 36-7, 27 ; Dev. 1878: 38, 29.

mind focusses. This unity exerts a regulative pressure that dissuades the Church from distorting revelation by seeing it through the prism of any one single dimension: for "there is no one aspect such, as to go the depth of a real idea, no one term or proposition which can duly and fully represent it …."[47]

EIGHT THESES ON THE PNEUMATOLOGICAL-CHRISTOLOGICAL CHARACTER OF *ECCLESIA*

The preceding presentation of Newman's phenomenology of ecclesial cognition permits the following argument to come to the fore: when he speaks of the idea of Christianity living within the mind of the Church because of certain principles, Newman equates, at a certain level, the principles perpetuating the idea of Christianity across time and space with the person of the Holy Spirit, and the idea of Christianity with the totality of the Christ-event continued in the Church. The validity of this theological reading [God-incarnate Word-Holy Spirit-Church] of his epistemological language [object-idea-principle-subject] is grasped when one comprehends how eight of his epistemological theses correlate with eight of his pneumatological-christological theses. Each thesis situates an aspect of his thought on the Holy Spirit and Christ within the logic of the isomorphism.

(1) Idea can be correlated with the mediation of the eternal Son and principle can be correlated with the animation of the Holy Spirit.

(2) Principle and idea relate to each other in a unified, complementary and distinct fashion, like the eternal Son and Holy Spirit.

(3) The principle-idea relationship resembles the perichoretic nature of the Holy Spirit- eternal Son relationship.

(4) The physical metaphor of inner-outer communicates similar meanings in the principle-idea and Holy Spirit-eternal Son relationships.

47 Dev. 1845: 34; Dev. 1878: 35.

(5) The idea is one, but the ultimate reality it both signifies and makes present has an infinite number of aspects, like the one God-man who is the inexhaustible fullness of divine revelation.

(6) Principle helps in the making present of idea, just like the Holy Spirit helps in the making present of Christ.

(7) Principle and idea, like the Holy Spirit and Christ, can be practically indistinguishable.

(8) Principle comes to light in virtue of knowing idea, like the Holy Spirit is known in virtue of knowing the God-man.

The pneumatological-christological likeness of principle-idea is now explored *via* these eight interpenetrating theses. Rather than illustrating theses according to their own array of texts, it is more consistent with the way in which they appear in the *Essay on Development* to treat them in clusters. The exception to the rule is Newman's association of principle-idea with the foundational task of mediation. This important thesis is addressed individually at the outset.

THESIS I: MEDIATION

In the *Essay on Development*, Newman speaks about the totality of the Christ-event in a manner that includes the origin, preservation and development of the Church by use of his term, "the idea of Christianity".[48] For example, he says that the "special and singular" "fact" of the Incarnation is the "antecedent of the doctrine of Mediation, and the archetype both of the Sacramental principle and the merits of Saints."[49] From this principle of mediation[50] originate atonement, holy eucharist, real presence, resurrection of the body, the cult of martyrs and saints, indulgences, purgatory, priesthood, celibacy and monasticism. From the sacramental principle originate the seven sacraments, the doctrine of justification, original sin, "the unity of the Church, the Holy See "as its type and centre, the authority of Councils" and "the

48 Dev. 1845: 152-55; 1, 94, 123, 146; Dev. 1878: 93-4; 3, 55, 84-5, 120.

49 Dev. 1845: 123, 154; Dev. 1878: 85; 93-4.

50 The "doctrine of Mediation is a principle". Dev. 1845: 123; Dev. 1878: 85.

sanctity of rites; the veneration of holy places, shrines, images, vessels, furniture and vestments."[51] In short, Newman derives Catholic Christianity from the incarnate Word who historically continues to communicate Himself in the idea of Christianity by virtue of mediatorial and sacramental principles. This sounds very much like the making present of the Christ-event by the ongoing work of the two hands of the Father, the incarnate Word and his Holy Spirit. Although Newman does not articulate the logic of how he relates these aspects of Catholic Christianity to each other, he stresses that these aspects of the Christian idea are part of the whole; and, that they definitely derive from the event of the one, full, personal mystery of the Word made flesh and sacramentally communicated through space and time:

> I observe, then, that if the idea of Christianity, as originally given to us from heaven, cannot but contain much which will be only partially recognized by us as included in it and only be held by us unconsciously; and if again, Christianity being from heaven, all that is necessarily involved in it, and is evolved from it, is from heaven, and if, on the other hand, large accretions actually do exist, professing to be its true and legitimate results, our first impression naturally is, that these must be the very developments which they profess to be .... These doctrines are members of one family, and suggestive, or correlative, or confirmatory, or illustrative of each other .... The Incarnation is the antecedent of the doctrine of Mediation, and the archetype of both of the Sacramental principle and of the merits of the Saints .... You must accept the whole or reject the whole; attenuation does but enfeeble, and amputation mutilate.[52]

This manner of speaking fits well with Newman's position articulated elsewhere regarding the mediatorial role of the eternal Son in the *synkatabasis*. According to his 1872 essay, "Causes of the Rise and Successes of Arianism,"[53] the cosmos is impressed with the filial stamp of Divine Wisdom because God's relationship to the created order is understood profitably in terms of the congruity between the eternal *gennesis* and the origin of creation: "He was born into the universe, as afterwards He was born in Mary, though not by any hypostatic union with it."[54] Consequently he speaks of the eternal Son as the "Archetype" or "**idea** in respect to typical order" of creation.[55]

51 Dev. 1845: 154; Dev. 1878: 93-4.

52 Dev. 1878: 93-4; Dev. 1845: 154.

53 TT 139-299.

54 TT 203.

55 TT 204-5. Emphasis added.

> Catholics, as we have seen in the extracts from Athanasius, were very explicit in teaching that the Divine Word was the **Living Idea**, the All-sufficient Archetype ... on which the universe was framed. The Son interprets and fulfils the designs of the Eternal Mind, not as copying them, when He forms the world, but as being Himself their very Original and Delineation within the Father. Such was the doctrine of the great Alexandrian School, before Athanasius as well as after .... Hence it was that He was fitted, and He alone, to become the First-born of all things, and to exercise a *synkatabasis* which would be available for the conservation of the world.[56]

The same understanding of the congruous relationship adhering between the eternal *gennesis* of the Son and his sacramental office in creation surfaces during Newman's 1833 examination of Catholic ante-Nicene theology[57] and informs his 1836 sermon statement that "Because our Lord is a Son, therefore it is that He could make Himself less than a Son .... His original Personality thus led on to His Temporal Procession."[58] Newman regards mediation as the personal office of the eternal Son and his affinity to the Alexandrian tradition strongly suggests that he is alive to the advantages of using the philosophical language of "idea" to express this mediatorial office. In this light, his identification of the idea of Christianity with the God-man in the *Essay on Development* comes as no surprise.

THESES 1-5: VIVIFYING-MEDIATORIAL; UNIFIED-COMPLEMENTARY-DISTINCT; PERICHORETIC; INNER-OUTER; ONE-MANY

Earlier it was established that Newman typically held life-giving to be the pneumatic *proprium* of the third person of Trinity in the economy of salvation, especially, in relation to the mission of mediation by the eternal Son. In the *Essay on Development* a corresponding relationship exists: principle(s) animates idea which mediates one's communion with the object of revelation. The pneumatological likeness of principle (animation) and the christological likeness of idea (mediation) pervade the text. Here it is apt to recall Newman's understanding of first principles as those basic judgments of mind which condition, direct or otherwise qualify one's acts of reasoning. They are not necessarily foundational in the sense that they are self-evidently indisputable

56 TT 218-9, emphasis added; TT 230-1.

57 Ari. 196.

58 PS vi 5: 58; see TT 185-6.

like the principle of indubitable certainty (*cogito ergo sum*) in Cartesian rationalism or the apodictic law of non-contradiction in Thomism (Walgrave 1975-76-77, 37). Rather, for Newman, any fundamental judgment about reality which guides the subject's decision-making process qualifies as a first principle. This explanation stands on the epistemological side of the isomorphism. From the theological side, Newman identifies ten first principles conditioning and enlivening the mind of the Church to ensure that the idea of Christianity lives, moves and has its being in history: dogma, faith, theology, sacramentality, the mystical interpretation of scripture, grace, asceticism, the recognition of the malignity of sin, the capacity of mind and matter to be sanctified and development itself.[59]

There is, however, much more to the isomorphism than the similarity between the animating role of principle/Holy Spirit and the mediatorial role of idea/Christ. The pneumatological and christological likeness of principle-idea comes to the fore in Newman's discussion of the power of assimilation as the third note of a genuine development of doctrine. One passage typifies how he invests principle-idea with pneumatological-christological significance. In this passage he treats principle and idea as distinct, complementary and unified; he associates them respectively with the work of animation and mediation; he reconciles them in perichoretic interplay that does not dissolve the poles of the one and many; and, finally, he uses the spacial metaphor of inner and outer to communicate this set of meanings. In the relevant passage, Newman indicates that the very "attempt" of an idea to grow relies upon the "presence of principle". He assigns principle the power of "stimulat[ing] thought". He also attributes the ability of the "living idea" to become "many", yet remain "one" to the operation of the stimulating principle within the idea which is its form. "Thus, a power of development is a proof of life, not only in its essay, but especially in its success; for a mere formula either does not expand or is shattered in expanding. A living idea becomes many, yet remains one .... The attempt at development shows the presence of a principle, and its success the presence of an idea. Principles stimulate thought, and an idea keeps it together."[60]

59 Dev. 1878: 324-6; see Dev. 1845: 319-96.

60 Dev. 1845: 74; Dev. 1878: 186.

Several observations about the pneumatological and christological character of principle and idea within this passage are in order. Principle acts distinctly as the vivifying source of the developing idea just like the Holy Spirit makes the eternal Son present in the *synkatabasis*. Obversely, idea acts distinctly as the incarnate form of life just like ontological constitution of the God-man is effected "by the power of the Holy Spirit" in the *synkatabasis*. The complementarity of the principle-idea relation is detectable in the distribution of the corresponding tasks of stimulus and concentration. In turn, these tasks resemble Newman's description of the work of animation by the Holy Spirit and the work of mediation by the eternal Son in the *synkatabasis*. The phrase, "living idea," presents a reciprocal relationship in which idea is enlivened by principle and principle is configured by idea. Newman is consistent in his use of this perichoretic terminology. Consider his 1870 turn of phrase, "vivifying idea". He twice uses this phrase in order to describe the "Image of Him who fulfills the one great need of human nature, the Healer of its wounds, the Physician of the soul, this Image it is which creates faith, and then rewards it."[61] This vibrant mutuality is strikingly similar to the theological doctrine of *circumincessio* favoured by Newman. That the "living idea becomes many, yet remains one" lends itself to a pneumatological interpretation in which there is unity in the midst of diversity. For example, Newman insists that the capacity of the risen Lord to become present in all places and times, yet remain one, is accomplished through the person of his Holy Spirit. As he remarks in his *Lectures on the Doctrine of Justification*, "Christ could not enter into the hearts of the ten thousand of the true Israel, till He came differently from His coming in the flesh – till He came in the Spirit."[62] In the same lecture, he subsequently describes the indwelling Christ made present to the baptized through the person-gift of his Holy Spirt as "a principle of life and a seed of immortality."[63] The unified, complementary, distinct and perichoretic nature of the interplay between principle-idea is also communicated *via* the spacial metaphor of inner and outer. Principles stimulate from the inside; ideas concentrate from the outside; successful principles are connected with the internal matter of development; successful developments issue forth in visible ideas. This is similar to Newman's manner of speaking

61 GA 299.

62 Jfc. 215-16.

63 Jfc. 217.

about the invisible and visible temporal missions of the Holy Spirit and eternal Son *via* the spacial metaphor of 'inner' and 'outer' to convey wholeness insofar as 'inner' and 'outer' require each other; complementarity insofar as 'inner' and 'outer' imply each other and distinction insofar as 'inner' and 'outer' are not each other. The possibility for this theological reading of Newman's epistemological language is established early in the *Essay on Development*. His foundational explanation of idea in his first chapter, "On the Development of Ideas,"[64] contains the same pneumatological and christological markers. At the outset, he speaks of an idea "interest[ing] and possess[ing]" many minds to become "a living principle within them" [vivifying/mediatorial; inner/outer];[65] he talks of the idea presenting "different aspects" in "different minds" to "persons variously circumstanced", yet he insists that these aspects "are capable of a mutual reconciliation and adjustment" without the idea ever "losing its substantial unity and identity" [many/one];[66] again, he refers to aspects of a real idea lying "in such near relation that each implies the others ... in that they have a common origin [distinct; complementary; unified].[67] One might object that this observation about the distinct-complementary-unified aspects of an idea is different than speaking about the same characteristics relative to principle-idea: for, after all, the first deals internally with the constitution of a single term [idea] while the second deals externally with the relation between two terms [principle-idea]. While this objection is valid from a certain perspective, it fails to operate from within the logic of the isomorphism. The vivifying role of principle extends into every dimension of idea and this triad of characteristics (distinctness, complementarity, unity) both reflects that penetration and testifies, from yet another angle, about the shared life of principle-idea. Each lives in and through the other. Finally, this manner of speaking is not *ad hoc*, isolated or elliptical. Newman regularly refers to the vivifying role of principle and the mediatorial role of idea,[68] the distinctness, complementarity and unity of their relation,[69] the tensile nature of

64 Dev. 1845: 30-39; Dev. 1878: 33-40.

65 Dev. 1845: 35; Dev. 1878: 36.

66 Dev. 1845: 31, 32; Dev. 1878: 34

67 Dev. 1878: 33-4.

68 Dev. 1845: 96, 112-3, 337-66; Dev. 1878: 57-8, 73-4, 355-82.

69 Dev. 1845: 67, 251-2; Dev. 178-9, 257-8.

this relation representing the mystery of the one and the many,[70] and the inner dimension of principle relative to the outer dimension of idea.[71]

THESES 6-8: 'MAKING PRESENT', 'PRACTICALLY INDISTINGUISHABLE' 'KNOWN IN LIGHT OF'

Further correspondences between 'principle' and 'the person of the Holy Spirit' are present in the text. On one occasion, Newman speaks of principles as "abstract", "general"[72] and "permanent"[73] and depicts them as "lying deeper in the mind" than developments of doctrine, "as being its assumptions rather than its objective professions."[74] He also interchanges the roles of idea and principle associating the former with "fecundity" and the latter with "generation".[75] Each of these descriptions readily transposes into a pneumatological key. The "abstract" nature of principle corresponds well to Newman's understanding of the Holy Spirit as the divine person who is capable of being known only indirectly through the revelation of Jesus Christ. The "general" nature of principle corresponds well to his sense of the Lord and Giver of Life fructifying without distinction all that the eternal Son sacramentally touches in the orders of nature and grace.[76] Insofar as assumptions tacitly, and even surreptitiously, underpin one's thought, Newman's epistemological characterization of principles as "assumptions rather than objective professions" resembles the theological commonplace that the "Spirit cannot be an object because we must be 'in' and 'using' the Spirit to understand the Spirit." (Hinze and Dabney, 2001, 262; *1 Cor* 12: 3b). In turn, this interpretation sheds light upon his location of principles "deeper" in the mind than the doctrines. For doctrines are made explicit upon principles energizing and acting in certain circumstances, which is to say that 'epistemological incarnation' is always a principle-idea event in which principle assists in the manifestation

70 Dev. 1845: 245, 258-9; Dev. 251, 265.

71 Dev. 1845: 96, 112-3, 258-9, 347-8; Dev. 1878: 57, 73-4, 265, 360-1.

72 Dev. 1845: 70; Dev. 1878: 178.

73 Dev. 1878: 178.

74 Dev. 1845: 368; Dev. 1878: 179.

75 Dev. 1845: 71; Dev. 1878: 180.

76 OS 186.

and development of idea.[77] In the theological arena, the incarnation of the eternal Son is a pneumatological-christological event in which the office of the Holy Spirit has an integral and ongoing place. In this passage, Newman also associates fecundity with idea and principle with generation. At first glance, this seems to invert his standard practice of identifying pneumatic life-giving with principle and christological mediation with idea as rooted in the Alexandrian patristic understanding of *gennesis*. However, the matter is one of exchange not inversion. In fact, this apparent deviation strengthens rather than undermines his usual association of christological mediation with idea and pneumatological life-giving with principle. Newman says that sometimes one practically cannot distinguish between the risen Lord and His Holy Spirit.[78] So too, one should expect that he sometimes identifies idea so closely with principle as to interchange their roles.[79]

On the basis of these eight theses about the pneumatological and christological likeness of principle-idea, one can reasonably argue that in the 1845 and 1878 versions of the *Essay on Development*, Newman invests his epistemological language with theological significance. True, the 1878 version of the text reveals some significant changes. Yet, relative to this immediate concern, the change is simply a matter of intensification. Newman more forcefully indicates in the 1878 version of the *Essay on Development* that the source from which prime ecclesial principles emerge is the incarnate Word.[80] As mentioned, he derives the principles of dogma, faith, theology, sacramentality, the mystical interpretation of scripture, grace, asceticism, the recognition of the malignity of sin, the capacity of mind and matter to be sanctified and development itself from his configuration of the Church to the form of the incarnate Word.[81] Each principle designates an activity traditionally associated with the agency of the Holy Spirit making the person and work of Christ real and present in the life of the Church. Although there is no correspondingly clear, concentrated passage in

77 Dev. 1845: 39, 96; Dev. 1878: 40, 58.

78 Ath. ii. 304; Jfc. 206-8.

79 TT 205.

80 See Dev. 1878: 324-6.

81 See Dev. 1878: 324-6.

the 1845 version of the *Essay on Development*, most principles are mentioned directly in the 1845 version.[82]

POST-1845 CONFIRMATION: 1847, 1868

The foregoing internal analysis of the 1845 *Essay on Development* correlating eight cognitional-theological theses effectively refutes the claim that Newman understands doctrinal development without proper reference to the Holy Spirit. Far from succumbing to what Frank Turner calls a naturalistic account of the Church's mission of communicating revelation in the Christian dispensation, the careful reader discerns that Newman possesses a potent pneumatic-ecclesiology which he often articulates via cognitional language. This conclusion, which stands on its own, is further strengthened by considering post-1845 evidence concerning Newman's view of the Holy Spirit, the Church, doctrinal development and the analogy of mind.

In 1847, Newman wrote a document entitled, "Whether the Catholic Church Has Advanced in its Knowledge of the Faith Once Delivered to it by the Apostles."[83] He composed the document in a terse, scholastic style of short numbered paragraphs organized into four chapters followed by twelve similarly structured theses. Newman submitted this document for theological commentary to the leading Roman theologian of the day, Fr. Giovanni Perrone SJ of the Pontifical Gregorian University. For this reason the document is popularly referred to as "The Newman-Perrone Paper." By this action, Newman hoped to lift the cloud of misunderstanding which swirled around the *Essay on Development*. Perrone returned the document with his margin notes.

In the Newman-Perrone Paper, Newman explicitly identifies the divine superintending of the dynamic of development of doctrine described in the *Essay on Development* with the office of pneumatic

82 For example, in the 1845 version, Newman also speaks of "Scripture and its Mystical Interpretation" (319-27), "Supremacy of Faith" (327-337), "Specimens of Theological Science" (388-96), "Dogma" (337-44) and its assimilating power (344-55), "The Assimilating Power of Sacramental Grace (355-69) and the "characteristic principle of Christianity" issuing forth in the doctrine that "Matter is susceptible of grace, or capable of a union with a Divine Presence and influence" (369-81; citation 370).

83 *Latin Papers*, 69-103.

animation. He speaks clearly of the Holy Spirit as "the author and giver of revelation, to whom it appears whole and entire in every respect". According to Newman, the Spirit illumines the "minds of the Apostles" and teaches them "all truth". This pneumatically originated-given revelation is borne "in the mind of the Church" as a gift received from Christ and transmitted by Popes, Ecumenical Councils, dogmas and the broader Tradition. Though revelation is spoken of as "the revealed word of God", "the deposit of faith," and "word of God", Newman pointedly compares it to "the ideas that occupy the mind of the philosopher, which he contemplates for many years, reflects upon, and leads to maturity; it is like a divine philosophy". At various junctures, he affirms the teaching, guiding, supervising and protecting role of the Holy Spirit in this ecclesial task of bearing revelation in history.[84] Further evidence that Newman understood the Holy Spirit to be the divine agent superintending the doctrinal development of the deposit of the faith committed to the Church, and described according to the cognitional analogy of mind, is found in his "Letter to Flanagan".[85] In 1868, Newman wrote an essay for the benefit of John Stanislaus Flanagan, parish priest of Adare in County Limerick, Ireland. Flanagan was a theologian, a former member of the Birmingham Oratory (1848-65), and he held Newman in high esteem as a spiritual father and a theological mentor. He was perturbed by a controversial exchange between Ignatius Ryder of the Birmingham Oratory and W.G. Ward concerning the latter's extreme views of papal infallibility, in which Ryder asserted that the revelation committed to Church was more, though not less, than a series of propositional truths guaranteed by the Church's gift of infallibility. Correctly suspecting that Newman stood behind Ryder's views, Flanagan was worried that he was at odds with Newman on a grave, theological matter. Newman's essay erased Flanagan's concerns and tutored him on the subject of how revelation was borne by the Church indwelt by the Holy Spirit.

In his 1868 letter, Newman describes the Church as a corporate person who knows revelation in a fashion similar to the manner in which a human knower understands a philosophy. He repeatedly refers to the "Mind of the Church" and a "Divine philosophy" which is

84 *Latin Papers*, 70, 76, 81, 86, 87.

85 TP ii 151-160.

"committed to her keeping ... in such a sense that the mind is possessed of it ...." Contending that the Church is, when necessary, able to know revelation "with fullness and exactness" because she lives "under the operation of supernatural grace", he presents her in a strikingly pneumatic-christological phrase as "a living, present treasury of the Mind of the Spirit of Christ."[86]

While the 1845 *Essay on Development*, the 1847 "Newman-Perrone Paper" and the 1868 "Letter to Flanagan" are distinctive literary projects, written at different historical moments, and distinguished by an array of theological themes, they share a common understanding of the Church as a sacramental, metaphorical person indwelt by the Holy Spirit who makes Christ present in her and who enables the Church faithfully to live in, articulate and communicate revelation across time and space. As Newman concludes in the final sentence of "The Letter to Flanagan,": "I put all this on paper with great diffidence, though it is the view I have entertained for so many years."[87]

CONCLUSION

Newman's *Essay on Development* possesses a potent pneumatic christology which is fundamental to his vision of the Church. By describing his phenomenology of ecclesial cognition in which theological meanings are communicated by his epistemological language of principle and idea, one demonstrates that the sacramental ecclesiology of the *Essay on Development* is penetrated by a powerful theology of the Holy Spirit and Christ. This effort reveals that the text is replete with a pneumatic christology which respects the dynamism of human consciousness and accounts for the personal, embodied, historical and social nature of Christianity based upon a communion between the Divine Mystery and humankind, a communion established through the total Christ event and made present in the corridors of history by the Lord Giver of Life. This theological reading of Newman's epistemological language draws upon the logic of his thought on the incarnation, the Holy Trinity, and pneumatic christology. In its own circumscribed manner, this cognitional-theological interpretation places the scholarly assumptions of several others concerning Newman's epistemology,

86 TP ii 158, 157-8.

87 TP ii 160.

theory of development, thought on revelation, and idea of the Church in the *Essay on Development* on firmer theological footings.

BIBLIOGRAPHY

PRIMARY SOURCES

Newman collected, revised and republished in his uniform edition from 1868-1881. Unless indicated otherwise, references to the uniform edition are taken from their final form as published by Longmans, Green and Co. between 1890-1940, except for Oxford critical editions of *Apologia pro Vita Sua, An Essay in Aid of a Grammar of Assent* and *The Idea of a University*. Initial unbracketed dates indicate the edition I have used for references. Dates in angled brackets < > indicate the years of original publication (of the whole or parts of the whole). Dates in rounded brackets ( ) indicate the year of inclusion into the uniform edition.

UNIFORM EDITION

Apologia pro Vita Sua: Being a History of His Religious Opinions. 1886. <1864> (1873). Edited with an introduction and notes by Martin J. Svaglic. 1967; Oxford: Clarendon Press.

The Arians of the Fourth Century. 1901. <1833> (1873).

Callista. A Tale of the Third Century. 1923. <1855> (1876).

Certain Difficulties felt by Anglicans in Catholic Teaching Considered. 1897. Vol. i: *In Twelve Lectures addressed to the Party of Religious Movement of 1833*. <1850> (1879). Vol. ii: *In a Letter addressed to the Rev. E.B. Pusey, D.D., on occasion of his Eirenicon of 1864; And a Letter addressed to the Duke of Norfolk, on occasion of Mr. Gladstone's Expostulation of 1874*. 1900. <1865-75> (1876).

Discourses addressed to Mixed Congregations. 1902. <1849> (1871).

Discussions and Arguments on Various Subjects. 1891. <1836-1866> (1872).

Essays Critical and Historical. 1919, 1897. 2 volumes. Vol. i: <1828-40> (1871). Vol. ii: <1840-42> (1871).

An Essay in Aid of A Grammar of Assent. 1889. <1870 uniform edition> Edited with an introduction and notes by I.T. Ker. 1985; Oxford: UP.

An Essay on the Development of Christian Doctrine. 1845, 1878. <1845> (1878).

Fifteen Sermons preached before the University of Oxford between A.D. 1826 and 1843. 1892. <1843> (1869).

Historical Sketches, 3 volumes. <1824-73> Vol. i: (1872). Vol. ii: (1873) Vol. iii: (1872). 1970 reprint; Westminster, Md.: Christian Classics.

The Idea of a University Defined and Illustrated: I. In Nine Discourses Delivered to the Catholics of Dublin; II. In Occasional Lectures and Essays Addressed to the Members of the Catholic University. <1852-1859> (1873). Edited with an introduction and notes by I.T. Ker. 1976; Oxford: Clarendon Press.

Lectures on the Doctrine of Justification. 1900. <1838> (1874).

Lectures on the Present Position of Catholics in England Addressed to the Brothers of the Oratory in the Summer of 1851. 1899. <1851> (1872).

Loss and Gain: The Story of a Convert. 1886. <1848> (1874). Edited with an introduction by Alan G. Hill. 1986 reprint; Oxford and New York: Oxford University Press.

Parochial and Plain Sermons, 8 volumes. 1868-70 (vol. i-vii), 1869 (vol. viii). <1834-43> (1869) Rivingtons. 1970 reprint; Westminster, Md.: Christian Classics.

Select Treatises of St. Athanasius in Controversy with the Arians. Freely translated, with an appendix [vol. ii] by John Henry Cardinal Newman. 1897, 1895. Vol. i: <1842> (1881). Vol. ii: <1844> (1881).

Sermons bearing on Subjects of the Day. 1901. <1843> (1869).

Sermons preached on Various Occasions. 1900. <1857> (1870).

Two Essays on Biblical and Ecclesiastical Miracles. 1901. <1826, 1842> (1870).

Tracts Theological and Ecclesiastical. 1902. <1835-72> (1874).

The Via Media of the Anglican Church. Illustrated in Lectures, Letters, and Tracts, Written between 1830 and 1841 in Two Volumes, with a Preface [1877] *and Notes*. Vol i: *Lectures on the Prophetical Office of the Church Viewed Relatively to Romanism and Popular Protestantism*. 1895. <1837, 1877> (1877). 1896. Vol. ii: *Occasional Lectures and Tracts*. <1830-45> (1877).

Verses on Various Occasions. 1903. <written 1818-65; published 1868> (1874) cited from *Prayers, Verses and Devotions*. 1989 reprint; San Francisco: Ignatius Press [PVD].

WORKS OUTSIDE THE UNIFORM EDITION

Catholic Sermons of Cardinal Newman. 1957. Edited at the Birmingham Oratory. Burns and Oates, London.

Correspondence of John Henry Newman with John Keble and Others. 1839-1845. 1917. Edited at the Birmingham Oratory. London: Longmans, Green and Co.

John Henry Newman: Autobiographical Writings. 1956. Edited by Henry Tristam of the Oratory. Sheed and Ward: London and New York.

Letters and Correspondence of John Henry Newman during his Life in the English Church with a brief autobiography. 1890. Edited by Anne Mozely. 2 volumes. London, 1890.

The Letters and Diaries of John Henry Newman. 1961-99. Edited by Charles Stephen Dessain *et. al.*, volumes i-viii (Oxford, 1978-99), xi-xxii (Edinburgh: Nelson, 1961-72), xxiii-xxxi (Oxford, 1973-77).

Meditations and Devotions of the Late Cardinal Newman (1893). 1989. Cited from the compilation of Newman writings, *Prayers, Verses and Devotions* [PVD] San Francisco: Ignatius Press.

My Campaign in Ireland, Part I: Catholic University Reports and other Papers. Edited by William Neville. 1896. Printed for private circulation only by A. King and Co., printers to the University of Aberdeen.

Newman the Oratorian: His Unpublished Oratory Papers. 1968. Edited with an introductory study on the continuity between his Anglican and Catholic Ministry by Placid Murrary, OSB. Leominster, Herefordshire: Fowler Wright Books, 1968.

On Consulting the Faithful in Matters of Doctrine. 1961. Edited with an introduction by John Coulson. Sheed and Ward: London.

On the Inspiration of Scripture. 1967. Edited by J. Derek Holmes and Robert Murray, SJ Washington, D.C.: Corpus Books.

Sermons on the Liturgy and Sacraments and on Christ the Mediator, vol. i of *John Henry Newman Sermons 1824-43.* 1991. Edited from previously unpublished manuscripts by Placid Murrary, OSB. Oxford.

Sermons on Biblical History, Sin and Justification, the Christian Way of Life, and Biblical Theology, vol.ii of *John Henry Newman Sermons 1824-43.* 1993. Edited from previously unpublished manuscripts by Vincent Blehl, SJ. Oxford.

The Philosophical Notebook of John Henry Newman. 1969-70. Edited by Edward Sillem. 2 volumes. Louvain, 1969-70.

Prayers, Verses and Devotions. 1989. San Francisco: Ignatius Press. This is a compilation of three reprints, the first translated and adapted by Newman, the other two being his own works: *The Devotions of Bishop Andrewes* (Oxford and London, 1843); *Meditations and Devotions* (London, 1903) and *Verses on Various Occasions* (London, 1903).

"Three Latin Papers of John Henry Newman: *Newman-Perrone on Development* (1847), *Theses on Faith* (1877) and *Proposed Introduction to the French Translation of the University Sermons* (1847)." 1995. Translated with introduction and commentary by Carleton P. Jones, OP. Dissertation for University of St. Thomas, Rome. The papers are found in the archives of the Birmingham Oratory at B.7.5.

Stray Essays on Controversial Points. 1890. Privately printed.

Sermon Notes of John Henry Cardinal Newman, 1849-1878. 1913. Edited by the Fathers of the Birmingham Oratory. London: Longmans, Green, and Co.

The Theological Papers of John Henry Newman on Biblical Inspiration and on Infallibility. 1979. Edited by J. Derek Holmes. Oxford.

The Theological Papers of John Henry Newman on Faith and Certainty. 1976. Edited by Hugo M. de Achaval, SJ, and J. Derek Holmes. Oxford.

OTHER

Beveridge, William. 1846. *Private Thoughts upon Religion, digested into Twelve Articles, with Practical Resolutions Formed Thereupon, Part I* and *Private Thoughts upon a Christian Life or Necessary Directions for its Beginning and Progress Upon Earth in order to its Final Perfection in the Beatific Vision, Part II* being part of volume VIII of *The Theological Works of William Beveridge, D.D.* Oxford: John Henry Parker.

Butler, Joseph. 1961. *The Analogy of Religion*, introduction by Ernest Mossner. 1736; New York: Frederick Ungar Publishing Co.

Burns, J. Patout SJ and Fagin, Gerald M. SJ, (eds.). 1984. *The Holy Spirit* volume 3 of *Message of the Fathers of the Church*. General editor, Thomas Halton. Wilmington, Delaware: Michael Glazier, Inc.

Gibson, Edgar C.S. Introduction and explanation. 1906. *The Thirty-Nine Articles of the Church of England*. 5th edition. London: Methuen &Co.

Hawkins, Edward. 1889. *A Dissertation upon the Use and Importance of Unauthoritative Tradition. Also Supplementary Extracts from his Bampton Lectures in Illustration of the Principle Advocated*. 1818; London: S.P.C. K.

Palmer, William. 1895. *Notes of A Visit to the Russian Church in the Years 1840, 1841*. Selected and Arranged by Cardinal Newman. London: Longmans, Green, and Co.

Scott, Thomas. 1814. *The Holy Bible containing The Old and New Testaments according to the Publick* Version; *with explanatory notes, practical observations and copious marginal references*. New edition with corrections by the author. Volume vi. London: L.B. Seeley, John Hatchard and Robert Baldwin.

Sumner, John Bird. 1839. *Apostolical Preaching Considered, in an Examination of St. Paul's Epistles*, 8th edition. 1815; London: Hatchard and Son.

Tracts for the Times 1833-41. 1969. Members of the University of Oxford. Volumes i-vi. Printed for J.G.F. & Rivington, 1841. Reprinted by AMS Press: New York and London.

Whately, Richard. 1830. *The Errors of Romanism traced to Their Origin in Human Nature*. London: B. Fellowes, Ludgate Street.

Wilberforce, Robert. 1848. *The Doctrine of the Incarnation*. London.

Wiseman, Nicholas. 1839. "Anglican Claim of Apostolic Succession," *Dublin Review* 13: 139-80.

SECONDARY LITERATURE

NEWMAN

Allen, Louis. 1975. *John Henry Newman and the Abbé Jager: A Controversy on Scripture and Tradition (1834-1836)*. New York: Oxford University Press.

Barbeau, Jeffrey. 2002. "Newman and the Interpretation of Inspired Scripture," *Theological Studies* 63: 53-67.

Biemer, Günter. 1967. *Newman on Tradition*. Translated and edited by Kevin Smyth. Freiburg: Herder; Montreal: Palm Publishers.

———. 1998. "A Vivified Church: Common Structures in the Ecclesiology of Johann Adam Möhler and John Henry Newman," *Sinnsuche und Lebenswenden: Gewissen als Praxis nach John Henry Newman, Internationale Cardinale-Newman-Studien*. Volume xvi. Edited by Günter Biemer, Lothar Kuld and Roman Siebenrock. Peter Lang: Berlin: 240-68.

Blehl, Vincent Ferrer, SJ. 1993. *The Whitestone. The Spiritual Theology of John Henry Newman*. Petersham, M.A.: St. Bede's Publications.

Bouyer, Louis, of the Oratory. 1982. *The Church of God. Body of Christ and Temple of the Holy Spirit*. Translated by Charles Underhill Quinn. Chicago: Franciscan Herald Press.

———. 1963. "Newman and English Platonism," anonymously translated by a monk of Our Lady of the Holy Cross Abbey. *Monastic Studies* 1: 111-31.

———. 1960. *Newman. His Life and Spirituality*. Preface, Mgsr. H. Francis Davis. New York: Meriden Books.

Boyce, Philip. 1988. "Holiness — the Purpose of Life according to Newman," *Newman's Teaching on Christian Holiness*. Edited by Günter Biemer and Heinrich Fries. *Internationale Cardinal-Newman-Studien*. Volume xii. Sigmaringendorf: regio Verlag Glock und Lutz: 43-51.

Brinkman, Marie. 1994. "Newman's Personal Principle at Its Source," *Personality and Belief: Interdisciplinary Essays on John Henry Newman*. Edited by Gerard MaGill. New York: University Press of America: 75-87.

Byrne, J.J. 1937. "The Notion of Doctrinal Development in the Anglican Writings of J.H. Newman," *Ephemerides Theologicae Lovanienses* 14: 230-86.

Cameron, J.M. 1974. "Editor's Introduction" to John Henry Newman, *An Essay on the Development of Christian Doctrine* (1845). Harmondsworth, England: Penguin Books: 7-50.

———. 1960. "The Night Battle: Newman and Empiricism," *Victorian Studies* 4: 99-117.

Chadwick, Owen. 1987. *Newman to Bossuet*. 2nd edition. London: Cambridge University Press.

Connolly, John. 1996. "Newman on Human Faith and Divine Faith: Clarifying Some Ambiguities," *Horizons* 23: 261-80.

Coulson, John. 1970. *Newman and the Common Tradition*. Oxford: Clarendon Press.

Coulson, John and Allchin, A.M. (eds.). 1967. *The Rediscovery of Newman: An Oxford Symposium*. London and Melbourne: SPCK and Sheed and Ward.

Daly, Gabriel. Review. 1984. "R. Strange, *Newman and The Gospel of Christ*," *Journal of Ecclesiastical History* 35: 289-90.

Davis, H. Francis. 1964. "Newman and the Theology of the Living Word," *Newman Studien* vi: 167-78.

Dessain, C.S. 1962. "Cardinal Newman and the Doctrine of Uncreated Grace," *Clergy Review* 47: 207-25, 269-88.

———. 1982. "Cardinal Newman's Teaching about the Blessed Virgin Mary," *Mary's Place in Christian Dialogue. Occasional Papers of the Ecumenical Society of the Blessed Virgin Mary 1970-1980*. Edited by Alberic Stacpoole, OSB. St. Paul Publications: 232-47.

———. 1966. *John Henry Newman*. London: Thomas Nelson and Sons.

———. 1977. *Newman's Spiritual Themes*. Dublin: Veritas Publications.

Dolan, Gerald. 1970. "The Gift of the Holy Spirit According to John Henry Newman (1828— 1839)," *Franciscan Studies* 30: 77-130.

Dragas, George. 1981. "John Henry Newman: Rediscovering the Catholicity of the Greek Fathers Today," *One in Christ* 17: 46-68.

Dulles, Avery, SJ. 1990a. "From Images to Truth: Newman on Revelation and Faith," *Theological Studies* 51: 252-67.

———. 1990b. "Newman, Conversion and Ecumenism," *Theological Studies* 51: 717-31.

———. 1990c. "Newman on Infallibility," *Theological Studies* 51: 434-49.

———. 1996. "Newman's Pneumatology: Ecumenical Considerations. " An unpublished paper presented 8 June 1996, *Catholic Theological Society of America*: 1-9.

Femiano, S. 1967. *The Infallibility of the Laity*. New York: Herder and Herder.

Gilley, Sheridan. 1990. *Newman and His Age*. Westminster, Maryland: Christian Classics.

Ker, Ian. 1989. "Foreword," John Henry Newman. *An Essay on the Development of Christian Doctrine*. 6th ed. Notre Dame: UP: xvii-xxvii.

———. 1985. "Introduction," John Henry Newman. *An Essay in Aid of a Grammar of Assent*. Oxford: Clarendon Press.

———. 1990a. *The Achievement of John Henry Newman*. Notre Dame, IN: University of Notre Dame Press.

———. 1993. *Healing the Wound of Humanity. The Spirituality of John Henry Newman*. London: Darton, Longman and Todd.

———. 1998. *John Henry Newman. A Biography*. Oxford and New York: Oxford University Press.

———. 1981. "Magisterium and Theologians," *Verantwoordelijkheden in de Kerk volgens John Henry Newman*. Druk: Dispuutgezel schap H.O.E.K.

———. 1990b. *Newman on Being A Christian*. Notre Dame, Indiana: University of Notre Dame.

———. 1990c. *Newman the Theologian. A Reader*. Notre Dame, Indiana: University of Notre Dame.

———. 1978. "Newman's Theory – Development or Continuing Revelation?," *Newman and Gladstone Centennial Essay on Developments*. Edited by James Bastable. Dublin: Vertitas Publications.

———. 1995. "The Influence of the Greek Fathers," *John Henry Newman: Selected Sermons*. Preface by Henry Chadwick. New York: Paulist Press: 28-40.

Ker, Ian and Hill, Alan G. (eds.). 1990. *Newman after a Hundred Years*. Oxford: Clarendon Press.

Graef, Hilda. 1967. *God and Myself. The Spirituality of John Henry Newman*. London: Peter Davies.

Jaki, Stanley, L., OSB (ed.). 1989. *Newman Today. Papers presented at a conference on John Henry Cardinal Newman. The Wethersfield Institute*. Introduction by Stanley Jaki. San Francisco: Ignatius Press.

Jost, Walter. 1989. *Rhetorical Thought in John Henry Newman*. Columbia, South Carolina: South Carolina UP.

Komonchak, Joseph. 1976. "John Henry Newman's Discovery of the Visible Church (1816-28)." Ph.D. Dissertation. Union Theological Seminary. New York.

La Delfa, Rino. 1997. *Personal Church? The Foundation of Newman's Ecclesiological Thought*. Palermo, Italy and Sao Paulo, Brazil: Italo-Latino-Americana Palma.

Lash, Nicholas. 1971. "Faith and History: some reflections on Newman's `Essay on the Development of Christian Doctrine,'" *Irish Theological Quarterly* 38: 224-41.

———. 1976. *Newman on Development: The search for an explanation in history*. Shepherdstown WV: Patmos Press.

Leroux, Guielmo F., SJ. 1959. "Divine Indwelling as found in the *Lectures of Justification*," chapter two of "The Inhabitation of the Holy Trinity in the Writings John Henry Cardinal Newman." Dissertation for the Pontifical Gregorian University. Rome.

Logan, Ian. 1998. "Shooting round Corners: Newman and Anselm," *New BlackFriars* 79: 544-50.

Magill, Gerard. 1992. "Newman's Personal Reasoning: The Inspiration of the Early Church," *Irish Theological Quarterly* 58: 305-13.

———. 1993. "Review of *Newman and Heresy: The Anglican Years* by Stephen Thomas," *Horizons* 20/1: 149-50.

Masson, Pierre, OP. 1982. *Newman and the Holy Spirit. Christian Life and the Church in our Times*. Translated by Sr. Mary-of-the-Trinity OP, Taipei.

McClelland, Allan, V. (ed.). 1996. *By Whose Authority. Newman, Manning and the Magisterium*. Bath: Downside Abbey.

McGovern, Thomas. 1992. "Newman and the study of the Church Fathers," *Homiletic & Pastoral Review* 92: 9-19.

McGrath, Alister E. 1983. "John Henry Newman's 'Lectures on Justificiation': The High Church Misrepresentation of Luther," *Churchman* 97: 112-22.

McGrath, Francis. 1997. *John Henry Newman. Universal Revelation*. Foreword by Gerard Tracey. Tunbridge Wells: Burns & Oates; Mulgrave: John Garratt Publishing.

McKeating, Colm. 1992. *Eschatology in the Anglican Sermons of John Henry Newman*. Lewiston/Lampeter: Mellen Research University Press.

Merrigan, Terrence. 1991. *Clear Heads and Holy Hearts: The Religious and Theological Ideal of John Henry Newman*. Foreword by Ian Ker. Louvain: Peeters Press.

———. 1990. "Review of *John Henry Newman. On the Idea of Church* by Edward Jeremy Miller," *Louvain Studies* 15: 77-9.

Miller, Edward Jeremy. 1987. *John Henry Newman. On the Idea of Church*. Foreword by Jan Walgrave. Shepherdstown, W.Va.: Patmos Press.

———. 1996. "Newman's Pneumatology From the Perspective of His Ecclesiology." An unpublished paper presented 8 June 1996, *Catholic Theological Society of America Proceedings* 1-3.

Misner, Paul. 1970. "Newman's Concept of Revelation and the Development of Doctrine," *Heythrop Journal* 11: 32-47.

———. 1976. *Papacy and Development: Newman and the Primacy of the Pope*. Leiden: E.J. Brill.

Murray, Scott. 1990. "Luther in Newman's 'Lectures on Justification,'" *Concordia Theological Quarterly* 54: 155-75.

Newsome, David. 1964. "Justification and Sanctification: Newman and the Evangelicals," *Journal of Theological Studies* ns 15: 32-53.

Neuhaus, Richard John. 1997. "Newman, Luther, and the Unity of Christians," *Pro Ecclesia* 6: 277-88.

Nichols, Aidan, OP. 1990. *From Newman to Congar. The Idea of Doctrinal Development from the Victorians to the Second Vatican Council*. Edinburgh: T&T Clarke.

Norris, Thomas, J. 1997. *Newman and his Theological Method*. Leiden: E.J. Brill.

———. 1996. *Only Life Gives Life. Revelation, Theology and Christian Living according to Cardinal Newman*. Blackrock, Ireland: the columba press.

Novak, Michael. 1960. "Newman on Nicaea," *Theological Studies* 21: 444-53.

O'Leary, Joseph S. 1991. "Impeded Witness: Newman Against Luther on Justification," *John Henry Newman. Reason, Rhetoric and Romanticism*. Edited by David Nicholls and Fergus Kerr, OP. Bristol, England: The Bristol Press, 153-93.

Pelikan, Jaroslav. 1979. "Newman and the Fathers: The Vindication of Tradition," *Studia Patristica* 18: 379-90.

Rowell, Geoffrey. 1990."Newman and the Anglican Tradition: Reflections on Tractarianism and the Seventeenth-Century Anglican Divines," *Louvain Studies* 15: 136-50.

———. 1983. *The Vision Glorious. Themes and Personalities of the Catholic Revival in Anglicanism*. Oxford: Oxford University Press.

Selby, Robin C. 1971. *The Principle of Reserve in the Writings of John Henry Cardinal Newman* London: Oxford University Press.

Sharkey, Michael. 1976. "The Christological Foundation" and "The Church" as excerpted from "The Sacramental Principle in the Thought of John Henry Cardinal Newman." S.T.D. Dissertation. The Pontifical Gregorian University. Rome.

Sheridan, Thomas. 1967. *Newman on Justification*. New York: Alba House.

Seynaeve, Jaak. 1953. *Cardinal Newman's Doctrine on Holy Scripture According to His Published Works and Previously Unedited Manuscripts*. Louvain: Publications Universitaires.

———. 1990. "Newman's Biblical Hermeneutics," *Louvain Studies* 15: 282-300.

Stern, Jean. 1969. "Le Saint-Esprit et Marie chez Newman et Faber," *Études Mariales* 26: 37-56.

Strange, Roderick. 1980. "The Development of Newman's Marian Thought and Devotion," *One in Christ*: 114-26.

———. 1981. *The Gospel of Christ*. New York: Oxford University Press.

———. 1988. "Newman and Athanasius on Divinization," *Newman's Teaching on Christian Holiness*. Edited by Gunter Biemer and Heinrich Fries. *Internationale Cardinal-Newman-Studien*. Volume xii. Sigmaringendorf: regio Verlag Glock und Lutz: 43-51.

———. 1990. "Newman and the Mystery of Christ," *Newman After A Hundred Years* 1990, 375-99.

Testa, Michael. "The Theological Anthropology of John Henry Newman." Ph.D. Dissertation. St. Louis University. Ann Arbor, Michigan, University Microfilms Int., 1993.

Thiel, John E. *Senses of Tradition. Continuity and Development in Catholic Faith.* Oxford: Oxford UP, 2000.

Thomas, Stephen. *Newman and Heresy: The Anglican Years.* Cambridge: Cambridge University Press, 1991.

Tolhurst, James. *The Church . A Communion — in the preaching and thought of John Henry Newman.* Leominster, Herefordshire: Fowler Wright Books Ltd., 1988.

Toon, Peter. "A Critical Review of John Henry Newman's Doctrine of Justification," *Churchman* 94 (1980) 335-44.

Walgrave, Jan Hendrik, OP. 1975-76-77. *J.H. Newman. His Personality, His Principles, His Fundamental Doctrines.* Katholieke Universiteit Leuven.

———. 1960a. "L'orignalité de l'idéé Newmanienne du dévelopment," Newman Studien iv: 83-96.

———. 1960. *Newman the Theologian, The Nature of Belief and Doctrine as Exemplified in His Life and Works.* Translated by A.V. Littledale. New York: Sheed and Ward.

———. 1972. *Unfolding Revelation. The Nature of Doctrinal Development.* Philadelphia and London: The Westminster Press and Hutchinson.

Weatherby, Harold L. 1973. *Cardinal Newman and His Age. His Place in English Theology and Literature.* Nashville: Vanderbilt University Press.

THEOLOGICAL AND PHILOSOPHICAL

Balthasar, Hans Urs von. 1993. *Mysterium Paschale.* Translated with an introduction by Aidan Nichols, OP. Grand Rapids, Michigan: W.B. Eerdmans.

———. 1992/98. *Theo-Drama. Theological Dramatic Theory.* Volumes iii and v. *The Dramatis Personae: The Person in Christ* and *The Last Act.* Translated by Graham Harrision. San Francisco: Ignatius Press.

Bienert, Wolfgang. 1981. "The Significance of Athanasius of Alexandria for Nicene Orthodoxy," *The Irish Theological Quarterly* 48: 181-93.

Bobrinskoy, Boris. 1984. "The Indwelling of the Spirit in Christ, 'Pneumatic Christology' in the Cappadocian Fathers," *St. Vladimir's Theological Quarterly* 28: 49-65.

———. 1999. *The Mystery of the Trinity. Trinitarian Experience and Vision in the Biblical and Patristic Tradition.* Translated by Anthony P. Gythiel. Crestwood, New York: St. Vladimir's Seminary Press.

Boulding, Mary Cecily. 1985. "The Doctrine of the Holy Spirit in the Documents of Vatican II," *The Irish Theological Quarterly* 51: 253-67.

Breck, John. 1990. "The Lord is the Spirit: An Essay in Christological Pneumatology". *Ecumenical Review* 42: 114-21.

Brown, David. 1989. "Trinitarian Personhood and Individuality," *Trinity, Incarnation, and Atonement. Philosophical and Theological Essays.* Edited by Ronald J. Feenstra and Cornelius Plantinga, Junior. Notre Dame: University of Notre Dame Press: 48-78.

Brown, Raymond, E. 1994. *An Introduction to New Testament Christology.* Paulist Press.

———. 1970. *The Gospel according to John* (XIII-XXI), *The Anchor Bible.* New York.

Campbell, Theodore. 1974."The Doctrine of the Holy Spirit in the Theology of St. Athanasius," *Scottish Journal of Theology* 27: 408-40.

Cantalamessa, Raniero, OFM Cap. 1994. *The Holy Spirit in the Life of Jesus. The Mystery of Christ's Baptism.* Translated by Alan Neame. The Liturgical Press: Collegeville, MN.

———. 2001. *The Mystery of Pentecost.* Translated by Glen S. Davis The Liturgical Press: Collegeville, MN.

Chirovsky, Andriy. 1988. "Orthodox in Communion with Rome: The Antinomic Character of Eastern Catholic Theology," *Logos: A Journal of Eastern Christian Studies* 39: 71-89.

Coffey, David. 1979. *Grace: The Gift of the Holy Spirit.* Sydney: Catholic Institute of Sydney.

Congar, Yves, OP. 1966. "Deification in the Spiritual Tradition of the East" and "The Human Person and Human Liberty in Oriental Anthropology," *Dialogue Between Christians.* Translated by Philip Loretz. Westminster, Maryland: Newman Press: 217-31; 232-45.

———. 1997. *I Believe in the Holy Spirit.* Translated by David Smith. Volumes i-iii. Geoffrey Chapman, 1983; New York: Crossroad, paper reprint.

———. 1973. "Renewed Actuality of the Holy Spirit," *Lumen Vitae* 28: 13-30.

———. 1967. *Traditions and Tradition. An historical and theologicial Essay on Development.* Translated by Michael Nasby and Thomas Rainborough. New York: The MacMillan Company.

———. 1986. *The Word and the Spirit.* Translated by David Smith. London: Geoffrey Chapman.

Crowe, Fred. 1983."Son and Spirit: Tension in the Divine Missions," *Science and Esprit* 25: 153-69.

———. 1989. "Rethinking God-With-Us: Categories from Lonergan". *Science et Esprit* 41: 167-88.

Davis, Stephen T. 1993. *Risen Indeed. Making Sense of the Resurrection*. Grand Rapids, Michigan: Wm. B. Eerdmans.

Davis, Stephen T., Daniel, Kendall SJ, and O'Collins, Gerald SJ. (eds.). 1998. *The Resurrection. An Interdisciplinary Symposium on the Resurrection of Jesus*. 1997; New York: Oxford University Press, paper reprint.

———. 2001. *The Trinity. An Interdisciplinary Symposium on the Trinity*. Oxford and New York: Oxford University Press.

De Lubac, Henri. 1988. *Catholicism. Christ and the Common Destiny of Man*. Translated by Lancelot C. Sheppard and Sister Elizabeth Englund, OCD. 1952; San Francisco: Ignatius Press, paper reprint.

———. *The Splendor of the Church*. Translated by Michael Manson. 1956; San Francisco: Ignatius Press, paper reprint 1986.

Del Colle, Ralph. 1994. *Christ and the Spirit. Spirit-Christology in Trinitarian Perspective*. New York and Oxford: Oxford University Press.

Dragas, George. 1979. "Holy Spirit and Tradition: The Writings of St. Athanasius," *Sorbornost* 1: 51-79.

Dulles, Avery, SJ. 1987. *The Catholicity of the Church*. Oxford: Clarendon.

———. 1978. *Models of the Church*. Garden City, New York: Image Books.

———. 1985. *Models of Revelation*. Garden City, New York: Image Books.

Dunn, James. 1975. *Jesus and the Spirit. A Study of the Religious and Charismatic Experience of Jesus and the First Christians as Reflected in the New Testament*. London: SCM Press Ltd.

Dunne, Tad. 1984. "Trinity and History". *Theological Studies* 45: 139-52.

Durrwell, F.X., CSSR. 1993. "A christology according to the Spirit," *Theology Digest* 40: 221-27.

———. 1960. *The Resurrection. A Biblical Study*. Translated by Rosemary Sheed and introduced by Charles Davis. New York: Sheed and Ward.

Farrow, Douglas. 1999. *Ascension and Ecclesia: on the significance of the doctrine of the Ascension for Ecclesiology and Christian Cosmology*. Edinburgh: T&T Clarke; Grand Rapids, Michigan: Wm. B. Eerdmans Publishing Co.

Fatula, Mary Ann, OP. 1990. *The Triune God of Christian Faith*. Collegeville, MN: The Liturgical Press.

Fortman, Edmund, J. 1972. *The Triune God: A Historical Study of the Doctrine of the Trinity*. Philadelphia: Westminster Press.

Galvin, John P. 1994. "From the Humanity of Christ to the Jesus of History: A Paradigm Shift in Catholic Christianity," *Theological Studies* 55: 252-73.

Galot, Jean. 1993. "L'Esprit Saint et la spiration," *Gregorianium* 74: 241-59.

Grillmeier, Aloys, SJ. 1975. *Christ in the Christian Tradition*. Volume. i. *From The Apostolic Age to Chalcedon* (451). 2nd edition. Translated by John Bowden. Atlanta: John Knox Press.

Hammond, David. 1989. "The Influence of Newman's Doctrine of Assent On The Thought of Bernard Lonergan: A Genetic Study," *Method: A Journal of Lonergan Studies*, 7: 95-111.

Hanson, R.P.C. 1988. *The Search for the Christian Doctrine of God. The Arian Controversy 318-381*. Edinburgh: T&T Clark.

Harmon, Nolan. 1989. "The Holy Spirit — Person and/or Presence," *Religion in Life* 29: 52-63.

Hinze, Bradford, E.and Dabney, Lyle (eds.). 2001. *Advents of the Spirit: An Introduction to the Current Study of Pneumatology*. Milwaukee, Wisconsin: Marquette University Press.

Hopko, Thomas. 1992. "Apophatic Theology and the Naming of God in the Eastern Orthodox Tradition," *Speaking the Christian God, The Holy Trinity and the Challenge of Feminism*. Edited by Alvin Kimel Jr. Grand Rapids, MI: W.B. Eerdmans; Leominster, England: Gracewing.

Hunt, Anne. 1997. *The Trinity and the Paschal Mystery. A Development in Recent Catholic Theology* Collegeville Mn.: The Liturgical Press.

Hussey, Edmund. "The Theology of the Holy Spirit in the Writings of St. Gregory of Nazianzus," *Diakonia* 14 (1979) 224-33.

Kannengiesser, Charles. "Athanasius of Alexandria and the Holy Spirit between Nicea I and Constantinople I," *The Irish Theological Quarterly* 48 (1981) 166-79.

Kasper, Walter. 1988. *The God of Jesus Christ*. Translated by Matthew J. O'Connell. New York: Crossroad.

———. 1976. *Jesus The Christ*. Translated by V. Green. London, England and Mahwah, N.J.: Burns and Oates and Paulist Press.

Kelly, J.N.D. 1978. *Early Christian Doctrines*. 5th edition. San Francisco: Harper & Row.

Loewe, William, P. 2000. "From the Humanity of Christ to the Historical Jesus," *Theological Studies* 61: 314-31.

Lonergan, Bernard, SJ. 1978. *Insight: A Study of Human Understanding*. San Francisco: Harper and Row.

———. 1988. *Collection* vol. 4, *Collected Works of Bernard Lonergan*. Edited by F.E. Crowe and R. Doran. Toronto: University of Toronto Press, 1988.

———. 1974. *Second Collection*. Edited by W.F. Ryan and B.J. Tyrrell. Philadelphia: Westminster Press.

Mackey, James, P. 1981. "The Holy Spirit: Relativising the Divergent Approaches of East and West," *The Irish Theological Quarterly* 48: 256-67.

Madsen, Norman. 1983. "Pneumatological Anthropology: A Proposal for a Theology of the Holy Spirit," *Reformed Review* 37: 13-24.

Maritain, Jacques. 1973. *On The Church of Christ: The Person of the Church and Her Personnel*. Translated by J.W. Evans. Notre Dame: Notre Dame UP.

Marsh, Thomas. 1978. "Holy Spirit in Early Christian Teaching," *The Irish Theological Quarterly* 45: 101-16.

———. 1994. *The Triune God: A Biblical, Historical and Theological Study*. Mystic, CT: Twenty-Third Publications.

Matsoukas, Nikos. 1983. "The Economy of the Holy Spirit: The Standpoint of Orthodox Theology," *Ecumenical Review* 41/3 (1983) 398-405.

McDonagh, Enda. 1982. "The Holy Spirit and Human Identity," *The Irish Theological Quarterly* 49: 37-49.

McDonnell, Kilian. 1982. "The Determinative Doctrine of the Holy Spirit," *Theology Today* 39: 142-61.

———. 1985. "A Trinitarian Theology of the Holy Spirit?" *Theological Studies* 46: 191-227.

———. 1998. "*Quaestio Disputata*: Irenaeus on the Baptism of Jesus – A Rejoinder to Daniel A. Smith," *Theological Studies* 59: 317-19.

McIntyre, John. 1997. *The Shape of Pneumatology: Studies in the Doctrine of the Holy Spirit*. Edinburg: T&T Clark.

Meredith, Anthony. 1981. "The Pneumatology of the Cappadocian Fathers and the Creed of Constantinople," *The Irish Theological Quarterly* 48: 196-211.

Mersch, Emile, SJ. 1962. *The Whole Christ. The Historical Development of the Doctrine of the Mystical Body in Scripture and Tradition*. Translated by John R. Kelly, SJ; 1936, 2nd French edition. London: Dennis Dobson.

Meyendorff, John. 1979. *Byzantine Theology: historical trends & doctrinal themes*. 2nd edition. New York: Fordham University Press.

———. 1975. *Christ in Eastern Thought*. Crestwood, NY: St. Vladimir's Seminary Press.

Meynell, Hugo. 1982. "Two Directions for Pneumatology," *The Irish Theological Quarterly* 49: 172-83.

Montague, George, SM. 1976. *The Holy Spirit: Growth of a Biblical Tradition: A Commentary on the Principal Texts of the Old and New Testaments*. New York: Paulist Press.

Nissiotis, Nikos. 1962-63. "Spirit, Church, and Ministry," *Theology Today* 19: 484-99.

O'Leary, Paul. 1979. "The Holy Spirit in the Church in Orthodox Theology," *The Irish Theological Quarterly* 46: 177-84.

Osborne, Kenan, B. 1997. *The Resurrection of Jesus: new considerations for its theological interpretation*. Mahwah, N.J.: Paulist Press.

Pelikan, Jaroslav. 1969. *Development of Christian Doctrine: Some Historical Prolegomena* (New Haven and London: Yale UP.

———. 1971 and 1989. *The Emergence of the Catholic Tradition (100-600)* and *Christian Doctrine and Modern Culture (since 1700)*. Volumes one and five of *The Christian Tradition: A History of the Development of Doctrine*. Chicago and London: The University of Chicago Press.

Pettersen, Alvyn. 1995. *Athanasius*. Ridgefield, CT: Moorehouse Publishing.

Prestige, G.L. 1952. *God in Patristic Thought*. 2nd edition. London: SPCK.

Prusak, Bernard, P. 2000. "Bodily Resurrection in Catholic Perspectives," *Theological Studies* 61: 64-105.

Rahner, Karl, SJ. 1965. "Some Implications of the Scholastic Doctrine of Uncreated Grace, *Theological Investigations*," vol. i. Translated with an introduction by Cornelius Ernst OP. Baltimore: Helicon Press: 319-46.

———. 1970. *The Trinity*. Translated by Joseph Donceel. Tunbridge Wells, Kent: Burns and Oates.

Ratzinger, Joseph. 1968. "The Ascension of Christ," *Sacramentum Mundi*. Volume i. General editor, Adolf Darlap. Montreal, New York and Great Britian: Palm, Herder and Herder and Burns & Oates: 109-10.

Robinson, John A.T. 1961. *The Body. A Study in Pauline Theology*. 1952; London: SMC Press, paper reprint.

Schwöbel, Christoph, (ed). 1995. *Trinitarian Theology Today: Essays on Divine Being and Act*. Edinburg: T&T Clark.

Smith, Daniel. 1998. "*Quaestio Disputata*: Irenaeus on the Baptism of Jesus – A Response to Kilian McDonnell," *Theological Studies* 59: 319-21.

Streeter, Carla Mae, OP. 1994. "The Lonergan Connection with Newman's *Grammar*," *Interdisciplinary Essays on John Henry Newman*. Edited by

Gerard Magill. New York and London: University of America Press: 172-83.

Theological-Historical Commission for the Great Jubilee of the Year 2000. 1998. *The Holy Spirit, Lord and Giver of Life*. Translated by Agostino Bono. New York: The Crossroad Publishing.

Welch, Lawrence. 1996. "Rahner's Trinitarian Axiom: Pre-incarnate Son or Christ?" *Église et Théologie* 27: 21-45.

Wilken, R.L. 1972. "The Interpretation of the Baptism of Jesus in the Later Fathers," *Studia Patristica*, vol. 11. Edited by F.L. Cross. Berlin: Akademie-Verlag: 268-77.

Wood, Susan, Roger Haight, Mary Ann Donovan, Barbara Finan. 1993. "Review Symposium of *God for Us: The Trinity and Christian Life* by Catherine Mowry LaCugna," *Horizons* 20: 127-42.

Worgul, G.S. 1977. "The Ghost of Newman in the Lonergan Corpus," *The Modern Schoolman*, 54: 317-32.

Wright, John. 1987. "The Church: Community of the Holy Spirit," *Theological Studies* 48: 25-44.

Zizioulas, John D. 1985. *Communion As Being. Studies in Personhood and the Church*. Foreword by John Meyendorff. Crestwood, New York: St. Vladimir's Seminary Press.

———. 1995. "The Doctrine of the Holy Trinity: The Significance of the Cappadocian Contribution," *Trinitarian Theology Today. Essays on Divine Being and Act*. Edited by Christoph Schwöbel. Edinburg: T&T Clarke: 44-60.

———. 1974. "The pneumatological dimension of the Church," *Communio* 1: 142-58.

HISTORICAL

Allchin, A.M. 1980. *Trinity and Incarnation in Anglican Tradition. A Paper Read to Romanian Orthodox Theologians*. 1977; Fairacres and Oxford: SGL Press, reprint.

———. *Participation in God: A Forgotten Strand in Anglican Tradition* (Wilton, Connecticut: Marlowhouse-Barlow, 1988) 48-62.

Brilioth, Yngve. 1933. *The Anglican Revival: Studies in the Oxford Movement*. London: Longmans, Green and Co.

Chadwick, Owen. 1975. *The Secularization of the European Mind in the Nineteenth Century*. Cambridge: Cambridge University Press.

Crouse, Robert. 1979. "'Devout Perusal': The Tractarian Revival of Patristic Studies", *Studia Patristica* 18: 328-34.

Elliott-Binns, L.E. 1953. *Early Evangelicals: A Religious and Social Study.* London: Lutterworth Press.

Härdelin, Alf. 1965. *The Tractarian Understanding of the Eucharist.* Uppsala: Acta Universitatis Upsaliensis, 1965.

Knox, E.A. 1934. *The Tractarian Movement, 1833-1845: A Study of the Oxford Movement as a phase of the Religious Revival in Western Europe in the second quarter of the nineteenth Century.* London and New York: Putnam.

McGrath, Alister. 1984. "The Emergence of the Anglican Tradition on Justification 1600-1700," *Churchman* 98: 28-43.

Newsome, David. 1966. *The Wilberforces and Henry Manning. The Parting of Friends.* Cambridge, M.A.: The Belknap Press of Harvard Univ. Press.

———. 1974. *Two Classes of Men. Platonism and English Romantic Thought.* London: John Murrary.

Prickett, Stephen. 1976. *Romanticism and Religion. The Tradition of Coleridge and Wordsworth in the Victorian Church.* Cambridge: Cambridge University Press.

Reynolds, J.S. 1975. *The Evangelicals at Oxford 1735-1871. A Record of an Unchronicled Movement with the record extended to 1905.* Appleford, Abingdon, Oxford: Marcham Manor Press.

REFERENCE

NEWMAN

Blehl, Vincent Ferrer. 1978. *John Henry Newman: A Bibliographical Catalogue of His Writings.* Charlottesville, Virginia: University Press of Virginia for the Bibliographical Society of the University of Virginia.

Coupet, Armel J. OP. 1966. *A Newman Companion to the Gospels. Sermons of John Henry Newman selected and schematically presented.* London: Burns & Oates.

Earnest, James David and Gerard Tracey. 1984. *John Henry Newman: An Annotated Bibliography of His Tract and Pamphlet Collection.* New York: Garland.

Ford, John T. 1982. "Newman Studies: Recent Resources and Research." *Thomist* 46: 283-306.

Griffin, John R. 1980. *Newman: A Bibliography of Secondary Sources.* Front Royal, Va.: Christendom College Press.

Rickaby, Joseph, SJ. 1914. *Index to the Works of John Henry Cardinal Newman.* London: Longmans, Green and Co.

Svaglic, Martin J. 1973. "Man and Humanist," *Victorian Prose: A Guide to Research.* Edited by David DeLaura. New York: Modern Language Association of America: 113-65.

OTHER

Brown, Raymond E. SS, Fitzmyer, Joseph A. SJ and Murphy, Roland E. O Carm. (eds.). 1990. *New Jerome Biblical Commentary.* Foreword by Carlo Maria Cardinal Martini, SJ. Englewood Cliffs, NJ: Prentice Hall, 1990.

Cross, F.L., Livingstone, E.A. (eds.). 1985. *The Oxford Dictionary of the Christian Church.* 2nd revised edition. Oxford: Oxford University Press, 1974; reprint with corrections.

Kittel, Gerhard, Friedrich, Gerhard (eds.). 1985. *Theological Dictionary of the New Testament.* Translated and abridged in one volume by Geoffrey W. Bromiley. Grand Rapids, MI and Exeter, Devon: William B. Eerdmans Publishing Co. and The Paternoster Press.

Komonchak, Joseph A., Collins, Mary and Lane, Dermot A. (eds.). 1987. *New Dictionary of Theology.* Collegeville, MN: The Liturgical Press.

O'Carroll, Michael CSSp. 1990. *Veni Creator Spiritus: A Theological Encyclopaedia of the Holy Spirit.* Collegeville, MN.: The Liturgical Press.

Ott, Ludwig. *Fundamentals of Catholic Dogma.* 1974. Edited by James Canon Bastible, D.D. and translated from the German by Patrick Lynch, Ph.D. 4th edition. 1960; Rockford, Illinois: Tan Books and Publishers, reprint.

SUBJECT INDEX

D

E

F

G

H

I

S

T

W

NAME INDEX

G

H

J

K

L

M

N

O

P

S

T

W

Z